APPEAL TO FORCE

American Military Intervention in the Era of Containment

Herbert K. Tillema

University of Missouri—Columbia

**THOMAS Y. CROWELL COMPANY
NEW YORK**
Established 1834

Copyright © 1973 by
THOMAS Y. CROWELL COMPANY, INC.
All Rights Reserved

Except for use in a review, the reproduction or utilization of this work in any form or by any electronic, mechanical, or other means, now known or hereafter invented, including photocopying and recording, and in any information storage and retrieval system is forbidden without the written permission of the publisher. Published simultaneously in Canada by Fitzhenry & Whiteside Ltd., Toronto.

L. C. Card 71-179778
ISBN 0-690-09508-2

Designed by Elliot Epstein
Manufactured in the United States of America

ACKNOWLEDGMENTS

So many persons gave generously of their time, attention, and information that there is not space to mention them all. I am particularly indebted to John D. Montgomery for his many helpful suggestions and for his careful reading of the study in its formative stages. Joseph Nye also made several important suggestions on the structure of the study.

The analysis of United States overt military intervention in the Dominican Republic would not have been possible without the assistance of Abraham Lowenthal. He took time from his study of the Dominican intervention to advise on sources, share the information he had gathered from his own extensive interviews, and make detailed comments on several drafts of the manuscript. Harry Shlaudeman also gave time and information on the Dominican crisis.

Basim Mussallam provided invaluable assistance in the analysis of the 1958 intervention in Lebanon. Mr. Mussallam shared information, made many helpful suggestions on both historical details and interpretation, recommended published sources, and arranged interviews with Dr. Charles Malik and Hisham Sharabi. Among the many others who shared their knowledge of the events in Lebanon were Admiral Arleigh Burke (ret.), Robert McClintock, Robert Murphy, Stewart Rockwell, Kemal Salibi, and Jack Shulimson.

All those who have given help must share in any credit, although they do not necessarily accept my conclusions, nor do they bear responsibility for any errors.

H.K.T.

APPEAL TO FORCE
AMERICAN MILITARY INTERVENTION
IN THE ERA OF CONTAINMENT

WILLIAM NEWMAN
Consulting Editor

CONTENTS

1
OVERT MILITARY INTERVENTION
1

The Puzzle of Overt Military Intervention, *4*
Intervention Past and Present, *8*
Some Theories of Postwar American Intervention, *16*
A Theory of Restraints on Intervention, *20*
Perception of Threat, *22*
Other Restraints on Intervention, *29*
Summary, *36*

2
THE FOUR INTERVENTIONS
41

South Korea, *41*
Lebanon, *45*
South Vietnam, *52*
The Dominican Republic, *60*

3
PERCEPTIONS OF THREAT
69

South Korea, *70*
Lebanon, *74*
South Vietnam, *83*
The Dominican Republic, *87*
Perception and Misperception, *91*

4
RESTRAINTS ON INTERVENTION
93

Fighting the Soviet Union, *94*

Avoiding the Use of Nuclear Weapons, *98*

Preventing a Nonpresidential Veto, *102*

Incremental Decisions, *108*

The Bases for Moral Justification, *117*

Restraints and the Expansion of Intervention, *127*

5
WHERE MILITARY INTERVENTION HAS NOT OCCURRED
131

Threats of Communist Government in "Special Interest Countries," *133*

Threats of Communist Government in "Communist-Threatened Regions," *142*

Threats of Communist Government in "Just Another Country," *162*

Threats of Communist Government in

"Disputed Territory at the Margins of Communist States," *168*

Threats of Something Other Than New Communist Governments, *170*

Developments in Communist States, *171*

Summary, *177*

6
THE PRESENT AND THE FUTURE IN THE UNITED STATES'S USE OF FORCE
179

The Critical Threshold of Overt Military Intervention, *183*

Inflexible Response, *189*

The Future, *193*

Appendix A
CONFLICTS, 1946–71, IN WHICH MILITARY OVERT INTERVENTION BY THE UNITED STATES DID NOT OCCUR
202

A-1: Threats of Communist Government in "Special Interest Countries," *204–5*

A-2: Threats of Communist Government in "Communist-Threatened Regions," *206–7*

A-3: Threats of Communist Government in "Just Another Country," *208–9*

A-4: Threats of Communist Government in "Disputed Territory at the Margins of Communist States," *210–11*

A-5: Threats of Something Other Than New Communist Governments, *212–15*

A-6: Developments in Communist States, *216–17*

CONTENTS

Appendix B
UNITED STATES OVERT MILITARY INTERVENTIONS, 1789–1940
218

SELECTED BIBLIOGRAPHY
227

INDEX
241

1

OVERT MILITARY INTERVENTION

Several times since World War II the United States has openly intervened with military force in the seemingly internal conflicts of other countries: Korea, Lebanon, the Dominican Republic, and Vietnam. Whether condemned or applauded, these interventions must be counted among America's best-known acts in world affairs. They carried with them more than transient significance, both for American politics and for international relations. Although none of these interventions improved a president's hold on his office, the larger of them —Korea and Vietnam—forced the war issue into the presidential campaigns of 1952 and 1968 and may have encouraged the incumbent presidents not to seek reelection in those years. To the world the interventions demonstrated American willingness to use conventional military force, but they sacrificed some of the United States's international image as a peaceful nation. The smaller actions in Lebanon and the Dominican Republic gave clear evidence of the mobility of American military forces but raised questions about the appropriateness with which those forces were used. The interventions in Vietnam and Korea, more controversial and more costly than the other two, commanded the attention of the world's elite, who wanted to know first whether the United States would win and later whether it would know when and how to withdraw.

The appeal to force has usually raised domestic controversy. Presidents Truman and Johnson paid high prices for their parts in Korea and Vietnam. The military intervention in Korea began under Truman in 1950 and preoccupied the last years of his Administration. He was beset by the political right for not attacking China after Peking sent troops to Korea and, by not doing so, for supposedly allowing the war to drag on without victory. He was attacked by some within his own party, who preferred withdrawal to continuance. Truman's popular prestige fell as the war continued. He chose not to run for reelection in 1952, and the populace elected a Republican, who pledged in his campaign that, if elected, he "would go to Korea."

President Johnson shared a similar fate. He did not begin the military action in Vietnam, but he greatly expanded it in 1965. The left attacked him for not withdrawing the troops; the right attacked him for not winning. In the spring of 1968 Johnson was challenged by rival candidates from within his own party, who attacked the war and sought the Democratic nomination for president. Presumably because of criticism of his role in the Vietnam War, Johnson declined to seek renomination that year. At the same time others demanded stronger action in Vietnam. In the election of 1968 one of the most effective third-party presidential campaigns in recent years was run by a team whose appeal was in part to those who wanted more drastic action—and victory—in Southeast Asia. To a much lesser extent the Dominican Republic intervention of 1965 also gave Johnson problems. It was a briefer, smaller act than that in Vietnam. Yet a number of those on the left who later attacked the intervention in Southeast Asia also condemned intervention in the Dominican Republic. Alone among the four military interventions, the Lebanon action of 1958 seemed without domestic controversy. Perhaps because the affair was so brief, because there was no real combat, and because no Americans were killed, President Eisenhower avoided the political attacks made upon other presidents who engaged in military intervention abroad.

The political price of military intervention, however, has not led presidents to abstain from the appeal to force. Every postwar president has had an intimate part in at least one of these actions. Truman had Korea. Eisenhower presided over the end of the Korean War, but he launched intervention in Lebanon. Kennedy approved the beginning of military intervention in Vietnam in 1961 when United States "advisers" first began openly to accompany the South Vietnamese army into battle. Johnson had the Dominican Republic, and he also expanded the war within South Vietnam and extended it to North Vietnam and Laos through air bombardment. Nixon continued the intervention in Southeast Asia, enlarging ground operations to include Cambodia and Laos.

Although every president has approved the use of force abroad, the interventions have not been of equal magnitude. All were large by nineteenth-century standards, but Korea and Vietnam were much larger than the others. Lebanon, the smallest, employed more than 14,000 troops; the Dominican action used about 22,000. Korea and Vietnam required several hundred thousand men each. The larger operations were also more costly in lives, dollars, and destruction. More than 33,000 American soldiers died in Korea, and the figure for Vietnam is several thousand higher. The Korean War cost at least $20 billion in direct expenditures, not including the lingering costs for veterans and interest on debts incurred. Vietnam has cost even more. During the peak years of 1967 and 1968, direct expenditures approached $25 billion a year. It is a major irony that the United States, which has contributed more than $100 billion in economic and military assistance to other countries in the postwar period, has spent even more on the direct and indirect costs of its military interventions. And the costs were not all American. In Korea total combat deaths were at least 2 million. Deaths among civilians may have been even higher. How many have died in Southeast Asia cannot yet be estimated, but the number must be high, because the United States has dropped more bombs on Southeast Asia than were dropped in all preceding wars put together.

Korea, Vietnam, the Dominican Republic, and Lebanon were distinctive events in postwar history. It is true that the United States intervened in different ways in the affairs of other countries in the period. In return for aid it shaped the military and economic development programs of many nations. United States military bases and American investments are scattered throughout the world, and in some places mere presence is influential. Covert part was taken in a variety of conflicts, from the support of the anti-Mossadegh coup in Iran in 1953 to the training and support of Cuban exiles who invaded Cuba's Bay of Pigs in 1961. But Korea, Vietnam, the Dominican Republic, and Lebanon received a blatant form of intervention—overt military intervention.

Overt military intervention is the open and direct use of military force by one country in another. The use of such force can be seen in four kinds of action. One is the deploying of combat-ready units to another country. "Combat ready" means the forces are prepared to move against possibly defended objectives without prior authorization from central military headquarters. Overt military intervention in Lebanon began in this way: on July 15, 1958, United States Marines landed on the beaches of Beirut. The 1965 military intervention in the Dominican Republic also began in this way, although the Marines arrived in helicopters rather than over the beaches. A second act of overt military intervention is shelling another country from ships at sea. No United States military intervention since World War II has begun this way, but naval shelling is a traditional use of military might. Although the interventions in Korea and Vietnam did not so begin, they eventually included naval bombardment. A third is bombing or firing missiles on another country from planes or missile sites. The intervention in South Korea began with bombing-strafing operations in the last week of June 1950. The fourth and last form of overt military intervention is providing close combat support to another country's forces in battle. "Close combat support" is a form of military assistance that occurs when a country provides essential nonmedical services at the scene of battle in such a way as to expose its own military personnel to combat. The military intervention in South Vietnam began with close combat support in December 1961, when the United States Air Force began flying units of South Vietnam's army into battle. By this definition there have been only four overt military interventions by the United States since World War II: in South Korea, later expanded to North Korea; in Lebanon; in South Vietnam, later expanded to North Vietnam, Laos, and Cambodia; and in the Dominican Republic.

THE PUZZLE OF OVERT MILITARY INTERVENTION

The blatancy of overt military intervention raises the question of its use. Why does the United States resort to it? America is supposed to be a peace-loving nation; at least many Americans like to think it is. The United States officially subscribes to the principle of national self-determination and to the United Nations Charter, which embodies that principle. Yet the use of military force in the affairs of other countries appears on its face to contradict the spirit of that principle and of the Charter. The appeal to force is often costly in lives, in dollars, and, for the incumbent president, in popular prestige as well. The countries that have experienced American military intervention do not seem to be intrinsically important ones. The postwar competition between the United States and the Soviet Union conferred some importance on Korea, Lebanon, Vietnam, and the Dominican Republic. Washington thought that each of these countries was threatened with Communist government. Nevertheless, it is puzzling that America resorted to force, since the arsenal of alternative actions is large, ranging from tolerance or the utterance of threats to covert action or the giving of money and armaments.

Why America resorts to force is but half the puzzle; the other half is why it does not do so more often. Open entry with military force into the conflicts of others four times in the space of a quarter-century is assuredly interesting. Yet it is equally interesting that the United States has openly intervened in only four of the more than one hundred conflicts threatening governments abroad since World War II (see Appendices A-1 to A-6). Conflict has been the common lot of nations in the postwar period. A number of wars have been fought between states. India and Pakistan battled more than once in Kashmir, fighting on a large scale in 1965; and they met again in East Pakistan in 1971, during Bangladesh's war for independence. China and India fought on their joint border from 1959 to 1962. Israel, France, and Britain invaded Suez in 1956; and Israel, Syria, Jordan, Lebanon, and the United Arab Republic engaged in brief but fierce war in 1967. The Soviet Union invaded Czechoslovakia in 1968. Other wars were less spectacular. Honduras and Nicaragua fought in 1957. El Salvador and Honduras were enemies in the "football war" of 1969. Nicaragua had a major border conflict with Costa Rica in 1955, and Morocco and Algeria had a similar dispute in 1962–63. Egypt invaded northern Sudan in 1958. In 1961 India seized Goa and the other Portuguese enclaves on the Indian subcontinent. China and the Soviet Union battled along the Ussuri River in 1969. Indonesia disputed with the Dutch over West Irian in 1962 and engaged in "confrontation" with Malaysia from 1963 to 1966. Ethiopia and Somalia conflicted sporadically on their border throughout most of the 1960's. In 1954 and 1958 the People's Republic of China bombarded offshore islands claimed by it and the Republic of China.

More than enough wars have occurred since World War II. Even more marked, however, has been the absence of domestic tranquillity, particularly in less-developed countries. Many disorders were struggles for independence from colonial powers. Algeria, Cyprus, Indonesia, Indochina, Kenya, Aden, Angola, Brunei, the French Cameroons, Madagascar, Malaya, Morocco, Mozambique, Palestine, Spanish Morocco, and Tunisia all suffered major armed conflict that could wholly or in part be ascribed to a struggle for independence from European colonial masters. Other conflicts arose in new nations recently independent. Laos, Cyprus, South Vietnam, the Congo, Indonesia, the Philippines, Burma, Rwanda and Burundi, India, South Yemen, Chad, and Nigeria each suffered protracted conflict shortly after gaining independence.

Older nations, too, suffered internal strife. Latin America has been turbulent throughout the postwar period. In the late 1940's and the 1950's revolts, civil wars, or contested coups occurred in Haiti, Bolivia, Costa Rica, Guatemala, Paraguay, Peru, Argentina, Colombia, Venezuela, and Cuba. The 1960's saw guerrilla wars in Bolivia, Brazil, Colombia, Guatemala, Panama, Peru, and Venezuela. Briefer disorders afflicted British Guiana in 1962, the Dominican Republic in 1961 and 1965, and Nicaragua, Argentina, and Venezuela in 1960. There were, in addition, brief invasions by exiles in Haiti in 1963 and Cuba in 1961. The Near East has also been noted for its instability. At one time or another since World War II most of the states of the region have been rent by domestic armed turmoil: Iran, Iraq, Jordan, Syria, the Sudan, Yemen, Muscat and Oman, and Egypt, not to mention Lebanon. Established nations in other regions have not been spared. Burma in the late 1940's and the 1950's, Thailand beginning in 1965, Cambodia in 1969 (fifteen years after independence), Pakistan in 1971 (more than two decades after independence), China, Greece, Hungary, and even Northern Ireland have suffered large-scale internal violence.

Several of these conflicts have had such clear significance that it is puzzling that the United States did not openly use military force in them. The Chinese civil war that had begun between Mao Tse-tung's supporters and Chiang Kai-shek's government before World War II continued after the war and ended in 1949 with Mao's victory and the Nationalist government's fleeing to Formosa. America's posture toward the People's Republic of China was less than unfriendly; for years the United States did not even deign to recognize the new government and worked actively to exclude it from the United Nations, to discourage trade with it, and to dissuade other countries from forming diplomatic ties with the Communist regime. During the civil war the Truman Administration provided large sums in military assistance to the Nationalist government—perhaps $2 billion in all—but did not commit United States forces to combat in the war. When Chiang's government "fell," Republican members of Congress immediately charged that the Democrats had given China away by not intervening militarily.

Indochina raises a similar question. The Viet Minh under Ho Chi Minh's leadership began systematically to battle the French and the

OVERT MILITARY INTERVENTION

French colonial government in 1946. The United States began to provide large-scale assistance to the French effort in 1950, and by 1954 America was paying the major portion of France's cost. But by the spring of 1954, with the encirclement of the French garrison at Dienbienphu, it became apparent that the Viet Minh were winning and that the French government was interested in withdrawing. Although a plan was formed for American air intervention at Dienbienphu, it was not used. No American combat forces were committed and North Vietnam passed to Ho Chi Minh's control. Not until years later, when conflict engulfed South Vietnam, did the United States appeal to military force. The question is obvious: If the United States would fight in South Vietnam in 1961, why would it not do so in Indochina in 1954?

The United States did not intervene in Hungary either, when a popular revolt broke out in Budapest at the end of October 1956. A rebel-formed coalition government under Imre Nagy appealed for help when Russian troops intervened to suppress the uprising. The Eisenhower Administration took no action, not even providing military equipment to the Nagy government. Inaction exposed Eisenhower to some of the same criticism leveled at Truman over China, although there was not so much of it.

The Kennedy Administration's behavior in the Bay of Pigs invasion of Cuba in 1961 is also puzzling. Fidel Castro assumed power in Cuba in 1959 after a three-year guerrilla war. Soon he announced that his was a socialist government. Yet America had taken no part in the war that preceded Castro's rise to power. The Eisenhower Administration did approve after 1959 a Central Intelligence Agency plan to covertly train Cuban exiles in military tactics and land them on Cuba's shore. With approval from the Kennedy Administration the plan was executed at the Bay of Pigs in April 1961. The venture was a failure, and the invaders were captured within a week. One wonders why so risky and ill-prepared an act was taken. Yet it is perhaps even more surprising that the Kennedy Administration took no military steps to back up the invaders once they began to lose. Why was Washington willing to support an invasion covertly but unwilling to support that move with overt force when the country at issue was too weak to resist effectively?

The same question must be asked of every other occasion on which the United States failed to respond with military force. Why did it not take action when Russia invaded Czechoslovakia in 1968? Why did it not intervene in the conflicts of Syria, Jordan, Iraq, or Iran, since it did so in Lebanon? Why did it resort to blatant military action only in the Dominican Republic among Latin American nations? Why did it not do so during the civil war in Cuba that led to Castro's assumption of power? Why has it taken no part in any of Haiti's disorders?

The full puzzle of American overt military intervention is why the United States resorts to force at some times and places but not others. Is there a pattern in America's appeal to force such that a theory can explain both military intervention and the more frequent absence of military intervention?

INTERVENTION PAST AND PRESENT

The question asked by this book—why has the United States appealed to open force in Korea, Lebanon, the Dominican Republic, and Vietnam but not elsewhere—presumes that there *is* a pattern to American overt military intervention since World War II. It is not assumed that there is one pattern to the entire history of American military action. Before World War II the conditions for the resort to force seem to have been different. One main difference is that postwar military intervention has occurred only when the top leaders of the United States perceived a threat that a new Communist party government might be established. Such a threat was perceived in Korea, Lebanon, the Dominican Republic, and Vietnam. There were many overt military interventions before 1941. Appendix B lists more than one hundred such acts. Yet in only two of these situations did Washington foresee the possibility of the formation of a new Communist government: in Russia and Nicaragua. United States troops joined forces with those of Great Britain, France, and Japan in northern and far eastern Russia in 1918 during World War I and remained until 1920. The joint forces occasionally fought Bolshevik units during those two years, when the Wilson Administration realized that a Communist regime was emerging in Russia. The United States also intervened in Nicaragua's civil war during the late 1920's and the early 1930's, when American Marines landed in 1926 and remained until 1933. United States policy-makers saw no Communist threat when troops were first dispatched; that came only later, when Augusto Sandino emerged as the opposition leader and began to attract international leftist support. The Nicaraguan campaign was thus unlike post-World War II interventions, where the perception of a Communist threat has preceded the resort to overt force. Yet even if one assumes that Nicaragua as well as Russia shared with the post-World War II actions a Washington perception of Communist threat, there were more than one hundred other prewar interventions in which communism was not seen as a threat. There are other differences, however, between pre-World War II and post-World War II interventions. Throughout most of the earlier period the use (and nonuse) of force by the United States exhibited central tendencies at particular times but no consistent pattern. The general inconsistency is most evident if prewar history is divided into segments and the periods are examined individually.

Between 1800, the year of the first overt military intervention by the United States, and 1865 American force was usually used under three kinds of conditions: the suppression of piracy, the suppression of slave trading, and, occasionally, the protection of American lives and property in conflicts in Latin America and the Far East. Some interventions, however, were inconsistent with these central tendencies. During the quasi-war with France, United States Marines and seamen in 1800 aided the Dutch at Curaçao to resist the encroachments of French forces. The same year, without Washington's direction, the crew of an American warship captured the Spanish fort at Puerto Plata, Puerto Rico, spiking the guns. The latter action was a curious one as neither piracy, slave trading, nor American lives were at stake, nor were Spain and France allies against the Dutch. Other hard-to-explain actions were the adventures of Captain John Williams in 1811–12 fighting Spaniards and Indians in Spanish Florida, and Andrew Jackson's similar expedition in 1818. Neither of these actions was explicitly directed by top United States leaders, and neither had to do directly with piracy, slave trading, or the protection of American lives. More curious yet were the two landings in Greece in 1827 to burn pirate towns. To be sure, these actions involved the suppression of piracy, but the Monroe Doctrine, released in 1823 at the time Greek rebels were seeking United States assistance in their war of independence, had pledged that America would not become involved in European conflicts—especially those in Greece. Perhaps most startling of all the interventions was Commodore Thomas Jones's seizure of Monterey in 1843. Jones thought that war with Mexico had begun and gave Monterey back upon realizing his mistake. There were also a number of interventions undertaken without Washington's approval in retaliation for acts against American seamen or consular officials. Commodore David Porter landed at Fajardo, Puerto Rico, in 1824, demanding reparations for insults and damages. Porter was later court-martialed for exceeding his authority. Lieutenant Charles Wilkes was more fortunate. On the return leg of a voyage that had verified the location of Antarctica, Wilkes's squadron stopped at several South Sea islands. At Fiji in July 1840, Samoa in February 1841, and Drummond Island in the Gilberts in April 1841, crewmen were killed by natives. Each time, one or more native villages were destroyed in retaliation. Other retaliatory actions were taken at Qualla Battoo, Sumatra, in 1839; Okinawa in 1854; and Fiji in 1858. But United States forces did not always retaliate when American seamen were injured or slain abroad. Incidents were common in the first half of the nineteenth century, and retaliation occurred only occasionally.

A major reason for the contradictions of the early nineteenth century was that local military commanders could and did use military force without the explicit approval of the president. Only in the twentieth century have top policy-makers habitually approved overt military intervention. This is understandable. For the president to insist that he must approve every overt act, there must be means for swift communication between Washington and United States military units stationed in other countries and at sea. The small number of navy ships before the Civil War, their dispersion, and their slowness made swift communication by ship-carried message impossible. The situation improved somewhat after the Civil War, when the navy had many more and newer vessels. Instantaneous communication has been possible only in this century—the radio telegraph was not invented until 1895. The relative freedom of local commanders in the earlier conflicts therefore created contradictions. Decisions to intervene were not made by one man or one small group of men at the top. The decisions were made by many men, acting individually, who had little contact with one another and whose notions of what was right and of what was practical in the use of force differed widely.

The period 1865 to 1928 embodies contradictions, too. The tendency during that time was to land troops when there was conflict in Latin America and the Far East. Usually, the forces merely seized control of those areas in key cities where American citizens lived or had possessions; sometimes, however, they also fought on the side of the established government against revolutionaries. But the United States did not intervene in all conflicts in Latin America and the Far East, and force was occasionally used elsewhere. United States Marines were used in conflicts at Alexandria, Egypt, in 1882, at Beirut, Syria, in 1903, and at Tangiers, Morocco, in 1904; but they were not deployed in any other of the many conflicts in the Near East and North Africa during the period. Some Latin American conflicts were conspicuously avoided. Among the major Latin American conflicts in which the United States did not intervene were Jamaica, 1865; Argentina, 1874–75; Colombia, 1876–77; the war between Chile, Peru, and Bolivia, 1879–83; Argentina, 1880; Brazil, 1892–94; Peru, 1894–95; and the war between the Dutch at Curaçao and Venezuela, 1908. Perhaps most striking is that no troops were sent to Cuba to protect American lives and property in the long and destructive revolution in Cuba, 1868–78, although the island was later invaded and placed under American rule in 1898, when internal strife was much less significant. The entry into World War I was also unprecedented. Although the act was publicly defended as protecting the lives of Americans traveling at sea, the war was primarily a quarrel among major European nations, and the United States had previously refrained from joining wars between major nations on the European continent.

After the American Civil War, and particularly after 1900, most military interventions were authorized in Washington. This permitted somewhat greater order in the use of force than had existed before, but until 1928, whether the United States intervened in a particular conflict seemed to depend on who was president. President Grant personally opposed intervention in Cuba, while President McKinley embraced it. No military force was used abroad under Rutherford B. Hayes. Theodore Roosevelt, however, threatened and demonstrated a readiness to use force all over the world, from Central America and the Caribbean to Korea, Morocco, and Syria. After 1928 the personality of the president was less conspicuous in where, or even whether, force was used. After 1928 there is no seeming link between a president's belligerence or pacificity and the resort to military intervention. President Hoover began no interventions but he continued those in Nicaragua and Haiti. One military intervention began under Franklin Roosevelt (World War II), Truman (Korea), Eisenhower (Lebanon), Kennedy (Vietnam), and Johnson (the Dominican Republic). As of mid-1972, Nixon had not started a new military intervention, although he enlarged the Vietnam war to include ground action in Cambodia and Laos. Nor is there an apparent relationship between a president's stated policies and America's use of force after 1928. Although President Eisenhower's secretary of state, John Foster Dulles, announced a policy to "roll back communism" in 1953, no military intervention began in a Communist state during Eisenhower's term of office. Although John Kennedy announced upon becoming president in January 1961 new cooperative policies for the United States in the world, close combat support began in South Vietnam in December of that year.

The period from 1928 to December 1941 is the first to exhibit an evident pattern in the use of overt military intervention. During that time no new interventions were begun, although the action already started in Nicaragua was continued until 1933, and Marine officers continued to lead the Gendarmerie d'Haiti in Haiti until 1934. The United States abstained from conflicts thought to threaten new Communist governments, as the Spanish civil war, 1936–39, and the Chinese civil war between the Kuomintang and Mao Tse-tung's forces that began in 1927. There was no overt military intervention in China despite the stationing of several thousand Marines in Shanghai, Peking, and the Tientsin area by early 1928. These Marines were not authorized to attack any objectives held by either Kuomintang or Communists. The United States also avoided the destructive Chaco War of 1930–35 between Paraguay and Bolivia, as well as the revolts in Brazil and Ecuador in 1932. American lives were threatened or lost and American property was damaged in all three of these Latin American conflicts. In an earlier era such threats to American lives might have led to the use of open force. Nor did American force counter the Japanese invasion of Manchuria that began in 1931—not even when Japan captured Shanghai, where United States Marines had often been used before—nor Italy's assault on Ethiopia in 1935–37, nor Germany's defeat of Poland in 1939 or its occupation of France and the Low Countries in 1940.

America from 1928 to December 1941 was both isolationist and noninterventionist. The United States consistently abstained from the resort to force in new conflicts. Neither before nor after these thirteen years did America abstain from military action for prolonged periods. Six years was as long as the United States had been able to restrain itself before 1928, and such periods occurred only twice after 1800: between 1876 and 1882 and earlier during the Civil War, 1860 to 1866. Even during other supposedly isolationist years, as 1920 to 1928, American military force was repeatedly used abroad.

World War II ended the thirteen-year era of nonintervention. In 1941–45 the United States fought the largest war of its history. Entry into war in December 1941 was not surprising, since Japan had blatantly attacked Pearl Harbor, thereby providing the occasion for American retaliation. Before the attack on Pearl Harbor, however, United States policy-makers ignored many lesser provocations; in the era of nonintervention nothing short of direct attack could spur the United States to the use of military force. After World War II America did not revert to the prewar habit of abstention. Although it was never attacked directly, nor threatened with the immediate prospect of such an attack, Washington authorized overt military intervention four times. One presumes that there is a precise pattern to these postwar interventions.

Periods of American history before 1928 fail to exhibit precise patterns in the use of military intervention. They show no more than central tendencies. Periods after 1928 do exhibit patterns, although the nature of the pattern is different for the years 1928 to December 1941 and the years after 1945. The centralization of decisions on the use of force contributed to this change. In the early nineteenth century, patterns were not possible because decisions were often made by local commanders who followed their own peculiar instincts. But the emergence of greater order in the practice of military intervention after 1928 is more closely associated with the decline in the importance of presidential personality. When presidents' personalities were important, patterns of intervention tended to end with a president's term; all that united longer periods were vague tendencies. This was the case before 1928; after 1928 it was not. Franklin Roosevelt continued one pattern begun under Herbert Hoover, and Presidents Eisenhower, Kennedy, Johnson, and Nixon, it is assumed, perpetuated a pattern begun under Truman.

One explanation sometimes offered for why it is that who is president no longer matters so much is that recent presidents are more like each other than were those in the past. The radical right and the new left in American politics both charge that key leaders of government are selected only from the middle of the political spectrum and that the public is not offered a true choice between competing personalities and ideologies. There is some truth to this charge. The true extremist rarely tries to get elected to high office, nor does he often seek appointment to a key post. Those who are at the margins of the middle —as George Wallace and Barry Goldwater on the right, and Eugene MaCarthy on the left—have sometimes sought the presidency, but they have been unsuccessful. To the extent that this has been true of leaders since Herbert Hoover, however, it was also true in earlier times. Andrew Jackson, elected in 1828, may have been the last and perhaps the only president whose values and cultural background were markedly different from those of the man who preceded him.

The great change that became evident after 1928 was not the narrowing of the group from which presidents are drawn; rather, that change was the altering of the president's role in decisions on foreign affairs. Before that time the president was more important in the process of making choices, making more of the decisions alone or in consultation with only his secretary of state. Presidents do not make their decisions alone any longer. Since the late 1920's there has been an increasing tendency toward group decision-making.[1] Especially since Franklin Roosevelt assumed office, there has been a dramatic growth in the machinery of the federal government at all levels, including the apparatus for top-level decision making. Even President Johnson, who reportedly liked to keep his own counsel, discussed intervention in the Dominican Republic in 1965 with a half-dozen other key policymakers before he approved it. When several persons are involved in the making of decisions on whether or not to employ force, the impact of the president's individual values and interests is diluted, and other influences can exert greater force.

The tendency toward group decision-making in foreign affairs became more marked after World War II, and several factors have led to this continued development. For one, the president has not always had so many advisers. Franklin Roosevelt was the first to create a White House staff of large size; before his Administration the president had only a few clerks. During World War II, with both the need for secrecy and the larger scale of presidential tasks, the White House developed a bureaucracy of its own.[2] Secretaries of state also were better able to inform presidents about the state of the world and of the activities of American diplomatic and military establishments. As late as 1913 the office building on the corner of Seventeenth Street and Pennsylvania Avenue, next to the White House, housed the Navy, War, and State departments. Today it can hold but a part of the Executive Office of the President. As the agencies grew, they came to do too many things for the secretary of state to know about all of them. The same agencies began to write too many reports about the state of the world for the secretary of state to assimilate them all. The growth in the volume of information on hand, the expansion in the number and size of programs administered by federal agencies in the area of foreign affairs, and the practice of security classification, which limits free exchange of information, have restricted every man's share of the total knowledge available, including the president's. Even if the president wished to make important decisions alone, he would not know enough to do it well. The same factors have made specialists of most of the key advisers, which means that the president cannot get all the infor-

[1] Joseph de Rivera's chapter "Interpersonal Relations: The Small Group" takes as its starting assumption the pervasiveness of group decision-making at top levels of American government since World War II. *The Psychological Dimension of Foreign Policy* (Columbus, Ohio: Charles E. Merrill, 1968), pp. 207–44.

[2] Richard E. Neustadt, "Approaches to Staffing the Presidency," *American Political Science Review*, Vol. 57 (December 1963), p. 859.

mation he wants from just one adviser, even an exceptionally able one. Nor can the president any longer know enough always to ask the right questions and thus be able to meet his advisers one by one. In order to bring to bear the wide range of information that is available, especially when time is too short to draft papers and circulate them for comment, the major leaders of government must meet as a group.

Not only is more information available today—more than a president alone can master—but information is also more necessary. Two changes have made the costs of wrong decisions greater than they were in earlier times. From the end of the War of 1812 until World War I the United States was an unchallenged insular power. Its acts did not have grave or obvious consequences for the state of the world as a whole. Since American leaders did not seek much influence outside the Western Hemisphere, they did not have to worry about challenges to global influence. After World War I the United States was a major power, while after World War II it became a global one, whether or not its people or leaders wanted it to be. Thereafter its actions had great impact on the rest of the world, and events abroad had direct significance for America's position of global power. Second, the creation of nuclear weapons radically increased the risks involved in unwanted war abroad. These two changes together may serve to undermine a president's confidence in making foreign policy decisions alone. They may make him more psychologically dependent on others in making major choices, which may partly explain why decisions on the use of force since World War II have generally been group decisions, with advisers not limited merely to proffering information to the president.

Not all top-level decisions since 1928, of course, have been group decisions. The president can and does sometimes act on his own. This happens occasionally even on military decisions. President Truman on June 30, 1950, approved by telephone, and without holding a meeting of advisers, a request from General MacArthur for the commitment to Korea of a regimental combat team of the United States Army. This was an expansion of the overt military intervention already taking place through air and naval action. President Johnson, too, reportedly made some choices on the conduct of the war in Southeast Asia either alone or in consultation with only one or two advisers. Nevertheless, decisions by the president alone generally have been relatively minor ones. Decisions regarded as critical have always been made in group meetings. The beginning of overt military intervention in a region has been regarded as a critical decision.

SOME THEORIES OF POSTWAR AMERICAN INTERVENTION

The differences between America's use of force before and after World War II make it difficult to explain the entire history with one theory. If the postwar period is the area of concern, as here, it is easier to build a theory only for this period. This has been done before, but the efforts are not fully satisfactory.[3] The popular theories tend to share a common failing: Most of them provide some reason for the military interventions that America has undertaken, but they do not adequately explain the more frequent absence of military action. To

---

[3] Most of the literature on American military intervention since World War II has been more concerned with what the United States ought to do than with explaining American actions. There have been some attempts to explain interventions, but most of these have been designed as condemnations at the expense of explanatory power, such as Richard J. Barnet, *Intervention and Revolution* (New York: World Publishing Company, 1968); Juan Bosch, *Pentagonism: A Substitute for Imperialism* (New York: Grove Press, 1968); Theodore Draper, *The Abuse of Power* (New York: Viking Press, 1967); Pierre Gallois, "U.S. Foreign Policy: A Study of Military Strength and Diplomatic Weakness," *Orbis,* Vol. 9 (Summer 1965), pp. 338–57; Gabriel Kolko, *The Roots of American Foreign Policy* (Boston: Beacon Press, 1969); Carl Oglesby and Richard Shaull, *Containment and Change* (New York: Macmillan, 1967); Merlo J. Pusey, *The Way We Go to War* (Boston: Houghton Mifflin, 1969); and Ronald Steel, *Pax Americana* (New York: Viking Press, 1967). Provocative ideas but no general theory of American use of force are to be found in Richard M. Pfeffer, ed., *No More Vietnams? The War and the Future of American Foreign Policy* (New York: Harper & Row, 1968), and Adam Yarmolinsky, "American Foreign Policy and the Decision to Intervene," *Journal of International Affairs,* Vol. 22 (Summer 1968), pp. 231–35. There have been some other efforts toward explaining military intervention by all states; these are interesting but they do not yet permit precise predictions. Among these are Karl W. Deutsch, "External Involvement in Internal War," in *Internal War,* ed. Harry W. Eckstein (New York: Free Press of Glencoe, 1964), pp. 100–10; James N. Rosenau, "The Concept of Intervention," *Journal of International Affairs,* Vol. 22 (Summer 1968), pp. 165–76; Urs Schwarz, *Confrontation and Intervention in the Modern World* (Dobbs Ferry, N.Y.: Oceana Publications, 1970); Oran R. Young, "Intervention and International Systems," *Journal of International Affairs,* Vol. 22 (Summer 1968), pp. 177–87; and several articles in *International Aspects of Civil Strife,* ed. James N. Rosenau (Princeton: Princeton University Press, 1964), including Karl W. Deutsch and Morton A. Kaplan, "The Limits of International Coalitions," pp. 170–84; Morton A. Kaplan, "Intervention in Internal War: Some Systemic Sources," pp. 92–121; George Modelski, "The International Relations of Internal War," pp. 14–44; and James N. Rosenau, "Internal War as an International Event," pp. 45–91.

put the point more formally, the popular theories tend to assert necessary but not sufficient conditions for military intervention.

Simpler theories posit motive forces to explain the action. What is taken as the motive force depends on whether the author is a defender or critic of American foreign policy. Defenders are kinder in the reasons they offer. One explanation sometimes heard even from official spokesmen is that the United States resorts to force in order to protect American lives and property—a time-honored defense of military intervention that has been used to legitimize force by other countries and in earlier times. It is true that the conflicts in which America intervened did threaten American lives and property. But in the postwar world American citizens and property repose in nearly every country, and almost any conflict threatens them. A different defense, and a common one, is that the United States intervenes to help other countries resist outside aggression, especially Communist aggression. That there was aggression by outsiders in the Dominican Republic prior to the landing of American Marines is exceptionable. That there was Communist aggression in Lebanon is also open to dispute. To cover all the instances of American overt military intervention, one has to include what Secretary of State John Foster Dulles called "indirect aggression"—the giving of money, equipment, leadership, or encouragement from other countries to insurgents. Indirect involvement by aid or leadership is commonplace in postwar conflicts, however. Its presence only rarely produces American military intervention. Nor is it enough to say that the United States intervenes to restore peace, for only seldom does it do so. Breaches of international peace as blatant as the Soviet Union's invasion of Czechoslovakia or El Salvador's war with Honduras and breaches of domestic peace as destructive of human life as the conflicts in the Sudan, Pakistan, the Congo, and Nigeria have failed to produce American military action. Also, the interventions in Korea and Vietnam prolonged wars that would probably have soon ended had America not joined them.

Unofficial defenders of American foreign policy can be more candid. They sometimes argue that the United States is engaged in a struggle with the "Communist bloc" and that military intervention is used to contain communism. That Washington perceived a risk of Communist government in each country where overt military action was approved gives some credence to this explanation. Yet as theory it has the same failing as the other defenses. From China to Chile there have been many countries where a Communist government was possible, but the United States has used direct force in only a few of them.

Critics of American foreign policy have been more inventive in asserting motive forces behind American use of military intervention, but they have not been more successful in explaining it. Some liberal critics have charged that America has lost the sense of her revolutionary origins and now acts as a conservative power to curtail change in the world. More radical critics may simply assert that the United States is an imperialist power that intervenes to protect its investments and economic dominance in other countries. But the United States does not use military force to curtail all change or even all revolutionary change. The charge of "American imperialism" is similar to the "to protect American lives and property" theory, only cast in condemnatory language.

Another explanation used by critics of American behavior focuses upon the means of international interaction as well the purposes of United States foreign policy. It suggests that the United States has formed the habit of using military tactics to solve its problems in the world either because it is too unimaginative or too unskillful to use less blatant techniques, or simply because traditional diplomacy has lately failed it. Theodore Draper and Pierre Gallois, among others, have expressed this thesis in interesting ways.[4] The notion is useful when applied to some questions. It helps explain why the United States used military might rather than negotiation in Vietnam and the Dominican Republic, but it cannot explain why forms of action other than military intervention are still the most frequently used tools.

Less satisfying are those attacks that claim some group prone to intervene dominates foreign policy decisions. The dominant group is sometimes asserted to be the armed services or, collectively, the "Pentagon." More popular among the new left is the argument that a "military-industrial complex" of high leaders in the armed services and business control American policy. Peculiar to Richard Barnet is the contention that a body of bureaucrats, labeled "national security managers," who think of America as the world's policeman make or vitally shape the choice of actions in world affairs.[5] There is, of course, an empirical question as to whether the posited groups do in fact make or control American foreign policy decisions. But even were the assertions correct, these theories would not answer our question. All that they can explain is why intervention happens; they cannot explain why it often doesn't. If some nefarious group habituated to intervention controls the decision-making process, the United States should take

[4] Draper, *op. cit.*; Gallois, *op. cit.*   [5] Barnet, *op. cit.*

drastic steps any time there is an appropriate stimulus from conflict, revolution, or a threat of communism abroad. It doesn't.

A theory that merely states a force impelling toward the use of intervention is inadequate to explain the frequent absence of military intervention. To work, a theory must include limits, too. More complex theories do include some kinds of countervailing factors. We may dismiss those theories that state that the limit is the need for drastic action and the ability of the United States to take it at that time and place. These theories beg the question of what constitutes "need" or "ability." Taken literally, the United States has had the ability to use military force nearly anywhere on the globe since World War II, and whether force was really needed is often known only after the fact. In retrospect one could say that military intervention was not really necessary in the Dominican Republic or Lebanon. Worse, one cannot say that the United States failed to intervene in China or Indochina because it was not necessary or because it did not have the means to do so.

More often, theories of intervention explain the absence of action by positing a geographical limit, such as a "sphere of influence." An example of such a theory is the one that asserts that the United States intervenes to contain communism within its sphere of influence. The concept of sphere of influence is fuzzy around its edges, however. It is certainly true that the United States is more likely to use force in some countries than in others, but the concept has traditionally meant much more than this. In the nineteenth century the major European nations delineated areas in Asia where each had the power, and the willingness, to use force to work its will. In their areas of influence the major powers not only threatened to use force against the encroachments of other major nations but they also dominated the local governments. American control over the Western Hemisphere today approximates this nineteenth-century phenomenon; the Soviet Union's control over Eastern Europe is similar. Outside these regions, however, it is most difficult to determine what is in America's or Russia's sphere of influence, because neither power has that traditional combination of dominance of local governments and ability and willingness to use force against others in most of the rest of the world. Thus the concept makes little sense when applied to some of the regions where the United States has intervened. If, for example, the United States did not intervene in China in the 1940's because China was outside America's sphere of influence, why was China's neighbor Korea inside it in 1950 when the United States intervened there? Theories that use a notion of a sphere of influence often define what the "sphere" includes in a circular manner. The sphere of influence is often taken to include those regions where the United States has demonstrated willingness to use force. Such definitions do not permit using the concept to explain military intervention. Definitions of geographical limit that avoid circularity are also usually inadequate. It is true that the United States is more likely to take *some* action in regions such as Europe and Latin America than elsewhere when it is thought that a country is threatened with Communist government. Theories that include only a geographical limit, however, do not illuminate why one kind of action is taken over another. The choice of military intervention over covert action, the giving of money or military equipment, a show of force, a verbal threat, or a diplomatic note is left unexplained.

A THEORY OF RESTRAINTS ON INTERVENTION

The puzzle of intervention can be approached either by looking for forces impelling toward intervention or by searching for factors that restrain its use. As it happens, most of the popular theories look for forces behind intervention. Herein lies their weakness. In order to predict a set of actions as different as those in Korea, Lebanon, the Dominican Republic, and Vietnam, the forces behind intervention must be stated broadly. Broadly stated forces tend to predict that the United States should have intervened where it did not. But many of the popular theories do offer plausible explanations for the interventions that happened. The desire to protect American lives does seem to be a force urging intervention, and it may be part of the motivation behind all four actions. So, too, "containment fever" seems a force for American military intervention, and also part of the motivation for each intervention that occurred. Other statements of the force behind intervention are also credible. There does seem to be some merit to the assertions that the desire to resist aggression, the desire to protect the peace, the desire to protect investments, and the intolerance of change all act to encourage the resort to force. As theories, these statements of motives behind intervention compete with one another, but as demands upon decision-makers, they are probably all present at one time or another. In fact, there are a host of demands for American military action, and most situations that gain international attention generate one or more.

The structure of world politics can generate demands. In the eyes of many Americans and in the view of some of America's allies, the United States engages the Soviet Union, the People's Republic of China, and other Communist states in a global struggle for control of the world. The expansion of a Communist state, the possibility of a new one, or the opportunity to overthrow or weaken a Communist government can stimulate demands for American intervention. Different demands may arise when communism is not involved. Since World War II the United States has assumed the posture of protector of the world's peace; at least, American presidents and secretaries of state have so often cited the United States's commitment to peace that many Americans and some foreign nations expect the United States to back that commitment with action. When peace is threatened, they may demand American action to protect it by punishing or defending against the aggressor or imposing a cease-fire on both belligerents.

America's friends and allies abroad constitute another source of demands. Many, but not all, were enlisted to help in the global contest with communism. But friendly and allied governments can become embroiled in regional conflicts unrelated to the global contest. When they do, they may demand American assistance to help them in their individual causes.

Other demands are encouraged by the nature of American politics. Americans traditionally expect their government to protect the economic well-being of individuals. Those who have invested abroad and suffered expropriation or restriction can demand that their interests be protected, and they may receive sympathetic support from other Americans. The national government is also expected to protect the lives of Americans abroad. When American lives are threatened, there is instant demand for military force to protect them. And when American "honor" is offended, as when North Korea seized the *Pueblo* or when Vice-President Nixon was stoned in Caracas, some popular sentiment can still be stirred to demand retaliation. Demands of this sort were more effective before World War II, when men in Washington were not so seriously concerned with the global implications of their actions. Yet these demands are still expressed, and they yet have some effect.

There were demands for intervention in Korea, Lebanon, the Dominican Republic, and Vietnam; but there were demands for intervention in many other situations, too. Indeed, nearly every conflict generates demands for American policy-makers to resort to force. If conflict abroad almost always engenders demands for American military action, it is not the demands or the forces or purposes that embody them that explain whether or not the United States intervenes. If we take for granted that there is always a push for American military action, it is the restraints upon intervention that determine whether or not it occurs. To put it crassly, we will assume that the United States is always tempted to go to war; what counts is what holds it back. This is an uncomfortable assumption. We do not like to think of ourselves as warlike. Yet, as Warner Levi has suggested, one reason we have found it difficult to explain the occurrence of war and violence may be our habit of always looking for the factors causing war rather than for those maintaining peace.[6]

One can imagine a large number of things that could restrain the use of force. To make the theory simple, however, we will suggest a short list of restraints. We will further hypothesize that any one of these alone is enough to prevent overt military intervention. If no restraint operates in a particular situation, the theory would predict intervention. If one or more does operate, the theory would predict that no overt military intervention will occur. The list of restraints comes from obvious sources. One is imposed by the manner in which American decision-makers perceive threats, while others come from the international system, the nature of the decision-making process, and the shared moral values of top American decision-makers.

PERCEPTION OF THREAT

The appeal to force being a blatant act, Americans and their leaders expect justification for its use. A threat to national security is common justification for the resort to overt military intervention. What matters, of course, are the threats perceived and what decision-makers take as legitimation, rather than the "real" nature of situations or the proper justification for force. The gap between what is in decision-makers' minds and what is in the world can be large, but the mental images have the greater impact upon choices made. Consistency is gained when decision-makers use over a long period the same standard for measuring threats to national security. American leaders seem to have done just that since the late 1940's. The standard for determining a threat serious enough to justify overt military intervention appears to be part of the top policy-makers' operational code.

[6] Warner Levi, "On the Causes of Peace," *Journal of Conflict Resolution*, Vol. 8 (March 1964), pp. 23–35.

The concept of the "operational code" is a useful one, permitting one to talk about values shared by a group and explaining both their general acceptance and persistence. An operational code is a set of imperatives and prohibitions concerning conduct, a set of "rules of the game" or norms held by a decision-making group.[7] It is essentially an instrument of social control, the means of group control over individuals. Yet, as with group norms generally, the individual decision-makers tend to make the values of the code so much their own that the norms become part of their personal value systems. The precepts of operational codes are sometimes written down, as the code of the Politburo of the Soviet Union found by Nathan Leites.[8] More often, though, an operational code is unwritten.

Most groups whose members have close contact with each other accept a set of norms or rules of the game that circumscribe behavior, and these norms or rules change slowly. A large body of sociological and anthropological literature is devoted to the particular rules of the game accepted by different groups. Two explanations—"differential recruitment" and "learning on the job"—are often offered to explain why these groups tend to accept particular operational codes. Differential recruitment suggests that only those persons who accept the particular code choose to join a group or are accepted by the group. Learning on the job, as Robert Merton some time ago described it, suggests that members of a group are taught to accept the code after they join.[9] Both explanations are useful. Of course, the members of a group could conceivably change the operational code or abolish the rules of the game altogether. Yet operational codes tend to exist because they serve to limit *post facto* opposition to actions taken and assure that the members may continue to act as a group. An operational code tends to persist over time because it is so well learned and so accepted that it is difficult to change.

One would expect the group of major United States foreign relations decision-makers to possess an operational code. The members form a group. They have to decide upon action. They have to continue

---

[7] Alexander George has suggested defining "operational code" somewhat more narrowly as shared beliefs on particular kinds of philosophical and policy questions. See his "The 'Operational Code': A Neglected Approach to the Study of Political Leaders and Decision-Making," *International Studies Quarterly*, Vol. 13 (June 1969), pp. 190–222.

[8] Nathan Leites, *A Study of Bolshevism* (New York: Free Press, 1953).

[9] Robert K. Merton, "Bureaucratic Structure and Personality," *Social Forces*, Vol. 17 (1940), pp. 560–68, in *Reader in Bureaucracy*, ed. Robert K. Merton, et al. (New York: Free Press, 1960), pp. 361–71.

to act as a group over a long period of time. Although the membership of the group changes, rarely does it change completely and at once. It is thus possible to teach the code to new members who do not at first accept it. There are also selective processes at work assuring that most persons who become major leaders have already accepted the precepts of the operational code. For the people to elect him, a presidential candidate presumably must demonstrate acceptable attitudes on questions of international strategy and morality. High-ranking members of Congress, too, presumably have to show their attitudes are acceptable in order to be reelected. Cabinet officers and other presidential advisers are screened by the president before they are appointed. Senior military officers emerge from a long and arduous selection process. Also, only a few Americans are seriously interested in holding these high offices. It is likely that only those persons confident of the appropriateness of their values are willing to pay the price necessary to gain membership in the group; and confidence is bred in part by continual reinforcement from other people.

The operational code of top policy-makers has apparently defined what constitutes a serious threat to the United States. It is accepted that imminent threats of invasion or annihilation and immediate threats to America's economic well-being or ideology are serious. Most states have seen these as menaces to national security. In addition, however, the operational code of American decision-makers has defined as serious a perceived long-range threat of gradual isolation and eventual succumbing to what are sometimes called "the forces of communism." This broad definition of a serious threat has assumed importance in the postwar world, since there have been no imminent threats to American independence, existence, economic well-being, or ideology. By traditional standards the United States has been unusually secure. At most, there have been long-range threats.

The importance of communism as a long-range threat was first articulately expressed in George Kennan's famous telegrams from Moscow of 1945 and 1946.[10] Kennan argued that the ideology of communism could spread globally and that the United States should "contain" communism and prevent the establishment of governments controlled by Communist parties in yet other countries. Kennan's subtle notion of containment by nonmilitary means was not generally accepted; however, the general concept of "containing communism" was.

[10] One of Kennan's telegrams was later published in abbreviated form as an article under the pseudonym "X": "The Sources of Soviet Conduct," *Foreign Affairs*, Vol. 25 (July 1947), pp. 566–82.

By the statements of succeeding presidents, secretaries of state, secretaries of defense, high-ranking members of Congress, and senior military officers, it would appear that since 1947 most of them have accepted the containment way of thinking.

The containment way of thinking possesses within itself a means for decision-makers to discriminate between those situations that are most threatening and those that are less so. The possibility of a Communist government in a country that does not have one is perceived to be a highly threatening situation. Developments within Communist-governed states, whether revolution or a rapid growth in military strength, are perceived as less threatening situations, because the containment way of thinking is oriented to the future, and the number of Communist states at any one moment is generally perceived to be not very threatening. Situations in non-Communist countries, when there is no thought that a Communist government might be established, are also perceived to be less threatening. Of course, American decision-makers must deal with many kinds of subtly different situations. A Communist government could be seen approaching in the Himalayan country of Bhutan. The same could be seen in store for Canada. It is not likely that decision-makers would regard the prospect of a Communist government in Bhutan as threatening as the same prospect in Canada. One can abstract a scale of seven classes used by American policymakers for measuring the relative importance of threats they perceive in different kinds of situations. Beginning with those situations seen as most threatening, the scale might appear as follows:

1. Imminent peril to American territory
2. Threats of Communist government in "special interest countries"
3. Threats of Communist government in "Communist-threatened regions"
4. Threats of Communist government in "just another country"
5. Threats of Communist government in "disputed territory at the margins of Communist states"
6. Threats of something other than a new Communist government
7. Developments in Communist states

When decision-makers perceive an imminent threat to American territory, they fear another Pearl Harbor, but never since World War II have they thought the United States faced an immediate and direct threat. Even the Cuban missile crisis of 1962 apparently alarmed the Kennedy Administration more for the future possibility that the Soviet Union could use missiles based in Cuba to blackmail the United States and for their propaganda value than for any immediate threat that the missiles would be launched. Nevertheless, decision-makers must realize that the United States could sometime again be attacked by another nation. If the United States were directly attacked, or if the political leaders perceived that it was about to be attacked, they would presumably see this threat as the most serious of situations.

When top policy-makers perceive a threat of Communist government in a "special interest" country, they fear a government controlled by a Communist party will take power in a country for which they feel unusually responsible. A country may be of special interest for any of three reasons. American leaders can believe there are long-standing ties of interest and affection between the United States and the people and territory of the country. This attitude is basically a paternalistic one that sees a direct relationship between the people of another country and the government of the United States, a relationship that does not necessarily rely on the country's government as intermediary. American decision-makers have long held this attitude toward all the peoples of the Western Hemisphere, particularly the people of Latin America. It has been expressed recurrently: in support for the anticolonial revolutions of the early nineteenth century; in the Monroe Doctrine; in some of the military interventions of the early twentieth century; in the reluctant self-discipline of the "Good Neighbor" policy; and in the rhetoric surrounding the Alliance for Progress. They perceive particularly close ties to the inhabitants of the Caribbean for their physical proximity; there they have been most paternalistic of all. United States Marines occupied the Dominican Republic from 1916 to 1924, restraining disorder that the local government could not prevent. Again in April 1965 Marines landed in the midst of internal strife.

A country can also be perceived to be of special interest if United States leaders have repeatedly declared they would defend the people and territory of the country as if they were America's own, and by those repeated statements bound themselves. In a sense this is true of all the Western Hemisphere, but it is also true of the North Atlantic Treaty Organization allies. More than other mutual security agreements, the NATO treaty has been supported by public assurances claiming that the Western European allies will be automatically defended. It is as if decision-makers saw a threat to Western Europe as very nearly equal to a threat to the United States.

OVERT MILITARY INTERVENTION

The third way a country can be perceived to be of special interest is by the United States's governing it. For a few years after World War II American military governments ruled Japan and part of West Germany, and the United States still governs Puerto Rico and a few South Pacific islands. Threats of Communist government in special interest countries are presumably regarded as more serious than similar threats to countries that are not of special interest.

American decision-makers seem to perceive threats of Communist government in Communist-threatened regions to be less serious than those in special interest countries. A Communist-threatened region is a geographic area in which top policy-makers believe the establishment of one Communist government would significantly increase the power or the likelihood of other Communist governments within the region. Communist-threatened regions are always perceived to be politically unstable, with strong Communist parties, weak military institutions, and a lack of natural boundaries between countries. United States leaders sometimes apply the "domino" theory to the regions, as President Eisenhower did to Southeast Asia. The domino analogy assumes that if one country in a region falls to communism, others in the region will automatically fall also. Those regions that have been regarded as Communist-threatened continually since World War II have been mainland Southeast Asia and the Fertile Crescent plus Iran. Sub-Sahara Africa apparently came to be perceived as Communist-threatened only in the late 1950's. Central America and the Caribbean have similarly been the object of concern since the early 1950's, but these regions are part of the Western Hemisphere special interest area, and threats there have been regarded as even more serious than those in Southeast Asia. Twice since World War II the United States has used open and direct military force in regions seen as Communist-threatened: in Lebanon in 1958, part of the Fertile Crescent; and in Vietnam beginning in 1961.

Only once since World War II have United States decision-makers used overt military intervention when they perceived a threat of Communist government in "just another country." That country was Korea. A non-Communist nation is just another country if it is not of special interest and its region is not seen as Communist-threatened. This category includes a wide range of nations, from the patently insignificant ones, as Gambia, to those seen as marginally important, as Korea was in 1950.

Situations in disputed territory at the margins of Communist states are perceived ambiguously—generally unimportant but sometimes possessing symbolic significance. Disputed territory includes those non-Communist lands that a neighboring Communist country claims by offering legalistic arguments: as West Berlin, Nepal, Sikkim, Bhutan, the northern borders of India and Burma, the Chinese offshore islands, and Tibet. West Berlin in particular has gained symbolic importance. Quemoy, Matsu, and the Pescadores among the Chinese offshore islands have also acquired symbolic significance in the struggle between the two Chinas. Taiwan itself is more than mere disputed territory, although Red China claims it, because the United States has come to consider it an independent state and an ally. Most of these territorial disputes are accepted with more tolerance than are threats to entire independent countries. Indeed, the United States has never used overt military intervention in disputed territory, even when Communist China invaded Tibet, seized a long stretch of land on India's northern border, or took control of some of the Chinese offshore islands.

Major United States decision-makers seem to see no threat to American security at all in those situations they think embody no real possibility of new Communist governments. The containment way of thinking seems to preoccupy American leaders so fully that they feel little threatened by other kinds of conflicts. Major conflict in the Sudan, Nigeria, or East Pakistan, resulting in the deaths of thousands, is regarded as morally deplorable but not threatening. Arab-Israeli tension in the Near East is considered threatening only when the Soviet Union's involvement suggests that Communist governments might develop. Accordingly, United States overt military intervention has occurred since World War II only when decision-makers perceived the possibility of a new Communist government.

American decision-makers have not seen great threat in what happens within Communist states. The Soviet Union's military interventions in Hungary and Czechoslovakia were apparently perceived as threatening to the United States only as they underlined the ever-present possibility that the Soviet Union might use military force in Western Europe. China's internal turmoil during the Great Leap Forward of the late 1950's and the Red Guard excesses of the mid-1960's generated less concern for the United States than hope for the downfall of Mao Tse-tung. The Soviet Union's first atomic detonation in 1949 was received less with fear than with outrage that it had pilfered the secret of how to do it. When China got the bomb almost two decades later, United States leaders discounted the threat posed by that weapon because they believed China could build only few bombs at a time and its delivery systems were primitive. Too, they thought an effective antimissile system would be simple and inexpensive to construct. Indeed, American decision-makers have never seemed to see any great threat to the United States in anything that has happened within a Communist-governed state. Threat has been seen only in the expansion of communism.

We will predict that the perception of true peril or a threat of Communist government is necessary for the approval of United States overt military intervention. The chance of Communist government may be seen in special interest countries, in Communist-threatened regions, or in other countries, but American leaders must perceive the threat of a new Communist government somewhere if they are to take direct action. Other threats are not deemed serious enough to justify the blatant use of force. The absence of a perception of true peril or the threat of a new Communist government acts to restrain the appeal to force.

OTHER RESTRAINTS ON INTERVENTION

The international system, the decision-making process, and that portion of the operational code that defines when intervention will be morally acceptable also impose restraints upon the use of military force. The relevant part of the international system is two tacit agreements between the United States and the Soviet Union. (A tacit agreement is an unwritten agreement, a bargain struck without full, direct communication and never recorded in any treaty.[11]) Since the end of World War II, the United States and the Soviet Union have been the two most powerful nations in the world, far stronger in military and economic terms than any other nation. The two countries have engaged in what resembles a contest of wills, but they have never fought each other directly despite the occasions they have had to do so in Berlin, Iran, Hungary, and Czechoslovakia. The Soviet Union has possessed nuclear weapons since 1949 and the United States since 1945, yet neither has used even tactical nuclear weapons against any country since World War II. The conscientious restraint of both the United States and the Soviet Union points to tacit agreements between them not to fight each other and not to use nuclear weapons and signifies that both countries have kept their part of the bargain.

---

[11] Thomas C. Schelling developed this concept of tacit bargaining in *The Strategy of Conflict* (Cambridge, Mass.: Harvard University Press, 1960).

It is not hard to understand why these two tacit agreements exist. There may be bargaining when two or more parties prefer an agreement to no agreement at all. It is in the interest of both the United States and the Soviet Union to avoid war with one another and to avoid a nuclear war with anyone. Even limited war between the superpowers risks grave destruction, and nuclear war anywhere risks escalation to holocaust. Tacit bargaining rather than explicit negotiation may occur when two parties seek agreement but cannot communicate fully with one another. Because ideological reasons make it difficult for either nation to openly discuss "outlawing" war against its presumed archfoe, and because the credibility of each nation's threat of nuclear retaliation against the aggression of the other is fragile, it is potentially costly to discuss openly what forces will willingly be used and what forces will not. Tacit bargaining can reach an agreement when there is some point so obvious that the parties can agree upon it without explicitly mentioning it. When the parties are bargaining to avoid war, the obvious point is the complete avoidance of direct military contact. When they are bargaining to avoid all-out nuclear war, the bargainers seize upon "no nuclear weapons" as the obvious point.

The consequence of these tacit agreements is straightforward. An act that would violate either of them is restrained. If intervention would require fighting the Soviet Union directly or entail the use of nuclear weapons, intervention is deterred. The theory predicts that for those situations where intervention would violate either agreement, overt force will not be used unless American leaders perceive true peril to the United States.

The decision-making process itself also imposes restraints. Since 1945 major decisions in foreign affairs in all Administrations have generally been made by a group of major decision-makers, not by the president alone. This practice, which began before World War II, became dominant after the war. The complexity of the modern world, the recognized need for "expert" knowledge to deal with it, and presidents' uncertainties about their own judgment in world affairs have each contributed to the pervasiveness of group decision-making. Who belongs to the group of major foreign affairs decision-makers varies somewhat over time and with the occasion. A man is a major foreign affairs policy-maker if the president permits him that role. Permission is in turn determined by the personality of the man, his relationship to the president, his interests, and his competencies. The president and his selected personal advisers are, of course, constant members of the group. Certain official positions also seem to confer membership.

Other members of the group usually include the secretary of state and senior officials of the State Department, the secretary of defense and senior civilian officials of the Department of Defense, senior military officers, the director of the Central Intelligence Agency, and high-ranking members of Congress. When major decisions impend, the group usually consults. Sometimes the group meets as a body, as it did when North Korea invaded South Korea in June 1950, during the Cuban "missile crisis" of 1962, and the morning of the Iraq coup, July 14, 1958. But the members need not all sit together. In the era of the telephone, an important policy-maker may convey his opinion by voice as did Senator Richard Russell in 1965 the night President Johnson was considering whether to intervene militarily in the Dominican Republic. A major decision-maker can also play a role even when he is neither seen nor heard; his views may be taken into account through the position he took at earlier meetings and the anticipation of what he would say were he present.

When major military action is discussed, all members of the group will not necessarily support it. If the president opposes it, the action is not likely to occur. Since he is commander-in-chief of the armed forces, his approval is presumably required. Whether other major decision-makers can prevent the action depends on the president. Theoretically, a president can direct military action when all other major policy leaders oppose it. In practice this does not happen. Postwar American presidents compulsively ask their secretaries of state, secretaries of defense, senior military officers, and other executive "experts" for advice on military matters and listen attentively. Sometimes presidents also ask the advice of senior members of Congress. President Eisenhower did so frequently. Often, when overt military intervention is discussed, the major decision-makers are all of the same mind, but this is not always the case. Sometimes some top officials oppose action while the rest favor it. Occasionally, the president will permit other major policy leaders to veto the use of military force, as happened in 1954 when President Eisenhower permitted congressional leaders to veto military intervention in Indochina. It is a rare event, but the possibility of a president granting another decision-maker a veto is a restraint of the decision-making process.

Another practice in top-level decision-making is reliance on incremental decisions; that is, many small steps are taken rather than a single giant stride. Incremental decision-making has been defined by Charles Lindblom as making a progressive series of decisions rather than making one large decision; within each decision in the series a choice is made between goal-action packages that differ relatively little from the behavior of the moment.[12] More crisply, Roger Hilsman described the incremental process as "the tendency to decide as little as possible" at any one moment.[13] Great problems that require action do not elicit great decisions plotting what the nation will do over the next several months or even the next several weeks. To calculate far ahead involves grave risks when information and time are limited, as they always are for top-level decision-makers. The complexity of situations must create uncertainty about the appropriateness of long-range or drastic plans. As a result, policy leaders divide the great questions into many small decisions, each of which is considered reversible by reason of its size. This offers top officials the opportunity to postpone more drastic actions until they have first tried something less extreme. The process of "escalation" in Vietnam from 1956 to 1967 demonstrated icremental decision-making. As each level of action failed to "solve" the Vietnam problem, one more step was taken. Had the United States "won" at any point, the escalation would presumably have stopped. In some situations incremental decision-making can serve to prevent overt military intervention. When a crisis erupts, United States decision-makers do not immediately choose direct military action, but first try something less drastic. At least, they first take lesser actions when true peril is not perceived. The first step may be a show of force, as in the several Berlin crises. Often the first step taken is the increase in the size of military assistance programs to the threatened countries, as during the several Latin American "wars of liberation" of the 1960's. The first step may "solve" the situation, or the situation may improve for other reasons. In either case, overt military intervention becomes unnecessary. Indeed, it can become unnecessary for three different reasons. First, the early steps can bring solution, as the shows of force in Berlin apparently deterred East German invasion. Second, another acceptable agent may take military action so that the United States does not need to do so. The United Nations assumed the military burden alone in Cyprus in 1964, and Great Britain did the same in the Malayan civil war. Third, sometimes after the United States takes a first step, the local actors show that they are strong enough to handle the situation with only limited American assistance. When guerrilla

---

[12] Charles E. Lindblom, "The Science of 'Muddling Through,'" *Public Administration Review,* Vol. 19 (Spring 1959), pp. 79–88.
[13] Roger Hilsman, *To Move a Nation* (Garden City, N.Y.: Doubleday, 1967), p. 548.

conflict erupted in Bolivia in 1965, the United States increased the size of its military assistance program. With this added aid the Bolivian army was able to contain the uprising and United States overt military intervention was unnecessary. Obviously, if lesser acts succeed either in ending or containing the threat, or if another acceptable agent intervenes in America's place, United States overt military intervention is restrained.

Decision-makers' attitudes on the morality of using force are also important to United States overt military intervention, and the operational code may control these attitudes. The Western Judeo-Christian cultural tradition creates for all its members a fundamental ambivalence on the use of force. In the Judeo-Christian tradition the use of force is simultaneously perceived as both wrong and justifiable—on the one hand, basically immoral, on the other, justifiable under certain circumstances. Most Americans share this ambivalence. It is part of the national character, and major United States officials are no exception. At least since the Kellogg-Briand Pact of 1929 "outlawing" war, they have consistently taken the public position that the use of military force is basically immoral because death and destruction will result. We have no particular reason to believe that the private attitudes of political leaders differ from their public utterances. Yet they have also said that certain military actions have been morally justified, particularly America's own interventions in World War II, Korea, Lebanon, Vietnam, and the Dominican Republic. How American officials believe military intervention gains moral legitimacy can have important consequences for action, given this fundamental ambivalence. Americans take their own morality so seriously that they demand their interventions be "moral" ones. In order to be justified, the interventions must presumably embody those features that lend moral legitimation.

Most Americans have a notion of what gives the use of force moral justification, a justification that transcends mere self-preservation. Robert Tucker has observed that to most Americans military action is just when it is taken "either in self-defense or in collective defense against armed attack." [14] This popular conception is a vague one, however. For a foreign affairs leader who must decide whether or not to use military force, it leaves unanswered questions. In modern guerrilla warfare, when sides are not clearly drawn and overt invasion across international borders is rare, what constitutes "armed attack"? In revolutionary wars where there are competing governments, with

[14] Robert Tucker, *The Just War* (Baltimore, Md.: Johns Hopkins Press, 1960), p. 11.

what governments can one legitimately join to carry on "collective defense"? And is preemptive intervention justified? Can one attack an ally's enemy first, before it has a chance to start a conflict?

The United States decision-makers' operational code appears to embody rules defining more specifically what lends moral legitimacy to overt military intervention. These rules can be inferred from those three moral justifications that decision-makers have repeatedly offered for every military intervention since World War II. The first constant justification has been that there was deadly conflict going on that should end. Each time the United States has begun overt military intervention, American leaders have pointed to armed conflict posing an evident threat to the government of the country receiving American intervention. The second constant justification has been that the host country's government requested United States intervention. The request came from unquestioned governments in South Korea, Lebanon, and South Vietnam. The Dominican Republic government that requested United States intervention in 1965, however, was one of questionable origin and questionable power. Nevertheless, United States decision-makers have always been able to point to a request from a government with some degree of *de facto* control in the country. The third constant justification has been that some other "outside" nation was already intervening in the situation.

Even more than the existence of conflict and the presence of a request, the intervention of others has been used by policy-makers as moral justification for United States overt military intervention. The "white papers" and official public statements released when United States military interventions have begun further imply that the intervention of others must possess two qualities if it is to lend moral justification to American military action. One is that United States policy-makers must be able to condemn the actions of the other intervening state, for it does seem to be the culpability of others that is used to justify American action. When the other outside country is an ally, as France was an ally when she intervened in Algeria, condemnation is difficult, if not proscribed, and moral justification is harder to find. The second requirement is that the intervention of others must be demonstrable, for a claim is suspect if United States leaders cannot prove it. When the intervention of others is well hidden, as is sometimes the case, it is more difficult to claim moral justification for American counterintervention.

One more thing affects the moral justification gained from the intervention of others. The involvement of others is not always of the same kind or degree. The intervention of others differs in this sense from the existence of a request and the existence of conflict: requests either exist or they are absent, and the kinds and degrees of conflict are hard to separate. But intervention may be divided into many different kinds of actions. As the United States can engage in overt military intervention, or in any of a number of other kinds of intervention, so can other countries. How blatantly others intervene in a situation presumably affects the amount of moral justification lent to American counterintervention. It is useful, therefore, to describe categories of intervention actions that differ in their blatancy or extremity. United States decision-makers seemingly separate these actions into three categories: overt military intervention, noncombat military assistance, and mere "support" to partisans in a conflict. Overt military intervention by another country, as North Korea's invasion of South Korea in 1950, is the most extreme form of intervention and presumably lends the greatest moral justification for American counteraction. Noncombat military assistance—the provision of money, weapons, ammunition, and military advisers on the scene—is next most blatant. North Vietnam engaged in this kind of intervention in South Vietnam until the mid-1960's, when it turned to overt military intervention. Least drastic is mere support, the tendering of training, advice, encouragement, and tactical guidance to partisans, from outside the country in conflict. Cuba's intervention in the Dominican Republic in 1964–65 was limited to this kind of action. Mere support lends much less moral justification to American overt military intervention; yet, as in the Dominican Republic, that justification sometimes suffices.

It may well be that the amount of moral justification needed to produce United States overt military intervention varies inversely with the perceived severity of the threat embodied in a situation. American policy-makers may be less concerned with morality when they think a threat is serious. One should not go so far as to suggest that a certain "legitimation sum" composed of "moral" and "security" parts is required to justify the resort to force. Yet it would appear that when policy-makers perceive a Communist threat to a special interest country, mere support by a condemnable other is enough to justify military intervention. In Communist-threatened regions intervention may be restrained unless others intervene, at least to the extent of providing noncombat assistance. When American officials see the chance of Communist government in "just another country," overt military intervention by another may be necessary to produce a parallel American response.

The decision-makers' operational code thus imposes three rules on American overt military intervention so that it can be morally justified: there must be armed conflict posing an evident threat to the government of the country to receive intervention, there must be a request from a government with some degree of *de facto* control in the host country, and there must be the necessary amount of demonstrable intervention by another country that United States decision-makers can condemn. Only one kind of situation can claim moral justification for United States overt military intervention without reference to these rules, and that is a direct attack on the United States itself. As it did on December 7, 1941, that kind of event of itself in United States leaders' eyes justifies immediate retaliation. But there has been no direct attack on the United States since World War II, nor is there an apparent prospect of one.

SUMMARY

This book offers a theory of overt military intervention by the United States since World War II. It seeks to explain why open military action is taken at some times and places but not others, although it does not try to explain all aspects of America's use of force. The theory assumes that there are restraints upon an ever-present tendency to resort to military force in crises and that intervention will occur unless it is restrained; but any one of the restraints can prevent the action. The several restraints are obstacles in the path of the tendency to intervene; they must be avoided if military action is to occur. The accompanying chart summarizes how the restraints can operate. For overt military intervention to occur, major United States decision-makers must perceive direct and imminent peril to the United States or see the threat of a Communist government being established in a country that does not already have one. When merely a "Communist threat" to a foreign country is perceived, there are additional requirements: military action must not require fighting the Soviet Union directly, and it must not require the use of nuclear weapons; intervention must not become unnecessary because of an early end to the threat, or the containment of the threat by local actors with no more than limited American assistance, or by another acceptable nation or international organization assuming the burden; the president must not permit other leaders, who oppose the action, to veto it; and the situation must contain a request, armed conflict, and an appropriate degree of interven-

HOW OVERT MILITARY INTERVENTION MAY BE RESTRAINED

Decision-Makers' Perception of Threat	Restraints That Can Prevent Intervention			
	International System	Decision-Making Process	Operational Code
1. True peril	None	None	None
2. Threat of Communist government in a special interest country	Need for nuclear weapons in the intervention Presence of Soviet forces so that United States would fight USSR	President permits veto Lesser acts successful Another nation assumes the burden Local actors strong enough alone	No active support from another nation for one side in the conflict No armed conflict No request for intervention
3. Threat of Communist government in a Communist-threatened region	Same as above	Same as above	No military assistance from another nation to one side in the conflict No armed conflict No request for intervention
4. Threat of Communist government in just another country	Same as above	Same as above	No overt military intervention by another nation No armed conflict No request for intervention
5. Threat of Communist government in disputed territory at the margins of a Communist state	Same as above Overt military intervention only if the territory has symbolic significance		Same as above
6. All other threats in non-Communist states	No overt military intervention—threat too unimportant to warrant drastic action		
7. Developments in Communist states	No overt military intervention—threat too unimportant to warrant drastic action		

37

tion by other nations the United States can blame in order to lend moral justification to American action. If but one of these requirements is not met, intervention will not occur. If all requirements are met, intervention occurs automatically.

The assumption is that these restraints have acted on all top-level United States decision-makers since World War II, no matter who has been president or secretary of state. It has not even mattered what official offices have been represented when the decision to intervene was made. The presence or absence of the director of Central Intelligence or the majority leader of the Senate, for example, has not been of much consequence. The theory also assumes that the tendency to overt military intervention and the restraints on it have been forces that work their way on American leaders, whatever may be the leaders' personal preferences respecting the use of military force. The theory contends that United States overt military intervention is fundamentally determined by the threats America's leaders perceive and by select conditions of the international system, top-level decision-making practices, and the shared moral values of major decision-makers. A president can manipulate the restraints on intervention only within narrow limits.

The following chapters test the validity of this theory. The criticism of popular theories is that they do not explain the use and nonuse of overt military intervention. If the proposed theory is to be better, it must perform effectively as explanation. Chapter 2 summarizes the four interventions of the United States to refresh the memory of these events, and may be skipped without detracting from the flow of the analysis. Chapter 3 begins to test the theory by looking at the four interventions in terms of the threats perceived by Washington in each situation. Obviously, if the theory is to work, it must explain when intervention happens. The first hypothesis of the theory is that the United States will intervene only when its leaders perceive a threat of Communist government (or true peril). Chapter 3 examines whether such perceptions operated for Korea, Lebanon, the Dominican Republic, and Vietnam. Chapter 4 continues testing whether the theory explains the interventions. According to the theory, none of the restraints on intervention should be operating when intervention occurs. If one restraint does operate, America is not supposed to resort to military force. Chapter 4 investigates whether any of the restraints were operating in these four situations. Chapter 5 tests the theory on the nonoccurrence of intervention. If the theory is to explain the absence of force, nonintervention, too, must be consistent with its predictions. According to the theory, intervention should occur unless at least one restraint operates. Chapter 5 looks at the instances of nonintervention to see whether there was at least one restraint operating in every situation. The task is made easier by limiting the number of situations to be examined. The theory predicts that United States overt military intervention requires that open conflict already have begun in order that American violence may be morally legitimized. This is an effective restraint—there has been no military intervention in the absence of conflict. Therefore, to see whether some other restraint operated, it is necessary to examine only those situations where there was armed conflict threatening a government. Chapter 6 explores some of the theory's implications for American foreign policy and speculates on how much longer the postwar pattern of intervention is likely to continue.

2

THE FOUR INTERVENTIONS

Overt military intervention by the United States has occurred four times since World War II: in Korea in 1950, Lebanon in 1958, Vietnam in 1961, and the Dominican Republic in 1965. In some respects each intervention has differed from the others. The four interventions occurred in regions so disparate as the Caribbean, the Far East, the Near East, and Southeast Asia. The actions were taken over a period of twenty years. Each was begun by a different president. Examined superficially, such differences make each intervention appear unique.

SOUTH KOREA

After World War II Korea was divided by circumstances. When Japanese forces surrendered in 1945, the Soviet Union accepted surrender in the area north of the 38th Parallel, and the United States accepted surrender in the south. As in Germany, a joint commission, composed of representatives of both major powers, was created to govern the country. Yet, as in Germany, the joint commission accomplished little. Korea was now two nations, in fact if not in law. In the south, the United States provided economic assistance, organized a South Korean army, supplied it with infantry arms, and formed and equipped a police force. The Soviet Union took similar steps in North Korea, but the army it built was a stronger, larger one. The United States and the Soviet Union were unable to agree on how to reunite the country. A United Nations Temporary Commission on Korea attempted to plan elections throughout Korea; unable to do so in the north, it scheduled elections in the south. These popular elections, held May 10, 1948, chose a national assembly. The assembly met, wrote a constitution, and elected Syngman Rhee president of the Republic of Korea. On August 15, 1948, the Republic of Korea was proclaimed and took over from the United States the functions of government in South Korea. Less than one month later, on September 9, the Democratic People's Republic of Korea was proclaimed in Pyongyang. That government, controlled by the Communist party, took over the functions of government in North Korea from the Soviet Union.

The new governments found it difficult to live in adjacent space. Each avowedly sought to reunify the country under its own control. In October 1948 the Republic of Korea experienced a series of internal uprisings. An uprising at Yosu, abetted by rebellious elements of the South Korean police, took the ROK army days to suppress. Syngman Rhee's government charged that North Korea had instigated these revolts, and indeed the Democratic Republic was probably intimately involved in them. There were also clashes between the opposing army units stationed on the 38th Parallel. These incidents, initiated by both sides, became common occurrences. Then, early on the morning of June 25, 1950, Seoul time (the afternoon of the twenty-fourth in Washington), North Korean troops crossed the border in strength at several points. The border crossing followed upon mortar and artillery bombardments that had begun about 4:00 A.M.[1]

These were at first ambiguous actions. Was this invasion or mere harassment? Uncertainty delayed the first reports to Washington. Not until late in the evening did Washington hear of the attack. Indeed, the first news of it reached the State Department when the United Press called to ask confirmation of a news correspondent's dispatch. The report of the United States ambassador to Korea, John J. Muccio, ar-

---

[1] Glenn Paige, *The Korean Decision, June 24–30, 1950* (New York: Free Press, 1968), p. 81. Paige's description of the decision to intervene in Korea is definitive. Other accounts are consistent with it but are not as detailed. Among these are Dean Acheson, *Present at the Creation* (New York: W. W. Norton, 1969), pp. 402–13; Beverly Smith, "Why We Went to War in Korea," *Saturday Evening Post*, Vol. 224 (November 10, 1951), pp. 22–23+; Harry S. Truman, *Memoirs*, Vol. II (2 vols.; Garden City, N.Y.: Doubleday, 1956), pp. 331–44; and Albert L. Warner, "How the Korean Decision Was Made," *Harper's*, Vol. 202 (June 1951), pp. 99–106. Alexander George has written an interesting article discussing the decision. "American Policy-Making and the North Korean Aggression," *World Politics*, Vol. 7 (January 1955), pp. 209–32. Joseph H. de Rivera discusses aspects of the decision at many different points in his book *The Psychological Dimension of Foreign Policy* (Columbus, Ohio: Charles E. Merrill, 1968).

THE FOUR INTERVENTIONS

rived somewhat later in the evening. The press inquiry instigated a series of telephone calls notifying the major decision-makers. The State Department public affairs duty officer notified the assistant secretary of state for Far Eastern affairs, Dean Rusk. Rusk told Secretary of the Army Frank Pace, Jr., who was attending the same dinner party that evening; Rusk later called Secretary of State Dean Acheson. Secretary Pace meantime informed Secretary of Defense Louis Johnson. At 11:20 P.M., a little more than two hours after news first reached the capital, Secretary Acheson telephoned President Truman in Independence, Missouri. When informed, the president suggested his own return to Washington, but Acheson discouraged him, suggesting there was still too little information to measure the seriousness of the situation. The group did decide to contact Trygve Lie, secretary-general of the United Nations, and in the early morning hours of the next day formally requested of him an emergency meeting of the United Nations Security Council.

Thereafter, the American response grew incrementally. The Security Council met at Lake Success the afternoon of June 25 and passed, with minor revision, an American draft resolution to "direct" the Democratic Republic of Korea to cease hostilities and withdraw north of the 38th Parallel. With evidence that the situation in Korea was worsening, President Truman decided to return that afternoon to Washington. On arrival he immediately sped to a prearranged meeting with Secretary of State Acheson, Secretary of Defense Johnson, the service secretaries, the Joint Chiefs of Staff, Assistant Secretary of State Rusk, and others at Blair House, the presidential guest house.

At Blair House, Acheson presented several recommendations, including more military equipment for South Korea, United States military planes to cover the evacuation of American women and children (Ambassador Muccio had already directed a partial evacuation), and authorization for the United States Far East Air Force to attack planes and tanks interfering with the evacuation. The first two recommendations, for more military equipment and for air cover for the Inchon evacuation, were approved. The third recommendation, to authorize planes to attack interfering tanks and aircraft, was handled with interesting ambiguity. Paige, in his definitive account of the Korean decisions, reports there was consensus among the decision-makers that American planes should have discretion in attacking North Korean forces.[2] But General Omar Bradley, chairman of the Joint Chiefs of Staff, opposed issuing a directive stating such authorization explicitly.

[2] Paige, *op. cit.*, p. 139.

Acheson also observed that attacking tanks would make the United States a belligerent in the conflict. No written directive was formulated at the Blair House conference. Nevertheless, according to Paige, General J. Lawton Collins, army chief of staff, and others who drafted the directive the Joint Chiefs of Staff sent to General Douglas MacArthur, attempted to convey the consensus that United States aircraft should have latitude in attacking interfering tanks. But they did avoid specific authorization.[3] Whatever the intent of the major decision-makers or the directive-drafters, United States overt military intervention did not occur under the inexplicit directive sent General MacArthur that night.

The situation in Korea became even more serious the next day, June 26. That evening the major decision-makers again met at Blair House, with approximately the same attendance as that of the night before. After a review of the military situation from General Bradley, including the reading of General MacArthur's estimate that South Korean collapse was imminent, Secretary Acheson presented more recommendations. Among them he recommended that United States naval and air forces assist the ROK army south of the 38th Parallel. The recommendation was accepted. Secretary of the Army Pace, Secretary of the Air Force Finletter, General Collins, General Vandenberg, and Admiral Sherman immediately went to the Pentagon and began a long-distance conference with General MacArthur, in which they authorized him to use air and naval forces in overt military intervention in South Korea. This time they were explicit.

It is not clear at just what hour United States overt military intervention began in South Korea, but sometime during the day of June 27 (Washington time) the Far East Air Force began bombing and strafing missions against North Korean military forces in the south.[4] At 3:00 P.M. on June 27 the United Nations Security Council met again and approved an American draft resolution recommending that United Nations members provide assistance to the Republic of Korea. Were it known just when United States overt military intervention began, it would be possible to determine whether that action followed or preceded the Security Council resolution. In either event, the timing was very close, and the authorization for the action preceded the resolution.

[3] *Ibid.*, p. 142.
[4] *Ibid.*, p. 207, and Robert F. Futrell, *et al.*, *The United States Air Force in Korea, 1950–1953* (New York: Duell, Sloan and Pearce, 1961), pp. 26–27.

THE FOUR INTERVENTIONS

After June 27 United States military intervention expanded, or "escalated" in the current jargon. On June 29 the major decision-makers authorized General MacArthur to extend air and naval operations to North Korea, and also to provide combat military assistance through United States Army service units. The next morning, June 30, President Truman authorized the commitment of United States combat units to Korea—first a regimental combat team, later in the day two full divisions. The first United States combat ground forces arrived at Pusan airfield on July 1.[5] In the following weeks United States combat forces in Korea increased to the two-division limit, and the limit was then increased. United States forces were assigned on July 8 to United Nations command, with General MacArthur designated the United Nations commander. The first month and a half was a period of defensive action as the garrison forces from Japan were transported to Pusan to maintain a toe hold on the peninsula. After an amphibious invasion at Inchon in September, behind the North Korean front line, United Nations and ROK forces took the offensive, chasing the North Korean forces north. That pursuit crossed the 38th Parallel in October 1950 and brought United Nations and ROK forces nearly to the Yalu River. There they were met by forces of the People's Republic of China, superior in number. United Nations and ROK units retreated until the opposing forces found a point of equilibrium near the 38th Parallel. There the conflict stalemated. The United States increased its troop strength, but the battle line changed little after March 1951. In 1953 an armistice was reached, leaving the battle line the boundary between North and South Korea. Most United States and Chinese forces withdrew. Not all American forces were withdrawn, however; a force of two divisions or stronger remained into the seventies.

LEBANON

Neither the situation in Lebanon in 1958 nor the American response to it bore much surface resemblance to those in Korea. Lebanon experienced civil strife in late spring 1958, although it was not very bloody. Its beginning was in 1957, however, when, in July, groups that opposed the government of President Camille Chamoun and Premier Sami Solh took to the streets in isolated acts of violence in Beirut

[5] Roy E. Appleman, *South to the Naktong, North to the Yalu* (Washington: Office of the Chief of Military History, Department of the Army, 1961), p. 61.

and Tripoli after supporters of President Chamoun won a decisive victory in the Chamber of Deputies elections in June.[6] Counterviolence by supporters of Chamoun followed, and the conflict expanded in 1958. Fighting between armed groups erupted in the Chouf and in southern Lebanon. Opposition elements greatly increased their activities after the editor of the leftist, anti-Chamoun newspaper *The Telegraph* was assassinated on May 8. Thereafter, the Moslem opposition in Beirut under Saeb Salaam consolidated its control over a section of the city, the Basta. In Tripoli, Rashid Karami, another opposition Moslem leader, established effective control over most of the city. Outside the cities opposition Moslem leaders were able with only limited bloodshed to expand the regions under their control until by late June they could deny the government access to nearly the entire eastern frontier of Lebanon.

Before May 8, 1958, elements of Lebanon's small army of 8,000 had suppressed the few mass uprisings that occurred, although it was ineffective in preventing isolated acts of violence. After May 8, when the opposition worked more regularly in large groups, the army no longer engaged opposition forces. Those who fought on behalf of the Chamoun government after May 8 were paramilitary groups, such as those directed by the PPS (Partie Populaire Syrienne) and those formed by individual pro-Chamoun politicians. The army under General Fuad Shehab contained the opposition in Beirut within the Basta but did not enter rebel-held territory. Outside Beirut the army maintained control of some of the major roads; on occasion it also limited armed conflict by placing itself between opposition forces and loyalist paramilitary forces.

The composition of the loyalist and opposition groups was exceptionally complex. It was only superficially a grouping of Christians on the one hand and Moslems on the other. A number of prominent Christians, including Maronite Patriarch Meuchi and the politician Henri Pharon, counted themselves among those opposing President Chamoun. The Communist party included many Christians, but it sided with the opposition. The PPS included many non-Christians, but

---

[6] This account of the background of the 1958 crisis is drawn primarily from conversations with Ambassador Robert McClintock, Dr. Charles Malik, Robert Murphy, Stewart Rockwell, Kemal Salibi, and Hisham Sharabi. Also useful were issues of the *Lebanese Press Review*, daily (U.S. Embassy–USIS Press, Beirut, Lebanon), 1957–58; Leila M. T. Meo, *Lebanon: Improbable Nation* (Bloomington, Ind.: Indiana University Press, 1965), pp. 130–87; and Kemal Salibi, *The Modern History of Lebanon* (New York: Praeger, 1965), pp. 199–204.

it fought on the side of the loyalists. Few Moslems not in the PPS, whether they were Shi'i (schismatic), Sunni (orthodox), or Druze (an independent sect), openly backed President Chamoun. Yet many Moslems, especially Shi'is, refused to give active support to the opposition leaders, the most prominent of whom were Sunni. The opposition was united only in seeking to force Chamoun and the Sami Solh government out of office. Some were Arab nationalists who wished closer ties to Egypt or Syria or who opposed Chamoun's and Foreign Minister Charles Malik's seemingly close ties to the United States. Some were politicians whom Chamoun had undermined in the June 1957 elections. Still others seemed to oppose Chamoun for his purported desire to stay in office beyond the constitutional six-year limit ending September 1958, or they opposed him for more personal reasons.

When the editor of *The Telegraph* was murdered May 8, the opposition gained a degree of unity it had not previously had. Violence increased strikingly, and the Chamoun government became markedly more concerned. Immediately, there were rumors that Syria would take advantage of the situation, sending or supplying guerrillas or perhaps invading with its First Army, which was stationed but a few hours from Beirut on the Damascus Road. In 1957–58 many people feared that Syria was close to becoming a Communist state. A Syrian invasion could thus threaten Lebanon with a Communist government. On May 13 Lebanon officially closed its border with Syria. That day, too, Chamoun called together the ambassadors of France, Britain, and the United States, asking them what they would do if he requested military help. The United States ambassador, Robert McClintock, cabled Washington of the inquiry.

President Eisenhower and Secretary of State John Foster Dulles, meeting with Allen Dulles, director of the Central Intelligence Agency, and others, decided that very day to tell Chamoun that they would honor a request for assistance under certain specific conditions. They also approved a speedup in the delivery of light arms under the military assistance agreement between the United States and Lebanon and agreed to provide a number of light tanks. All this equipment was gathered from stocks in West Germany and sent immediately; but United States troops, although alerted at that time, were not sent to Lebanon. The civil war continued for two more months before United States overt military intervention began.

In the meantime, in June, Lebanon claimed before the United Nations Security Council that the United Arab Republic was assisting the opposition with men and supplies through Syria. The United Nations

Observation Group in Lebanon (UNOGIL) was dispatched to investigate the complaint,[7] and the first week in July it filed a preliminary report with the Security Council. The report said UNOGIL had found little evidence to support Lebanon's claim and that the bulk of men and arms involved in the conflict were Lebanese.[8] The Chamoun government immediately protested, pointing out that the observation group had never visited the Syrian frontier.[9] Indeed, the group had not, for the frontier was not in government hands and the opposition refused access to it.[10]

Simultaneously with the UNOGIL preliminary report, fresh plots were uncovered in Jordan against King Hussein. Iraq, under the Arab Union agreement signed in February with Jordan, agreed to send troops to help Hussein. Then, on the morning of July 14, 1958, as Iraqi troops passed through Baghdad on the way from the eastern to the western front, a coup d'état was executed against King Faisal and Premier Nuri es-Said's government. The coup in Iraq was unexpected, and it was at first unknown outside Iraq who had led the coup, what kind of government had been formed, and whether there was internal resistance to it. President Chamoun called together the ambassadors of the United States, Britain, and France and asked them to commit forces to his country.

The major decision-makers in Washington met in hurried sessions on the morning of July 14 to discuss the Iraq coup.[11] They anticipated a Lebanese request for assistance and began their discussions even before it was received. Ambassador McClintock's cable reporting Chamoun's request arrived in midmorning. By late afternoon the leaders

---

[7] United Nations, Security Council, *Complaint of Lebanon: Resolution of the Security Council*, June 11, 1958, S/4023.

[8] United Nations, Security Council, *First Report of the United Nations Observation Group in Lebanon*, July 3, 1958, S/4040.

[9] United Nations, Security Council, *Official Comments of the Government of Lebanon on the First Report of the United Nations Observation Group in Lebanon*, July 8, 1958, S/4043.

[10] Fahim I. Qubain, *Crisis in Lebanon* (Washington: The Middle East Institute, 1961), pp. 133–53, has analyzed the question of whether or not there was substantial Syrian intervention. He concludes that although most of the men and arms in the conflict were Lebanese, there was Syrian participation. The observation group did not see it because it did not have access to the border and most of the infiltration occurred before the group's arrival.

[11] Eleanor Lansing Dulles, *American Foreign Policy in the Making* (New York: Harper & Row, 1968), pp. 273–78; Dwight D. Eisenhower, *Waging Peace* (Garden City, N.Y.: Doubleday, 1965), pp. 269–75; Fletcher Knebel, "Day of Decision," *Look*, Vol. 22 (September 16, 1958), pp. 17–19; and "Story of a Decision," *U.S. News and World Report*, Vol. 45 (July 25, 1958), pp. 68–70.

THE FOUR INTERVENTIONS

had chosen overt military intervention. President Eisenhower authorized General Nathan Twining, chairman of the Joint Chiefs of Staff, to direct a landing of United States Marines on the beaches of Beirut, and later to dispatch an army battle group from Europe. The president also authorized the sending of a Composite Air Strike Force of fighter planes, reconnaissance planes, and other aircraft to Turkey for use in the Lebanon area.

The first Marine battalion executed an amphibious assault on Red Beach south of Beirut at 3:00 P.M., July 15, 1958, Beirut time (9:00 A.M. in Washington).[12] The Marines landed wholly without incident. As they stormed ashore, weapons loaded, they met, not armed force, but curious Beirut sunbathers and Coca-Cola vendors. The Beiruti were accustomed to both the United States Navy and the Marines—Beirut was one of the Sixth Fleet's regular ports of call. The first battalion surrounded the airport adjacent to the beach, and twelve hours later a second Marine battalion landed north of the city, also without incident. Two days later a third arrived. The Composite Air Strike Force arrived at Incerlik air base near Adana, Turkey, a few planes at a time; it was several days before all arrived.[13] The army battle group sent from Europe was diverted in flight to Incerlik, where it sat for a few days. On July 19 the battle group was sent to Beirut. At no time during the military exercise did United States military forces engage in combat beyond a few exchanges with snipers.[14] Unlike Korea, it was a bloodless intervention.

While the military deployment was in progress, other actions were taken. On July 17 British forces deployed to Jordan on the request of King Hussein; the United States provided logistic support to British forces once they were in Jordan but did not directly participate in the

---

[12] Jack Shulimson, *Marines in Lebanon 1958*, Marine Corps Historical Reference Pamphlet (Washington: U.S. Marine Corps Headquarters, G-3 Division, Historical Branch, 1966), p. 12.

[13] Peter Braestrup, "Limited War and the Lessons of Lebanon," *Reporter*, Vol. 20 (April 30, 1959), pp. 25–27; James P. O'Donnell, "Operation Double Trouble," *Saturday Evening Post*, Vol. 231 (September 20, 1958), p. 42 +; Albert P. Sights, "Lessons of Lebanon: A Study in Air Strategy," *Air University Review*, Vol. 16 (July–August 1965), pp. 28–43; and Henry Viccellio, "The Composite Air Strike Force 1958," *Air University Review*, Vol. 11 (Summer 1959), pp. 3–17.

[14] Harry A. Hadd, "Orders Firm but Flexible," *U.S. Naval Institute Proceedings*, Vol. 88 (October 1962), pp. 81–89; Harry A. Hadd, "Who's a Rebel? The Lesson Lebanon Taught," *Marine Corps Gazette*, Vol. 46 (March 1962), pp. 50–54; Sydney S. Wade, "Lebanon," *Marine Corps Gazette*, Vol. 49 (November 1965), p. 86; and Sydney S. Wade, "Operation Bluebat," *Marine Corps Gazette*, Vol. 43 (July 1959), pp. 10–23.

exercise. The next day Deputy Under-Secretary of State Robert Murphy arrived at Beirut. Secretary Dulles had suggested Murphy be sent, and the secretary and President Eisenhower gave him two tasks. First, he would be adviser to Admiral James L. Holloway, commander-in-chief, Specified Command Middle East, overseeing the operation; he was charged with establishing smooth relations between American military and civilians on the scene.[15] Second, he was instructed to do what he could to settle and stabilize not only the Lebanese situation but also that of the Middle East at large.[16] These directives were not explicit; Murphy was not told precisely what to do, nor was he extensively briefed. On arriving, he announced his role as that of observer only. He was within a few days, however, an active participant in Lebanese politics. He held a series of discussions with Lebanese politicians and other influential persons, soon concluding that settlement could best be accomplished by electing a new Lebanese president. From this election, it was thought, solutions to the other problems would follow. Murphy therefore suggested to the State Department soon after his arrival that the United States seek an immediate election, leave other questions aside, and not attempt to maintain Camille Chamoun as president.[17] The State Department accepted the recommendation.

Murphy also participated in the selection of the new president. He and Ambassador McClintock concluded that General Fuad Shehab, commander-in-chief of the army, was the preferred candidate. Shehab had organized a provisional government in 1952 after President Khoury was finally forced to resign several years after his constitutional term had expired. A number of moderate Lebanese had recommended Shehab do so again in the 1958 crisis before United States troops landed. And on May 22 in a meeting with United States Ambassador Raymond Hare,[18] President Nasser of the United Arab Republic had reportedly recommended a Shehab provisional government. After Murphy's arrival, McClintock had asked President Chamoun who could succeed him and be able to end the conflict; Chamoun thought only Shehab could do so.[19] In the following days the diplo-

[15] Robert D. Murphy, *Diplomat Among Warriors* (Garden City, N.Y.: Doubleday, 1964), p. 398.

[16] John Foster Dulles Oral History Project, Princeton University Library, Interview with Robert Murphy, Section II, June 8, 1965, p. 53.

[17] Murphy, *op. cit.*, p. 404.

[18] *The New York Times*, May 24, 1958, 4:3; Miles Copland, *The Game of Nations* (London: Weidenfeld and Nicolson, 1969), p. 201.

[19] Interview with Ambassador Robert McClintock.

THE FOUR INTERVENTIONS

mats found that Shehab was acceptable to a large number of Lebanese. Although the hard-core loyalists wished to retain Chamoun, Shehab was acceptable to many of the opposition and to the army. Murphy and McClintock thus proposed to the State Department that the United States support the election of Fuad Shehab as president.[20] The department again agreed.

In Lebanon the president is elected by the Chamber of Deputies. An election was scheduled for July 31. In the last week of July some loyalists and some of the opposition were still recalcitrant, and Americans on the scene went to considerable lengths to assure that an election would be held. President Chamoun has claimed that "the commanding Admiral of the Sixth Fleet" threatened to withdraw American forces from Lebanon if the Lebanese did not reach an agreement among themselves.[21] (Chamoun presumably meant Admiral Holloway, not Admiral Brown, the actual commander of the Sixth Fleet.) American military personnel helped the Lebanese army make security arrangements so that violence could not disrupt the election on the scheduled date. The election was held that day and Shehab was elected. He would take office September 24, the day President Chamoun's term expired. Chamoun, it was planned, would complete his term. With the election over, Admiral Holloway was authorized to begin planning the withdrawal of American forces and on August 13 one battalion of Marines left Lebanon in a token gesture.

Violence broke out again in late September. When Fuad Shehab was inaugurated September 24, he named a cabinet headed by Rashid Karami, one of the Moslem opposition leaders, with whom Shehab had had a series of discussions beginning even before American intervention. The cabinet Shehab proposed included only persons who had opposed Chamoun; no loyalists were included. The loyalists were incensed. The loyalist Phalangist party called a general strike and lockout and also supplied paramilitary groups, which took to the streets against the Karami government. For the predominantly Christian Phalangist party's role, this episode is often called the "Christian counterrevolution."

Ambassador McClintock inserted himself into this conflict as a mediator, meeting with members of the Karami government, with Phalangists, and with other opponents of the new regime. McClintock's concern was that Chamoun was seeking to return to the presidency.[22]

[20] Interview with Robert Murphy.
[21] Camille Chamoun, *Crise au Moyen-Orient* (Paris: Gallimard, 1963), p. 428.
[22] Interview with Ambassador Robert McClintock.

For his mediating efforts the ambassador reaped criticism from both sides in the conflict. But the general strike and paramilitary attacks persuaded Shehab and Karami to alter their position. Shehab expressed concern that United States troops not be withdrawn while his appointed government was under attack, but he was given no assurances—troop withdrawal had already been planned, approved, and was under way. Then, on October 14, Shehab announced a new cabinet. Rashid Karami was still premier, but two loyalists were named to balance the two members of the opposition in the new four-member cabinet. One of the loyalists named was Pierre Gemayel, leader of the Phalangist party. The counterrevolution immediately ended. The Chamber of Deputies approved the new government, and it was established. The United States continued withdrawing its troops, completing the process on October 25, 1958.

SOUTH VIETNAM

The military intervention in South Vietnam, which later expanded to North Vietnam, Laos, and Cambodia, began under circumstances much more bloody than those in Lebanon, but it was not initially as massive as the intervention in Korea. Also, conflict in Indochina was one of the enduring features of the postwar world. Lebanon's conflict was but a year old when United States overt military intervention began; Korea's, but a few days. Vietnam, however, had known almost continuous internal conflict since before World War II, many years before the beginning of American military intervention in December 1961. There were conflicts between nationalists and French authorities in the late 1930's, there was World War II, and then in 1946 the "Indochina War" began. In the beginning the Indochina War was fought between France and the official colonial governments of the several Indochina states on the one hand, and Ho Chi Minh, the Indochinese Communist party (participating covertly, for it had been announced disbanded in 1945), the Viet Minh, and the Democratic Republic of Vietnam government on the other. Actually, isolated acts of violence involving the Viet Minh had begun in 1945, shortly after Ho Chi Minh and the Viet Minh first returned to Vietnam from their sanctuary in China.

During World War II President Roosevelt reportedly made many efforts to prevent the return of the French colonial rule to Indochina

THE FOUR INTERVENTIONS

at war's end.[23] For a few years after Roosevelt's death, and even after the Indochina War began, the United States gave France no direct military assistance in that fight, although it did not assist the opposition either. France, however, was unable to defeat the Viet Minh alone. In February 1950, after Mao Tse-tung's Communist government established control over the entire Chinese mainland, and after Vietnam, Cambodia, and Laos had been made Associated States in the French Union, the United States began officially to provide economic and military assistance to France and the Associated States for the prosecution of the war. On June 27, 1950, three days after North Korea attacked South Korea, President Truman approved an increase in the volume of that assistance. In July a small military assistance mission was established in Indochina. This mission was not involved in combat, nor even in training the "native" troops of the French Union forces. It oversaw the supply of United States equipment and gave initial instruction in its use.

From 1950 to 1954 the United States increased the extent of its assistance. Overall, the amount for those five years was substantial— $2.5 billion by one accounting.[24] In 1953 French General Henri Navarre devised a plan to defeat the Viet Minh by luring them into open battle. This necessitated the strengthening of French Union forces, and on September 30, 1953, the Eisenhower Administration agreed to provide additional dollars for the military buildup. Estimates of the proportion of the war's cost the United States was bearing by 1954 varied widely, but at the time Hanson Baldwin offered a median figure—two-thirds.[25] By 1954 there had also been some qualitative changes in the American military assistance program. The United States Military Assistance and Advisory Group still did not operate in combat areas, nor did it train the native troops. But by early 1954 American transport planes and crews were moving French paratroopers from France to bases in Indochina outside the combat zones.

For reasons that will be explored later, the United States did not begin overt military intervention in 1954, even though Washington considered doing so. After a devastating defeat of her elite forces at Dienbienphu, France sought to disengage. An international conference on Indochina and Korea began in Geneva at the end of April 1954 at

[23] Bernard B. Fall, *The Two Vietnams* (New York: Praeger, 1963), pp. 40–59.
[24] Robert Scigliano, *South Vietnam: Nation Under Stress* (Boston: Houghton Mifflin, 1963), p. 11.
[25] *The New York Times*, February 7, 1954, IV, 5:1.

APPEAL TO FORCE

which an agreement on Indochina was reached two months later. The northern zone of Vietnam was left in the hands of the Viet Minh, and South Vietnam, Cambodia, and Laos became separate states without Viet Minh control. French forces were withdrawn. New governments were formed in the new states. Ho Chi Minh formed a Communist government in North Vietnam, a young politician named Ngo Dinh Diem became head of government in South Vietnam, and the royal houses were restored to full power in Laos and Cambodia.

In 1954 South Vietnam looked particularly unstable. As Assistant Secretary of State for East Asian and Pacific Affairs William Bundy observed years later, few people in 1954 expected the independent government of South Vietnam to survive.[26] If that government did not fall of its own, the elections planned in the Geneva agreements would likely defeat it. The North was more populous, and it could be expected to vote unanimously for Ho Chi Minh. President Eisenhower has noted that as early as 1952 it was generally accepted that Ho Chi Minh could win an election in all of Vietnam.[27] This particular possibility was averted when Diem, with the support of the United States, failed to hold the elections envisaged at Geneva. Another possibility was that the Viet Minh might overthrow the Diem government. Under the 1954 agreements, all combatants sympathetic to the Viet Minh were to move to North Vietnam; all those opposed were to move to South Vietnam. A two-way migration followed, but it was not complete. The Democratic Republic (North Vietnam) found it necessary to institute extensive purges in 1955–56. The South, too, had its dissidents. Some Viet Minh remained in the southern countryside, and some Viet Minh "agents" in responsible public positions also remained. There were also many caches of Viet Minh arms left hidden in South Vietnam. In consequence, the Viet Minh had the means for effective insurrection.

Yet to the surprise of some, Diem's government did survive its first few years. In a sense this development gave United States decision-makers a "second chance" in the region, since they had forgone the first chance to prevent Communist governments in 1954. Beginning in 1955–56 the United States undertook major efforts to strengthen the government, economy, and armed forces of the South. From fiscal year

---

[26] William P. Bundy, *The Path to Viet-Nam: A Lesson in Involvement,* East Asian and Pacific Series No. 166, Department of State (Washington: Government Printing Office, 1967), p. 3.

[27] Dwight D. Eisenhower, *Mandate for Change* (Garden City, N.Y.: Doubleday, 1963), pp. 337–38.

1955 through fiscal year 1960 the United States officially obligated more than $1.8 billion to the Republic of Vietnam in loans, grants, and surplus food sales, including military assistance. Another $225 million was obligated in fiscal year 1961.[28] The United States undertook to build, supply, and train a 150,000-man army plus police units (called the Civil Guard and the Self-Defense Corps) of 50,000 men each from the 250,000 Vietnamese troops remaining in the South after partition. A United States military assistance mission of just under 700 men was formed in the mid-1950's to help train these forces and oversee the supply of equipment. The military assistance mission was not a combat force. Most of its members were not even in direct contact with South Vietnamese troops; instead, they handled paperwork or trained South Vietnamese instructors, who in turn trained South Vietnamese troops and administrators. The military assistance group was not expanded until 1961.

The situation in South Vietnam began to deteriorate toward the end of the 1950's. Violence in the provinces increased; in particular, growing numbers of village officials were assassinated. Persons trained in agitation, propaganda, and guerrilla tactics infiltrated from North to South Vietnam. In mid-1959 the Democratic Republic reportedly made a decision to build an organization in South Vietnam to control and direct revolutionary activities there.[29] By 1961 there was an elaborate control structure, including a front organization, the National Liberation Front, which drew together a variety of dissident groups, not all of whom were Communist party members or adherents. By spring 1961 the Kennedy Administration was aware that the situation in South Vietnam was becoming more serious. In May Secretary of State Dean Rusk told a news conference that the armed strength of the Viet Cong in South Vietnam had grown from 3,000 in 1954 to 12,000 in May 1961.[30]

During the winter of 1960 a plan for the extensive reform of the Diem government had been prepared at planning levels of the United States government. Reform was considered necessary if the insurgency was to be contained. President Kennedy named a special Vietnam Task Force in April 1961 after giving general approval to the reform proposal. The Task Force accepted the plan and made forty specific recommendations for reform, which were discussed and favorably re-

[28] John D. Montgomery, *The Politics of Foreign Aid* (New York: Praeger, 1962), p. 284.
[29] Douglas Pike, *Viet Cong* (Cambridge, Mass.: M.I.T. Press, 1966), pp. 77–84.
[30] *The New York Times,* May 5, 1961, 10:1.

APPEAL TO FORCE

ceived by President Kennedy and his chief advisers in late April and early May. The Task Force also recommended that preparations be made for the possible use of American troops in Vietnam.[31]

In May Vice-President Lyndon Johnson undertook a mission to Southeast Asia and the Far East. The trip had several functions, among them communication with the Diem government. In a Saigon speech the vice-president announced the United States's willingness to increase the size of South Vietnam's military forces. The vice-president also urged Diem to accept the reforms recommended by the Washington Task Force. When Johnson returned to Washington, he recommended a substantial increase in the assistance provided the Diem government. He did not, however, recommend a large-scale commitment of American combat troops. In late May, Administration leaders agreed to increase the size of the United States military advisory mission from 700 to 1,650. The increase was more than a quantitative change though, since some of the advisers were now routinely to accompany Vietnamese units into combat. This development still was not overt military intervention, however, because United States advisers were not providing essential services at the scene of battle.

Viet Cong activity increased substantially in the fall of 1961. In September they briefly controlled a provincial capital near Saigon, and on September 29 President Diem requested through United States Ambassador Frederick Nolting a security treaty with the United States.[32] Diem did not ask for American combat troops, but several plans for their use surfaced to top levels in Washington. One plan involved the stationing of American units at strategic points around Southeast Asia, another proposed barricading the Laos-South Vietnam border against infiltration, and a third considered the use of United States combat teams in the dual role of training South Vietnamese units and active combat, if needed. The most prominent of these plans envisaged the employment of an American combat force of from twenty to twenty-five thousand men.[33] On October 11, 1961, President Kennedy announced that General Maxwell Taylor and Walt W. Rostow, assistant secretary of state for policy planning, were to go to

---

[31] Theodore Sorensen, *Kennedy* (New York: Harper & Row, 1965), p. 652.

[32] U.S. Congress. House. Committee on Armed Services, *United States-Vietnam Relations, 1945–1967*, Sec. IV.B.1, Vol. 2 (12 vols.; Washington: Government Printing Office, 1971), p. 52.

[33] *Ibid.*, p. 76; *The New York Times*, October 8, 1961, 1:4, and October 12, 1961, 1:4.

South Vietnam to survey the situation before any decisions were made.

When the Taylor-Rostow mission returned to Washington, it offered three sets of recommendations.[34] The first was for reform of the Diem government. The second was for substantially increased military assistance in the form of more equipment, including helicopters, more advisers to train the South Vietnamese in the use of the new equipment, and advisers to operate the new equipment until the South Vietnamese were trained. The third was for a ground force of about 8,000 men to raise Vietnamese morale, help Vietnamese military and flood relief operations, conduct independent combat operations, and act as a reserve force and a possible advance force were the plans for the use of larger numbers of American forces approved. It is perhaps important that the last of the three proposals did not appear in the formal report of the mission widely distributed in the United States government, but rather in telegrams marked for "the eyes only" of the president, secretary of state, and secretary of defense.

There was no question about approving the recommendations for reform. For months, at State Department insistence, Ambassador Nolting had been urging Diem to make reforms. The problem was one of implementation; Diem was not doing much reforming. The government was not making the changes in the civilian and military bureaucracies that Washington recommended. The recommendations for increased military assistance were also seemingly uncontroversial, but the proposal to send troops was the subject of extended discussion among the major decision-makers of the Kennedy Administration. At a National Security Council meeting on November 15, 1961, the recommendations for reform and increased military assistance were formally approved, that approval stated in National Security Action Memorandum No. 111 dated November 22.[35] The policy-makers authorized more training personnel, and the sending of American advisers in guerrilla war, logistics, communications, engineering, and intelligence. They also approved overt military intervention by authorizing the dispatch of United States helicopter teams, with helicopters piloted by American military men, to fly South Vietnamese army units into battle. Finally, President Kennedy directed contingency planning for the

[34] U.S. Congress. House. Committee on Armed Services, *op. cit.,* Sec. IV.B.1, Vol. 2, pp. iv–v and pp. 94–108; Roger Hilsman, *To Move a Nation* (Garden City, N.Y.: Doubleday, 1967), p. 420; and James W. Fulbright, ed., *The Vietnam Hearings* (New York: Random House, 1966), p. 171.

[35] U.S. Congress. House. Committee on Armed Services, *op. cit.,* Sec. IV.B.1, Vol. 2, p. 133; *The New York Times,* November 17, 1961, 1:6.

possible direct introduction of the large United States combat units recommended in the Taylor-Rostow report, but he did not authorize the deployment of such units at that time.

On December 15 President Kennedy and President Diem executed a public exchange of letters. Diem formally requested further United States aid against the insurgents (without specifying the form of assistance) and pledged himself to reform. Kennedy agreed in his letter to increase United States assistance.[36] Diem's pledge to reform government administration was part of a bargain reached in negotiations with United States Ambassador Nolting. United States overt military intervention began almost immediately. The first combat support unit, 40 H-21C helicopters and 400 crewmen, arrived in Saigon on December 11, and within a week of its arrival began transporting South Vietnamese army units to the scene of combat, authorized to fire if fired upon.[37] The intervention expanded incrementally thereafter. By January 1, 1962, 3,000 United States military personnel were in South Vietnam. By March 1965 the number had gradually increased to 27,000, and the "advisers" provided increasingly more combat support services to the South Vietnamese army.

The radical expansion of United States forces came in 1965. Beginning in March, entire combat units arrived, and by June had actively joined the battle. More units were sent, until by 1968 there were more than 500,000 military personnel in Vietnam, plus a large contingent in Thailand. Also in 1965, in early March, American military aircraft began bombing the Ho Chi Minh Trail in Laos, a guerrilla supply route into South Vietnam. This, too, was overt military intervention, as was the bombing of North Vietnam. North Vietnam was first bombed in retaliation for alleged attacks on United States vessels in the Gulf of Tonkin in August 1964. The North was bombed continuously from March 1965 through 1968. The bombing was restricted to the southern portion of North Vietnam in spring 1968; then later the constant air strikes ended with the beginning of formal negotiations in Paris between representatives of the United States, South Vietnam, North Vietnam, and the National Liberation Front. In 1969 the United States began withdrawing combat troops from South Vietnam, turning over ground combat responsibilities to the Army of the Republic of Vietnam under a program President Nixon called "Vietnamization." The bombing of Laos continued, however, directed primarily against infiltration routes into South Vietnam. But from the beginning of the

[36] *Ibid.*, December 17, 1961, 1:7.   [37] *Ibid.*, December 20, 1961, 1:1.

bombing in 1965 some missions were flown against Pathet Lao and North Vietnamese troop concentrations in northern Laos. These latter missions supported America's covert paramilitary involvement in Laos against the Pathet Lao.

In 1970, however, the area of the intervention was enlarged even as the numbers of United States troops in Vietnam were being reduced. For several years some Viet Cong and some North Vietnamese troops had used sanctuaries in Cambodia on the South Vietnamese border. When American forces and Viet Cong had clashed in Vietnam near the border, and the insurgents had withdrawn to the sanctuaries, or fire had been directed upon Americans from these areas, United States aircraft had sometimes retaliated. Such incidents were infrequent. Then, in early March 1970, Prince Sihanouk, the neutralist leader of Cambodia, demanded that Viet Cong and North Vietnamese forces leave the country. They did not. The prince journeyed to Moscow to talk to Russian leaders, during which time a military coup on March 18 deposed his government. A new government, more anti-North Vietnamese than the previous one, was formed under Lieutenant General Lon Nol. Prince Sihanouk vowed to return, and Hanoi made statements in support of him. The Cambodian army immediately began a sweep through the sanctuaries on the South Vietnamese border. Americans quickly became involved, but at first only on a limited scale. American planes provided, on occasion, reconnaissance for Cambodian army commanders at the border. South Vietnamese army units, sometimes with United States advisers present, crossed the border to invade the sanctuaries. The Cambodian attack on the sanctuaries was unsuccessful. In April the Lon Nol government requested a large grant of military equipment from the United States, and Washington agreed to provide small arms. Then, on April 30, President Nixon announced a massive assault by United States ground forces against the Viet Cong, the North Vietnamese, and their supplies in the Cambodian sanctuaries. When this offensive was completed in six to eight weeks, he announced, American forces would withdraw. At the same time Washington announced that a limited number of air strikes was again being flown against targets in the southern border regions of North Vietnam. The troops were withdrawn from Cambodia, but sporadic air strikes over North Vietnam continued. The number of United States military personnel in South Vietnam continued to decline through 1970 and 1971, but at the beginning of February 1971 American planes and ground troops took active part in a brief South Vietnamese army incursion into Laos. In the spring of 1972, the United States resorted to

APPEAL TO FORCE

the mining of harbors in North Vietnam and the resumption of massive air strikes in the north, but the removal of American ground forces continued.

THE DOMINICAN REPUBLIC

In one way the military intervention in the Dominican Republic in 1965 resembled that in Lebanon—it was a small operation, involving only about 20,000 men. Unlike Lebanon, however, effective government had collapsed in the Dominican Republic when United States forces arrived; and very unlike 1958, United States forces became involved in combat. Also, armed conflict began only four days before United States overt military intervention; in this respect it was similar to the Korean intervention. In its own way the Dominican conflict was unique—American intervention and the Dominican strife itself were wholly limited to the capital city, Santo Domingo.

Revolt began in the Dominican Republic on April 24, 1965, when Armed Forces Chief of Staff General Rivera Cuesta confronted three Dominican army officers who were allegedly plotting against the national government. The national government was formally a triumvirate, but by April it included only two men, Donald Reid Cabral as senior partner and Ramon Caceres Troncoso. Sometime between 11:00 A.M. and noon at army headquarters at Camp 27th of February outside Santo Domingo, General Rivera asked the three officers to resign their commissions.[38] The officers refused, and with the support of army units at the camp they arrested Rivera and took control of the headquarters. Later in the day another group of military officers took control of another camp near Santo Domingo, and a Santo Domingo radio station began broadcasting reports of a successful coup against Reid.

The capture of the army camps was not spontaneous. A coup had been planned for April 26, but it was launched prematurely on the twenty-fourth when Rivera confronted some of the plotters. John Bartlow Martin has suggested that the plot was narrow in focus, having as its aim the return of Juan Bosch to the presidency (Bosch had been

---

[38] These details of events on April 24 primarily reflect the accounts of John Bartlow Martin, *Overtaken by Events* (Garden City, N.Y.: Doubleday, 1966), and of the Center for Strategic Studies, Georgetown University, *Dominican Action—1965* (Washington: Center for Strategic Studies, 1966). Other accounts differ on some details.

president in 1962–63 but had been removed by a military coup in 1963), but this may be an oversimplification. J. I. Quello and Narcissa Isa Conde, the latter a prominent member of the Dominican Communist party, have suggested that the planned overthrow was supported by different persons for different reasons. Some wanted the immediate return of Bosch, while others supported a coup against Reid but wished to establish a junta to hold elections. Still others wished a coup merely to purge the armed services.[39] The coup probably was complex rather than single-minded. Reid, like Chamoun in Lebanon, had enemies on several sides. He was opposed by some for the meagerness of his social welfare programs, and by others, in the military services, for his efforts to limit the actions of the military establishment.

When the revolt began on April 24, United States Ambassador W. Tapley Bennett, Jr., was in Georgia on his way to Washington for conferences. William Connett was deputy chief of mission in Santo Domingo and chargé d'affaires in Ambassador Bennett's absence. Connett sent a series of cables to Washington describing the situation. His first reports apparently cited large numbers of persons milling in the streets and the radio proclamations that Reid's government had been overthrown. Later reports from the deputy chief of mission said that military forces loyal to Reid had regained control of Radio Santo Domingo and limited the revolt to its original sites, the two army camps. Reid's government was in difficulty but not yet overthrown. Early the next morning, April 25, Connett cabled the State Department of growing disorder in Santo Domingo and the possibility of great bloodshed. Senior officials, including Thomas Mann, under-secretary of state for economic affairs and former assistant secretary for inter-American affairs, and President Johnson were for the first time notified of the events.

The Dominican situation deteriorated rapidly over the next four days as the conflict became more complicated and effective government disappeared. The morning of April 25, Dominican military leaders met in informal conference. They did not agree among themselves. Some of them favored naming Rafael Molina Urena, a leader of Juan Bosch's Dominican Revolutionary party, provisional president until Bosch returned from Puerto Rico. Other officers wanted a government to be formed under former President Joaquin Balaguer, and still oth-

---

[39] J. I. Quello and Narcissa Isa Conde, "Revolutionary Struggle in the Dominican Republic and Its Lessons," *World Marxist Review*, Vol. 8 (December 1965), p. 97.

ers favored a military junta. No one, however, expressed vocal support for the continuance of Reid's government.[40] The meeting ended without agreement. By late morning Reid and Ramon Caceres were placed under "arrest" by revolutionary officers at the presidential palace. Revolutionaries were now in control of the Santo Domingo television station, and unscheduled programming began, consisting of miscellaneous criticism against the establishment, much of it extreme and inflammatory. There were also reports of Dominican police officers killed in the streets, although many of these reports later proved erroneous. By midday April 25 the Boschist revolutionaries had decided to install Molina Urena as provisional president, scheduling the ceremony for 1:00 P.M. at the palace. The anti-Boschist military officers were as opposed to Molina Urena in the afternoon as they had been in the morning. After the installation General Jesús de los Santos Céspedes, air force chief of staff, and other air force officers issued an ultimatum: the revolutionaries had to submit to a military junta or be attacked. The anti-Boschists set 4:30 P.M. as the deadline for submission. The hour came and passed. Air force planes strafed the presidential palace.

April 25 and April 26 saw the revolutionaries seemingly grow in strength within Santo Domingo and the anti-Boschists become more militant. The revolutionaries captured army stores of small arms and distributed these to followers. The morning of April 26 anti-Boschist military officers began plans for a counteroffensive. Brigadier General Elias Wessin y Wessin organized an armored operation, using the elite armored unit under his command. His offensive started from San Isidro air base and moved toward downtown Santo Domingo, but it met resistance at the outskirts of the city and halted. On April 27 General Salvador Montas Guerrero committed himself to the anti-Boschists and began to move his forces into the outskirts of the city from the west, across Santo Domingo from Wessin's unit. General Montas, too, stopped at the edge of the city. Communications between the two anti-Boschist forces were almost nonexistent.

The afternoon of April 27 members of Bosch's PRD party and other revolutionaries contacted the United States embassy. They held several meetings that afternoon with Ambassador Bennett, who had

[40] Theodore Draper, "Dominican Crisis: A Case Study in American Policy," *Commentary*, Vol. 40 (December 1965), p. 38. Draper published a revised account of the Dominican intervention in *The Dominican Revolt* (New York: Commentary, 1968). The revised account is slightly more complete but less restrained than the earlier one. All references to Draper's work that follow are to the earlier version.

returned from Washington at noon, and with First Secretary Benjamin Ruyle. The last of these meetings began at the embassy shortly before 4:00 P.M. Molina Urena, Lieutenant Colonel Miguel Angel Hernando Ramirez, and Colonel Francisco Caamano Deno, two prominent revolutionary military officers, spoke with Ambassador Bennett. After this meeting Molina Urena took asylum in the Colombian embassy rather than return to the palace. Colonel Hernando went to the Ecuadorian embassy. Only Colonel Caamano returned to the revolutionary forces in the streets. This left the Dominican Republic momentarily with no government at all, but the gap was filled late the next morning, April 28, when a military junta was finally formed, with a middle rank air force officer, Colonel Benoit, as the key figure. The junta claimed to be the government of the Dominican Republic, but in fact it controlled only San Isidro air base and its immediate environs.

American involvement increased as the situation deteriorated. Early in the conflict United States military attachés and members of the United States Military Assistance Advisory Group established close contacts with senior Dominican military officers. Most of the senior Dominican officers were anti-Boschist. The American officers provided a two-way channel of communication between the American embassy and the anti-Boschist Dominican officers. The morning of April 25 Connett reported to the State Department the possibility of a military junta formed of anti-Boschist but anti-Reid officers. He recommended that the department support such a junta rather than continue support for Reid. The State Department Caribbean Country Director, Kennedy M. Crockett, agreed.[41] The afternoon of April 25, after the anti-Boschists gave the revolutionaries the ultimatum to submit to a junta or be attacked, anti-Boschist Dominican army, navy, and air force officers contacted Connett individually. Connett later reported to Washington that he had agreed to their plans to prevent Bosch's return even if that required the use of force. Connett's cable emphasized the need to prevent Bosch's return and also the Communist role in the conflict. He again recommended that the State Department back a military junta.

Meanwhile, late in the morning of April 25, United States Atlantic Fleet headquarters ordered Naval Task Force 44.9, commanded by Captain James A. Dare, to proceed to the vicinity of the Dominican Republic. Task Force 44.9, the Caribbean "ready group," carried a

---

[41] See Abraham Lowenthal's definitive study of the Dominican conflict and American intervention, *The Dominican Intervention* (Cambridge, Mass.: Harvard University Press, 1972), p. 70.

Marine battalion.[42] It is interesting that the entire task force was deployed. One or two ships of the six in the force would have been enough to evacuate American nationals, as Captain Dare himself has observed, but sending the entire ready group provided capability for a wide range of actions from "civil action, to show of force, to assault."[43]

Intelligence reports received in Washington, beginning on the twenty-fifth, mentioned Communist activities in the conflict: meetings, observations of Communists involved in street incidents, and reports that Communists were among those distributing the weapons captured from army stores. Connett himself reported in cables the morning of April 26 that the anti-Boschist military leaders were weakening. He also reported that there was a serious danger of a Communist government, that an American "show of force" might later be useful although it was not then needed, and that he was advising American citizens to prepare for evacuation. The State Department responded, directing Connett to request an immediate cease-fire of both revolutionaries and anti-Boschists to permit the evacuation. Connett received assurances from both sides. That same morning, April 26, United States military attachés at San Isidro air base told Connett that the anti-Boschists planning offensives against the revolutionaries needed communications equipment, a request Connett may not have relayed to Washington.

Early the next morning, April 27, American citizens began gathering at the Hotel Embajador in Santo Domingo for evacuation. By noon there were a thousand, and trucks and buses took them to the port of Haina for pickup by the ready group. Two ships of the group landed at the pier. Unarmed Marines and helicopters landed to assist in the loading, which began at 2:15 P.M. Ambassador Bennett asked Captain Dare to move two other ships of the ready group in close to downtown Santo Domingo, six miles from Haina but also directly on the coast. Captain Dare complied with this request, later calling it a "show of force."

Other decisions were made in Washington on April 27. The 82nd Airborne Division of the Strategic Army Command at Fort Bragg, North Carolina, was alerted for possible deployment to the Dominican

---

[42] R. McC. Tompkins, "Ubique," *Marine Corps Gazette,* Vol. 49 (September 1965), p. 34; and Center for Strategic Studies, *op. cit.,* p. 15.

[43] James A. Dare, "Dominican Diary," *U.S. Naval Institute Proceedings,* Vol. 91 (December 1965), p. 38.

Republic. The major decision-makers also decided to request a meeting of the Inter-American Peace Committee of the Organization of American States. The committee did meet that day and did discuss the Dominican situation, but it took no action. A careful cable of instructions was prepared for the State Department to send the embassy. The cable stated multiple objectives: restore law and order, protect the lives of American citizens, and prevent the establishment of a Communist government. The cable instructed the embassy to gain agreement from both sides toward these ends and toward forming a provisional government. Given the situation of the twenty-seventh, a "provisional government" meant a military junta.

That afternoon Ambassador Bennett met Molina Urena, Colonel Hernando, and Colonel Caamano in the meeting already mentioned that seemingly led Molina Urena and Hernando to seek diplomatic asylum. Precisely what the ambassador told this group is the subject of dispute. It is generally agreed that he informed the revolutionaries that their movement had been infiltrated by Communists and that he criticized the revolutionaries for their conduct. He also declined to use his good offices for formal negotiations toward a cease-fire, saying the Dominicans should reach agreement among themselves. Further, as Colonel Caamano has claimed, he may have told the assembled revolutionaries that their movement could no longer succeed. After the meeting Molina Urena and Hernando went to foreign embassies. Still later in the evening Ambassador Bennett cabled the State Department, emphasizing the role of Communists in the situation and stressing the uncontrolled nature of the revolutionary movement after the departure of Molina Urena. Meanwhile, ships carrying evacuees left Santo Domingo, but the flagship of the ready group, with two rifle companies aboard, remained offshore. More foreign nationals gathered at the Hotel Embajador for evacuation the next morning.

Early the next morning, April 28, General de los Santos again asked the embassy for walkie-talkies. The ambassador had sent the head of the United States Military Assistance Advisory Group to San Isidro that morning, and that officer reported to Bennett that Wessin's offensive had halted and that the anti-Boschist military were in disorder. Ambassador Bennett recommended to Washington that walkie-talkies be provided. The State Department, however, was apparently opposed and at first prevented such an action. United States representatives at San Isidro may also have been active in forming the Benoit junta announced later that morning. Senator Joseph Clark charged that the junta was formed "at the instance of the C.I.A." [44] Americans may also have been involved in a request Benoit made for United States assistance. In a noon telephone conversation Benoit told Ambassador Bennett that the military could no longer protect American lives. About 2:00 P.M. Benoit telephoned Bennett again to request 1,200 Marines to help restore order.[45] The specificity of Benoit's request is interesting. The ready group carried approximately 1,200 combat Marines, and an American officer may have supplied the appropriate number for Benoit to request. That afternoon Ambassador Bennett communicated through cable and telephone with Washington, recommending communications equipment and later urging direct military action. It was agreed to provide the walkie-talkies. Later, about 6:00 P.M., President Johnson and several of his key advisers approved overt military intervention.

Before the major decision-makers approved such intervention, Ambassador Bennett made a direct request of Captain Dare for Marines to "guard" the polo field of the Hotel Embajador where foreign nationals were gathered awaiting evacuation. An unarmed pathfinder unit and a platoon of Military Police were dispatched by helicopter. Then the ambassador recommended that helicopters evacuate the foreign nationals directly from the polo field, an action that was not immediately undertaken. Bennett also requested a platoon of Marines to reinforce the embassy guard; these were sent, also by helicopter. Then, at 6:53, Captain Dare received authorization from the Defense Department to land 500 Marines; Ambassador Bennett was authorized to request the same. They contacted each other and the landing was decided. Two rifle companies of Marines, armed and combat ready, were dispatched to the Hotel Embajador polo field by helicopter. The Marine reinforcements for the embassy landed first, but their arrival was not overt military intervention. They were not combat ready—to get to the embassy they traveled in private automobiles and taxicabs. The airborne envelopment of the polo field by the two Marine rifle companies was the beginning of overt military intervention.

The night of the twenty-eighth was a quiet one for the Marines. Despite a few alarms they had no difficulty controlling the polo grounds perimeter. They engaged in no combat. The helicopters that brought the Marines carried evacuees to the ships on their return trips. The next day the State Department cabled Ambassador Bennett that the

[44] Senator Joseph Clark, *Congressional Record,* Senate (daily), September 17, 1965, p. 23366; quoted in Draper, *op. cit.,* p. 46.
[45] Center for Strategic Studies, *op. cit.,* p. 35.

Marines were not to expand their perimeter at the polo field and that aggressive action could be authorized only by President Johnson. The cable also agreed with Ambassador Bennett's interpretation of the revolutionaries—communicated to Washington the night before—that extremists had captured control of the movement. The State Department recommended that the ambassador use United States military officers to assist the San Isidro military in planning a "mop-up" campaign through revolutionary-held areas of Santo Domingo. Later in the day Ambassador Bennett reported that revolutionary victory could mean Communist government, but that the anti-Bosch military were taking no action. He suggested that more Marines would be needed, and also that the Marine perimeter be expanded. The afternoon of April 29 the major decision-makers in Washington decided to land the rest of the Marines aboard the ready group, thus increasing the number ashore to 1,200. Bennett was told to drop the plan to assist the anti-Bosch military in preparing an offensive. After further communications with Ambassador Bennett, the major decision-makers decided on April 29 to send paratroops from the 82nd Airborne Division in addition. American military forces were further expanded in the following days as the entire 82nd Airborne was committed.

The Council of the Organization of American States had met on April 28 at the request of the United States ambassador to the council, Ellsworth Bunker, but it had adjourned without action. The council met again the night of April 29–30, voting then to ask the papal nuncio in Santo Domingo, dean of the diplomatic corps there, to help arrange a cease-fire. The council also passed a resolution calling for a cease-fire and urging the Dominicans to accept an "international zone of refuge" in Santo Domingo, a neutral zone in the part of the city housing most of the foreign embassies, most of the foreign residences, and the Hotel Embajador. On April 30 United States Marines moved out from the polo field and paratroops moved out from San Isidro air base, where they had landed. When more paratroops arrived to complete the operation, these deployments created the international zone of refuge and at the same time encircled the revolutionary-held areas of downtown Santo Domingo. Carrying out the operation, United States forces met resistance from the revolutionaries and suffered their first casualties.

The afternoon of April 30 John Bartlow Martin, United States ambassador to the Dominican Republic in 1962–63, flew to Santo Domingo on behalf of President Johnson and the State Department to discern the situation and to recommend solutions. The Council of the

Organization of American States the same afternoon voted to send Jose Mora, secretary-general of the OAS, to assist the papal nuncio in effecting a cease-fire. On May 3 Ambassador Martin began discussions with General Antonio Imbert, who had remained aloof from the anti-Bosch military and from the revolutionaries, toward a coalition government including General Imbert and Colonel Caamano. On May 7 General Imbert formed a "Goverment of National Reconstruction" that did not include Caamano. On the fifteenth the general undertook an offensive in the area north of the American lines surrounding downtown Santo Domingo, effectively dispersing revolutionary forces in that area. The same day, McGeorge Bundy, President Johnson's special assistant for national security affairs, Under-Secretary of State Thomas Mann, Deputy Secretary of Defense Cyrus Vance, and Jack Hood Vaughn, assistant secretary of state for inter-American affairs, went to Santo Domingo. Ambassador Martin was told to stop his efforts to form a coalition between Imbert and Caamano. McGeorge Bundy's group entered discussions toward forming a government under Antonio Guzman, but no government resulted from these discussions.

In mid-May the Council of the Organization of American States voted to establish an Inter-American Peace Force to command all foreign troops in the Dominican Republic. Brazil contributed a small number of men and General Hugo Panasco Alvim of Brazil was named commander of the inter-American force. Then a three-man commission from the OAS, including United States Ambassador Ellsworth Bunker, began yet another set of negotiations.

On September 3, 1965, a provisional government under Hector Garcia-Godoy was officially established—the product of the last set of negotiations. United States forces, which had in May reached more than 20,000, were by October reduced to 8,500. The provisional government scheduled presidential elections to be held June 1, 1966. Joaquin Balaguer, former president under Trujillo; Rafael Bonnelly, former president of the Council of State that governed the Republic in 1962; and Juan Bosch all ran. Balaguer won and was inaugurated July 1, 1966. Thereafter, most of the remaining American troops were withdrawn.

3

PERCEPTIONS OF THREAT

The four postwar American interventions obviously show many differences. Although in no sense could they be called identical, yet they were not wholly dissimilar. One similarity is the threat major United States decision-makers saw in the situations. In each instance, American leaders envisioned the threat of a new Communist government before they approved overt military intervention. The decision-makers' operational code may require that they perceive such a threat if they are to use direct military force.

Overt military intervention is a drastic kind of action. It is often costly both in human life and in material well-being. The number of Americans killed or wounded in Vietnam exceeded even the number killed or wounded in World War I, and casualties among the Vietnamese were far greater than those among Americans. Few died in the actions in Lebanon and the Dominican Republic, but many died in Korea. The economic costs of war for North and South Vietnam, as well as for North and South Korea, were too large to be calculated easily. The United States paid a high price for Vietnam and Korea, too. But Americans imagine themselves to be a peaceful people who would not wantonly inflict the wounds of combat on themselves or others. Since the use of force is destructive, Americans expect that force will not be used capriciously; they expect that the costs of American involvement in war will be justified by the circumstances of the action. Major United States decision-makers, those who make the final decisions whether or not to approve overt military intervention, seemingly share this expectation. In the post-World War II era, that group's operational code has included two sets of rules meant to assure that any direct military action the United States undertakes may be justified in moral terms and also justified as a protection of American security. The rules for moral legitimation and the rules rating perceived threats are probably equally important in determining whether United States overt military intervention occurs. The absence of a perception of high threat or the absence of sufficient moral legitimation may each prevent the use of military force. Yet the discernment of threat comes first in one sense. If United States political leaders saw no threat to the United States, how could they justify even considering military action? Indeed, they rarely do discuss using force unless they perceive a threat to American security.

The operational code provides major American decision-makers with a scale to measure the significance of the different threats they see. The scale, which marks seven kinds of threats foreign policy leaders may perceive in situations and grades them for significance, we have already delineated on page 25.

One element of the pattern in United States overt military intervention since World War II is that direct military action has been begun in a region only when decision-makers envisioned the possibility of a new Communist government. It would seem that only threats high on the scale justify for foreign affairs leaders the drastic act of military intervention. They saw in the Dominican Republic the threat of a Communist government in a "special interest" country. They saw in Lebanon and South Vietnam threats of Communist governments in "Communist-threatened" regions. And they saw in South Korea the threat of a Communist government in what was then to them "just another country."

SOUTH KOREA

The threat of Communist government in Korea was obvious. The military forces of the People's Republic of Korea invaded the south. The government of the People's Republic was Communist; if its forces won, they could be expected to form a Communist government in South Korea. The Truman Administration discerned the Communist threat as soon as it realized that the North Korean border crossings of June 24, 1950, constituted an invasion. But it apparently envisioned Korea at that time as just another country, rather than a country of special interest or as part of a Communist-threatened region. There

PERCEPTIONS OF THREAT

was no opportunity to perceive Korea as part of a Communist-threatened region because there were no other insecure non-Communist countries near it. Mainland China had been lost to Mao Tse-tung by the winter of 1949. Formosa, occupied by Chiang Kai-shek and the Kuomintang forces driven from the mainland, was insulated from Korea by the distance between them. The Philippines was even further from Korea; and although it had internal conflict, what happened in Korea could make little direct difference to the outcome of that conflict. Japan was relatively secure because the American military occupation still continued. It is true that after the North Korean invasion had begun, the Joint Chiefs of Staff did suggest, at the second Blair House conference, June 27, that a Communist Korea would be a threat to Japan. This view, however, had not been expressed at the first Blair House conference; the Joint Chiefs seemed to form the opinion just before they stated it, and the threat to Japan was not a major topic of discussion at the second conference. Even the Joint Chiefs of Staff seemed to discount the significance of the threat, for they continued to insist on June 27 that Korea was not of strategic importance to the United States.[1]

In addition, the major foreign affairs leaders had chosen not to consider South Korea a special interest country. A country is envisioned to be of special interest if policy-makers see close ties between the United States and the people of the country, if political leaders have declared they would defend that country as if it were part of the United States, or if the United States governs it through occupation. The perceptions of Korea in 1950 fit none of these conditions. It is conceivable that some decision-makers observed close ties with the Korean people stemming from the years of American presence, 1945–49, but that attitude was apparently not generally held, and it was not comparable to the intense attitudes about ties to Latin Americans and West Europeans. The United States did occupy Korea, but when American forces withdrew in 1949, no assurance was given that the United States would defend the Republic of Korea as if it were an extension of Los Angeles. Indeed, a series of decisions in 1948–49 suggested disinterest in Korea.

Following a visit to the Far East in the summer of 1947, General Albert C. Wedemeyer recommended that United States forces occupying South Korea be withdrawn. The general argued that, in the event of major war in the Far East, forces in Korea would be a liability

[1] Glenn D. Paige, *The Korean Decision, June 24–30, 1950* (New York: Free Press, 1968), p. 175.

rather than an advantage, because the United States would be unable to support them. Yet the ports and air bases of South Korea could be of use to a potential enemy; thus, Wedemeyer recommended that United States withdrawal be keyed to Soviet withdrawal from North Korea. The Joint Chiefs of Staff made the same recommendations to Secretary of State Acheson in a letter dated September 25, 1947.[2] In preparation for possible withdrawal the United States in 1948 committed itself to equipping and training the South Korean army as a modern infantry. In December 1948 the Soviet Union announced it had unilaterally withdrawn all of its own forces from North Korea. By spring 1949 the American equipping of South Korea's army had begun, although it included no artillery, no tanks, and, in the beginning, no aircraft. That spring the United States began withdrawing its own combat troops, completing the process by the end of June 1949. When the combat troops had been withdrawn, the only American military men who remained were the 482 members of the military assistance group assigned to assist the republic's security forces in their continued development.

The Truman Administration had also apparently decided that in the event of conflict in South Korea it would not use military force to support the republic. Secretary of State Acheson delivered a major public address on January 12, 1950, in which he repeated information he gave the Senate Foreign Relations Committee two days before.[3] The secretary spoke in general terms about the Far East; he did not focus on Korea alone. Yet he made statements relevant to Korea. Among other things Acheson suggested that outside military force could not stop the "subversion and penetration" to which some Far Eastern countries were susceptible because of the weakness of their governments. That statement seemed to imply that he would not support overt military intervention in a guerrilla war in the Far East, including one in Korea. Acheson also described the American "line of defense" in the Far East, a line reportedly developed by the Joint Chiefs of Staff and the National Security Council in 1948–49 when United States forces were withdrawn from Korea.[4] The line of defense in-

[2] Harry S. Truman, *Memoirs,* Vol. II (2 vols.; Garden City, N.Y.: Doubleday, 1956), pp. 325–26.

[3] Dean G. Acheson, "Crisis in Asia: An Examination of U.S. Policy," address before the National Press Club, January 12, 1950, *Department of State Bulletin,* Vol. 22 (January 23, 1950), pp. 111–18.

[4] Richard H. Rovere and Arthur M. Schlesinger, Jr., *The General and the President, and the Future of American Foreign Policy* (New York: Farrar, Straus and Young, 1951), p. 101.

cluded those places where United States forces were stationed, such as Japan, Okinawa, and the Philippines, but excluded Formosa and Korea. Those countries outside the line, were they attacked, would have first to rely on their own military forces; then, the secretary suggested, they might expect the assistance of other nations under the United Nations Charter. In describing this line of defense, Acheson seemed to say that United States military forces would not likely join immediately and unilaterally in a conflict between North and South Korea. In his memoirs, written years later, Acheson neither repudiated his words, nor did he see anything surprising or new in them. They were, he still believed, consistent with the thinking of the Joint Chiefs of Staff. He did clarify that he was not speaking explicitly of Korea, but of Asia in general, although Korea was included. Still, the fundamental point of the speech was that the United States alone could not control events on the continent, and the future of Asia would have to depend heavily upon the decisions of Asians themselves.[5]

Secretary Acheson's speech suggested to Koreans and to others that the leaders of the United States were not deeply committed to the protection of the Republic of Korea.[6] Although probably ideologically committed, they were not committed to always using force to protect it. It was, in their view, "just another country." Underlying this attitude was the view that Korea would not be important in a major war with the Soviet Union. The possibility of major war with Russia seemed to preoccupy decision-makers' thoughts in 1950. Consonant with this lack of concern, the United States Far East command possessed no contingency plans for military intervention to defend South Korea against attack or to assist it in a guerrilla war. The only plan on hand was one for the protection and evacuation of American nationals.[7]

Nevertheless, when North Korea blatantly attacked South Korea on June 24, 1950, the United States did intervene. That act of overt military intervention by North Korea offered the moral justification that is required for United States action in a nation regarded as just another country. What happened after United States military intervention began in South Korea is significant to the theory. The intervention was quickly expanded into North Korea. The first open military move by

[5] Dean Acheson, *Present at the Creation* (New York: W. W. Norton, 1969), pp. 354–57.
[6] Paige, *op. cit.*, pp. 66–69.
[7] Robert F. Futrell, *et al., The United States Air Force in Korea, 1950–1953* (New York: Duell, Sloan and Pearce, 1961), p. 8*n*.

the United States was the beginning of air strikes against North Korean troops in South Korea. The act was approved on June 26 and strikes began on June 27. Two days later, on June 29, the Truman Administration approved the extension of air strikes and naval bombardments into North Korea. Thus, United States overt military intervention was expanded to North Korea even before the first American combat troops were deployed in the South! In October ground troops also entered North Korea. This action is important in that North Korea was not threatened with a Communist government—it already had one. Military action will not be begun in Communist states, but it can be expanded into a Communist state from a nation threatened with a Communist government. This distinction is apparently an important one for American leaders, for only under this condition has the United States used military force in a Communist country. It does demonstrate, however, that the rules governing the initiation of United States overt military intervention do not necessarily control what America does in the region thereafter.

LEBANON

The perception of threat in Lebanon in 1958 was more complex than that in Korea. In part, this reflects the greater ambiguity of the Lebanese conflict. There was no overt invasion. Major American decision-makers did discern the threat of Communist government, but they saw that threat primarily in the possibility of a Syrian invasion, an invasion that never occurred. The perception was different in another way. The Eisenhower Administration envisioned the Fertile Crescent as a Communist-threatened region; it did not consider Lebanon a country of special interest. Yet another difference was that once United States troops arrived, the foreign affairs leaders appeared to change their minds about the threat to Lebanon. Once committed, they no longer took the threat so seriously.

The objective conditions that may encourage the perception of a Communist-threatened region had existed for years in the Fertile Crescent. Governments in Jordan and Syria had been notoriously unstable since the end of World War II. Syria's was particularly so: it experienced three successful coups d'état in 1949 alone and bloody uprisings in the Druze Mountains during an army revolt in 1954, and the composition of the ruling group was susceptible to sudden major change from within. Military establishments in Iraq, Jordan, Syria, and Lebanon were relatively weak compared to those in Egypt, Turkey, and Israel. There were few natural boundaries between countries; indeed, Syria and Lebanon had been united under French mandate before World War II. Also, the Communist parties in the Fertile Crescent were among the largest in the Near East during the 1950's. By 1957 the State Department's Bureau of Intelligence and Research estimated the Syrian and Lebanese Communist parties had together between twenty and twenty-three thousand members; more populous Egypt had only an estimated four to five thousand; and Saudi Arabia was thought to have less than one hundred. The Jordanian party, the bureau estimated, had only three hundred members, but it was thought to be strong and effective for its five to six thousand active supporters.[8] These Communist parties may have been more significant than the numbers of their members suggest. As Walter Laquer observed in 1955, Near Eastern Communist parties tended to be stronger for their size than European Communist parties because there were few other parties in the Near East that could command many militants.[9]

The key decision-makers of the Eisenhower Administration were seemingly fearful that Communist governments might arise in the Near East. One obvious way they could arise would be through the military intervention of the Soviet Union. Accordingly, President Eisenhower requested of Congress in January 1957 a joint resolution on the Middle East authorizing American military action upon request from any country in that area attacked by forces of any nation controlled by "international communism." Congress passed the resolution, and the mass media dubbed it with a name that stuck—the "Eisenhower Doctrine." There was also concern that a Communist government could arise in the Near East from internal "subversion," even if there were no direct military intervention by the Soviet Union. President Eisenhower apparently saw potential for Communist governments in many Near Eastern nations, but he was particularly worried about Syria in 1956–59 because of the weakness of its government.[10] Parker T. Hart, deputy assistant secretary of state for Near Eastern and South Asian affairs, described, a year after the Lebanese intervention, how he thought Communist governments could be established in the Near East

---

[8] U.S. Department of State, Bureau of Intelligence and Research, *World Strength of the Communist Party Organizations,* Annual Report No. 10 (Washington: Department of State, 1958), pp. 47, 98.

[9] Walter Z. Laquer, "The Appeals of Communism in the Middle East," *Middle East Journal,* Vol. 9 (Winter 1955), pp. 21–22.

[10] Dwight D. Eisenhower, *Waging Peace* (Garden City, N.Y.: Doubleday, 1965), p. 197*n*.

through subversion. He may very well have expressed the thoughts of the major decision-makers. In a May 1959 policy address, Hart asserted that there were "Communist" plans for takeover in the area. The Soviet Union had allied itself with indigenous, nationalist groups in Near Eastern countries, and at the same time it had built cohesive and separate Communist parties in those countries. In the midst of turmoil, Hart said, the Communist parties would seize power from the nationalists. But this was not the only method he saw the Soviet Union using. The Greek civil war, the demands made of Turkey after World War II, the street violence in Syria in 1957, and developments in Iran in 1953 all represented for him "Communist" attempts to seize government.[11]

By late 1957 major United States decision-makers seemed to see the possibility of Communist government in Syria as imminent, if not already in process. A new Syrian cabinet was formed in January 1957, which the Central Intelligence Agency reported as leftist but not Communist-oriented.[12] In August 1957 the government appeared to move much further left, when the Syrian defense minister signed an economic and technical assistance agreement with the Soviet Union on the sixth of that month. A week later the government charged an American plot to overthrow it and expelled three United States representatives. Then the commander-in-chief of the armed forces, Nizam al-Din, was replaced on August 17 by 'Afif al Bizri, an officer suspected of being pro-Soviet. It appeared to United States leaders that Syria might become, if it had not already become, a satellite of the Soviet Union. In President Eisenhower's words: "The entire action was shrouded in mystery but the suspicion was strong that the Communists had taken control of the government." [13]

President Eisenhower and Secretary of State John Foster Dulles held crisis discussions August 19 on the Syrian situation, including conversations with the British ambassador.[14] But United States overt military intervention did not follow. Those factors that decision-makers think lend moral legitimation to military intervention were clearly absent: there was no open conflict in Syria, there was no request from a Syrian government, and there seemed little hard evidence of Soviet

---

[11] Parker T. Hart, "Tensions and U.S. Policy in the Near and Middle East," address before the Foreign Policy Association of Pittsburgh, May 1, 1959, *Department of State Bulletin,* Vol. 40 (May 18, 1959), p. 717.

[12] Eisenhower, *op. cit.,* pp. 196–97.   [13] *Ibid.,* p. 196.

[14] Patrick Seale, *The Struggle for Syria* (London: Oxford University Press, 1965), p. 295.

military assistance in the presumed "takeover." President Eisenhower and Secretary Dulles did, however, send a message to Turkey saying that if Syria's neighbors took action against the Syrian government, the United States would accelerate planned arms deliveries and replace any equipment lost in combat, as well as restrain any Israeli action against Arab countries.[15] Units of the Sixth Fleet were also moved to the Eastern Mediterranean, and some American tactical aircraft were sent from Europe to Incerlik air base near Adana, Turkey.

Syria's neighbors failed to take action. Loy Henderson, deputy under-secretary of state, then flew to Ankara, where he talked to Prime Minister Menderes, King Faisal of Iraq, and King Hussein of Jordan. He went on to Lebanon, where he talked to President Chamoun. Henderson returned to Washington on September 4, reporting that rivalry among the Arab states made joint action against Syria unlikely. Lebanon seemed interested in joint action, but the other states did not. Turkey, a non-Arab state, also seemed interested; at least its political leaders did—the military were more reluctant. After Henderson's report the United States apparently used undercover means to encourage the reluctant Turkish military to maintain a posture of readiness on the Syrian frontier.[16]

The situation quieted toward the end of 1957. The Syrian government persisted, however, unchanged in its composition until January 1958, when Syria united with Egypt to form the United Arab Republic. The formal documents of union were signed on February 1, 1958. Those in American intelligence circles, Charles D. Cremeans for one, later realized that anti-Communist Syrians, not Nasser or Syrian Communists, forced the union.[17] But United States policy-makers apparently misperceived the union at its inception. As President Eisenhower later wrote, they were unsure of President Nasser's political leanings, and they wondered whether the union was Communist-promoted but assumed the "Communists" were going along with it.[18] The American political leaders seemed to assume that the union would be to "Communist" advantage.

Jordan's government was unstable too, and major United States decision-makers also seemed to see there a susceptibility to Communist

---

[15] Eisenhower, *op. cit.*, p. 199.

[16] Emmet John Hughes, *The Ordeal of Power* (New York: Atheneum, 1963), pp. 253–54.

[17] Charles D. Cremeans, *The Arabs and the World* (New York: Praeger, 1963), p. 161.

[18] Eisenhower, *op. cit.*, p. 262.

government. King Hussein's position was precarious: he lacked broad public support and the Palestinian refugees opposed him because he was moderate both in his efforts to improve social welfare and in his behavior toward Israel. The king was dependent on the army to maintain his position and was therefore to a degree at the mercy of military officers. The Jordanian cabinet of ministers was to some extent autonomous; King Hussein could not easily appoint whomever he would nor always remove those he opposed. In early 1957 the king made attempts to reorganize the cabinet, and his first efforts in February were immediately followed by rumors of plans for coups d'état and some public demonstrations. On the basis of reports provided by CIA Director Allen Dulles, President Eisenhower apparently believed these disturbances were precipitated by "Communists." [19] In April Hussein tried again, replacing the premier (whom Eisenhower considered pro-Soviet) with a conservative. The United Arab Republic issued a series of denunciatory statements over radio, and there were more rumors of plots. At this juncture Eisenhower approved sending units of the Sixth Fleet to the Eastern Mediterranean, and the White House released a statement emphasizing the importance the president and Secretary Dulles placed on the continued independence and integrity of Jordan. When this crisis abated, and no coup occurred, the Sixth Fleet task force withdrew westward. However, the uncovering of plots and rumors of plots against the king's government remained a fact of life in Jordan.

The fear of a Syrian invasion of Lebanon was reflected in the military contingency planning of May and June 1958. On May 13, a few days after the editor of *The Telegraph* was assassinated, Marine Corps Brigadier General Sydney S. Wade was ordered to the Mediterranean and placed in command of all Marines with the Sixth Fleet.[20] On his arrival General Wade expanded the existing Marine contingency plan for intervention in Lebanon. Neither the existing nor the expanded plan was directed toward containing Lebanese insurgents; both assumed the major military threat to be from the Syrian First Army stationed a few hours from Beirut across the border. Military contingency plans for the Fertile Crescent had been revised in late 1957 during the period of greatest concern over developments in Syria. In November

---

[19] *Ibid.*, p. 194.
[20] Sydney S. Wade, "Lebanon," *Marine Corps Gazette*, Vol. 49 (November 1965), p. 86; and Jack Shulimson, *Marines in Lebanon 1958*, Marine Corps Historical Reference Pamphlet (Washington: U.S. Marine Corps Headquarters, G-3 Division, Historical Branch, 1966), p. 7.

1957 the Joint Chiefs of Staff directed the formation of a "shadow" command for the region, the Specified Command Middle East, which could be activated under Admiral James L. Holloway in the event of United States military action in the Fertile Crescent. Admiral Holloway was directed to develop contingency plans for military intervention in Jordan and Lebanon. In January 1958 he asked the Marine battalion with the Sixth Fleet to prepare a plan for landing at Beirut. (United States Army–Europe also developed contingency plans for the Fertile Crescent in November 1957 and revised them extensively in February 1958. There was little coordination, however, between Marine and army planning until May 1958.)

On May 22, after General Wade arrived in the Mediterranean, he met on Cyprus with Brigadier John A. Read, commander of the British Third Infantry Brigade and Brigadier General David W. Gray of the United States Eleventh Airborne Division in Europe to coordinate United States contingency planning and develop a joint United States-British plan for military intervention in Lebanon. The two-nation plan that emerged was called BLUEBAT. Since the plan assumed the major threat to be from the Syrian First Army, United States-British objectives were the Beirut airport, the Beirut docks, and the roads leading to Beirut from the direction of the Syrian army. Under the plan two United States Marine battalions would land at Beirut, one on Red Beach south of the city by the airport, the other on the beach north of the city and near the Damascus Road. When the airport was secure, British paratroops were to fly in from Cyprus. United States Army battle groups in Europe were to have no role in BLUEBAT. The joint plan was accepted in Washington, and most of the transport planes sent to Europe in mid-May for possible transport of army troops to Lebanon were returned to the United States. BLUEBAT was in fact the plan used in the July 15 intervention, with two important modifications. The first was that a United States Army–Europe battle group was substituted for the British paratroops. The second was that the two Marine battalions did not land simultaneously. An immediate presence was ordered, and the second battalion, farther away from Beirut, landed several hours after the first.

That decision-makers had for so long feared Communist governments in the Fertile Crescent makes understandable the language President Eisenhower chose to use in explaining the intervention in Lebanon to the American public. The Iraq coup of July 14 was apparently interpreted by the Eisenhower Administration as a Communist coup, and the major decision-makers apparently feared that Communist government was also imminent in the Lebanese conflict. So when, on July 15, the president delivered a radio-television address at the precise moment that United States Marines landed on Beirut's beaches, he spoke in grandiloquent terms of the threat in the Near East:

> What we now see in the Middle East is the same pattern of conquest with which we became familiar in the period 1945 to 1950. This involves taking over a nation by means of indirect aggression; that is, under the cover of a fomented civil strife the purpose is to put into domestic control those whose real loyalty is to the aggressor.
>
> It was by such means that the Communists attempted to take over Greece in 1947. That effort was thwarted by the Truman Doctrine.
>
> It was by such means that the Communists took over the mainland of China in 1949.
>
> It was by such means that the Communists attempted to take over Korea and Indochina, beginning in 1950.[21]

The perception of a Communist threat declined almost as soon as American troops arrived. After the decision to intervene was made, American leaders received more information on the Fertile Crescent situation. They learned that no hostile forces met the Marines as they landed and that the troops encountered only occasional sniper fire after they took control of the BLUEBAT objectives. It was also soon learned that there was no civil war in Iraq and that the new government was not Communist. By July 18 it was known that Premier Nuri as-Said and King Faisal of Iraq were dead. Intelligence reports received by President Eisenhower indicated that the new regime appeared to have effective control of the country. By July 19 there were intelligence reports that Iraq wished to establish "good terms" with the United States and Britain.[22] Further, intelligence dossiers on the leaders of the new government indicated that they were neither Communists nor Nasserites, most being Iraqi nationalists. And with each day

---

[21] President Dwight D. Eisenhower, radio-television message, July 15, 1958, *Department of State Bulletin*, Vol. 39 (August 4, 1958), p. 185. Eisenhower states the situation in dramatic terms. According to Miles Copland, however, the Central Intelligence Agency did possess information that the Iraq coup was part of a "three-pronged operation" aimed also at King Hussein in Jordan and President Chamoun in Lebanon. Miles Copland, *The Game of Nations* (London: Weidenfeld and Nicolson, 1969), pp. 202–3.

[22] Eisenhower, *Waging Peace*, p. 278.

that United States forces met no opposition in Lebanon and consolidated their positions, a Syrian invasion of Lebanon became less plausible. It is no doubt indicative of changed perceptions that when President Eisenhower recorded a message on July 19 for servicemen on duty in Lebanon, he said nothing about maintaining military readiness. If the president had still feared a Communist government, he might have been expected to say something to counter the passiveness of the Lebanese, which was presumably destructive of fighting morale. Instead, he warned the troops that they would be assailed by propaganda and that there might be deliberate efforts to involve them in incidents that could later be exaggerated by propagandists.[23]

Changes in action came quickly with the change in perceptions. Army Task Force Alpha, en route to the Near East from Germany and rigged for a parachute drop, was ordered on July 16 to land at Incerlik air base. That the force was rigged to drop, rather than land, delayed the unloading at Incerlik. Instead of departing immediately for Beirut, Alpha remained at Incerlik until July 19. From there it could move into either Lebanon or Iraq. Jordan's King Hussein discovered new army plots against his government as United States forces first arrived in Lebanon. He formally requested British assistance, charging that Syria was infiltrating arms and that Jordan faced a threat of Syrian invasion. The British cabinet approved military intervention; it planned to send paratroops from Cyprus. With Task Force Alpha at Incerlik, the British forces were no longer needed as reserves. Both Prime Minister Harold Macmillan and Foreign Secretary Selwyn Lloyd, who arrived in Washington on July 17, attempted to persuade President Eisenhower to make the Jordan operation a joint American-British action. But the president, while approving the British plan and offering logistic support, refused to permit American forces to participate directly. The British intervened in Jordan alone on July 17. Foreign Secretary Lloyd, in conversations with President Eisenhower and Secretary Dulles on July 17, reportedly reached agreement not to extend military intervention to Iraq.[24] On July 17, also, General Shehab asked Brigadier General Wade, now in charge of United States ground forces in Lebanon, to group these forces so that they would not appear to be occupation troops. Wade agreed.[25] By July 21, Shehab informed Wade that he was placing Lebanese army troops between the positions of United States forces and those of the

---

[23] *The New York Times,* July 20, 1958, 14:6.
[24] *Ibid.,* July 18, 1958, 1:6.   [25] Shulimson, *op. cit.,* pp. 22–23.

APPEAL TO FORCE

Lebanese armed opposition. On July 19 Task Force Alpha was sent to Lebanon, where it was stationed on the roads leading into Beirut from the north. After July 19 no more combat units were sent. The second army battle group alerted in Germany was kept there. A few more combat Marines arrived later, but these were replacements. The number of United States military personnel in Lebanon eventually swelled to 14,000 only after the arrival of supply and support units needed to maintain the combat forces.

About July 17, two days after American forces first landed, major decision-makers seemingly focused their attention on finding a solution to the Lebanese crisis through a negotiated settlement among the Lebanese. That day Under-Secretary of State Robert Murphy was dispatched to the scene. Murphy apparently assumed that a settlement negotiated among the Lebanese combatants would be the most satisfactory solution. He did not believe that Communists were active in Lebanon, and on July 19 he and Admiral Holloway could agree that "communism" was not a direct participant in the conflict between the Lebanese.[26] Consequently, Murphy encouraged the Lebanese to negotiate a settlement, and recommended to Washington that it support General Shehab for president. Shehab was not the only man available; a pro-Chamoun politician could have been installed and maintained by American troops. Indeed, Shehab must have been distasteful to the Eisenhower Administration, since President Nasser had recommended in May that the Lebanese general take over the government. Yet, although the choice of Shehab was a quasi-Nasserite solution, it permitted American disengagement. At the price of a less than ideal regime the United States could withdraw its troops—for Shehab had the Lebanese army and a large popular following behind him. American policy-makers accepted Shehab as a presidential candidate and facilitated his election.

Thus the Eisenhower Administration perceived in Lebanon on July 14, 1958, the threat of the establishment of a Communist government. Once American troops landed, however, events and new information modified that view. The quick change in Washington's attitude toward the conflict in Lebanon has led some observers to wonder whether President Eisenhower's statement of July 15 about the Communist danger in the Near East was not mere rationalization. It was certainly more than that. The military contingency plans used for the Lebanon

[26] Robert Murphy, *Diplomat Among Warriors* (Garden City, N.Y.: Doubleday, 1964), p. 404.

intervention were specifically designed to prevent a takeover of Lebanon by a Syrian invasion, and the Eisenhower Administration believed that Syria was becoming a Communist state. The plans had been developed at the direction of the United States Joint Chiefs of Staff and approved by them once formulated. The use of these plans was specifically approved by President Eisenhower; and while British troops were excluded from the initial deployment by the choice of top leaders, the military objectives—airport, docks, and the road to Damascus—were not altered. Those objectives, especially control of the Damascus Road, were important primarily to the containment of a Syrian assault; they had only secondary significance for the containment of conflict among Lebanese. The rapid change in perceptions once intervention had begun demonstrates instead that the impressions of top leaders of American government are fortunately not immutable. They can sometimes be affected by information and events.

The rapid change in Washington's view of the Lebanese situation has suggested to other observers that the "real" threat perceived might have been one to the Western supply of oil from the Near East. It is indeed likely that the Eisenhower Administration believed the oil supply to be endangered by the conflict in Lebanon and the coup in Iraq. Major oil pipelines cross both Iraq and Lebanon. A threat of Communist government and a threat to oil (or any other natural resource), however, are not mutually exclusive perceptions. The policy-makers probably perceived both threats at the same time. Most crises involving complex events do pose multiple dangers, and it would be surprising should American leaders see only one at a time. The theory of military intervention does not require that a threat of Communist government be the only impression in the minds of American decision-makers; all that is necessary is that it be one of them.

SOUTH VIETNAM

The threat of Communist government in South Vietnam was more obvious than the threat in Lebanon. In consequence, Washington's perceptions of Vietnam were simpler than those of Lebanon. From the time they took office in January 1961, President Kennedy and his advisers assumed that the Viet Cong were fighting for control of the government in South Vietnam. The Administration believed that if the Viet Cong should win, a Communist government would emerge, allied with Ho Chi Minh and North Vietnam.[27] This view of the situation was so deeply held and widely shared that there was no one at top levels to question it and it did not have to be mentioned or justified in meetings. It had been assumed in Washington from the time conflict resumed in South Vietnam in the late 1950's that the insurgents were "Communists." The assumption was not inaccurate. The term "Viet Cong" was coined by the Diem government as a name for the opposition. Until 1960 the opposition was too disunited to have a name for itself; then it formed the "National Liberation Front." Not all Viet Cong or National Liberation Front members were Communists. Nevertheless, most of the opposition leadership admired Ho Chi Minh, sought reunification with North Vietnam, and received moral support, supplies, and some direction from the government of North Vietnam and its official Lao Dong (Communist) party. In addition, many of the leaders of the Viet Cong had fought with the Viet Minh in the war against the French.

Washington also believed that Vietnam was part of a Communist-threatened region, a perspective the Kennedy Administration had inherited from the Eisenhower Administration. The belief that Southeast Asia was a Communist-threatened region may have originated in the late 1940's when wars of liberation erupted simultaneously in nearly all the countries of the area. The view was not publicly enunciated, however, until the 1950's.

Hanson Baldwin, military affairs correspondent for *The New York Times,* was among the first to talk about the perceived Communist threat. In early 1954 he noted that major American political leaders regarded Indochina as the "key" to Southeast Asia, where the neighboring countries of Thailand, Burma, and Malaya were militarily weak.[28] United States leaders began to speak for themselves after the Viet Minh began their devastating attack on Dienbienphu in March 1954. On March 29 Secretary of State John Foster Dulles delivered an address to the Overseas Press Club in which he stated that if Communist forces won control of Indochina, they would then attack the other "free peoples" of Southeast Asia.[29] Secretary Dulles repeated this view before the House Foreign Affairs Committee on April 5, saying that

[27] Arthur M. Schlesinger, Jr., *A Thousand Days* (Boston: Houghton Mifflin, 1965), pp. 320–23 and 536–40; Theodore C. Sorensen, *Kennedy* (New York: Harper & Row, 1965), pp. 648–61; Roger Hilsman, *To Move a Nation* (Garden City, N.Y.: Doubleday, 1967), pp. 419–24.

[28] *The New York Times,* February 7, 1954, IV, 5:1; and March 28, 1954, IV, 5:1.

[29] *Ibid.,* March 30, 1954, 4:1.

he saw China's aim to be not merely the takeover of Indochina but of all Southeast Asia, including Malaya, Thailand, Indonesia, the Philippines, Australia, and New Zealand.[30] Then President Eisenhower, at an April 7 press conference, described the analogy to dominoes that has since become so famous: "You had a row of dominoes set up, and you knocked over the first one, and what would happen to the last one was the certainty that it would go over very quickly." [31]

There is reason to believe that the President's off-the-cuff and grammatically confused remark overstated the decision-makers' perception of threat to the region. Secretary Dulles assured a May 11 news conference that the "domino theory" did not have automatic effects; if the free nations of Asia would unite, they could prevent their own fall.[32] Eisenhower, too, was more cautious in writing his memoirs than he had been at the April 7 news conference. In describing, in the memoirs, his views of Southeast Asia of 1954, he merely said that the fall of Indochina would threaten Burma and Malaya and bring added risks to East Pakistan, South Asia, and Indonesia.[33]

It is not important here whether policy-makers of the Eisenhower Administration really believed in the domino theory. Whether or not their views were so extreme, they did believe that a Communist government in Indochina increased the probabilities of Communist governments being formed in other countries of the region. The geographic range of the threat is ambiguous and is reflected in the differing statements of 1954. Interpreting the statements narrowly, however, it can be said that the top leaders perceived mainland Southeast Asia, including Indochina, Burma, Thailand, and Malaya, as a Communist-threatened region.

The United States did not intervene at Dienbienphu. At the Geneva conference that followed France's defeat, Indochina was partitioned. One of the new nations—North Vietnam—gained a Communist government, and most of the other states of the region retained Communist insurgent groups. The Geneva settlement did not give stability to Southeast Asia. It would be more accurate to say that the "Communist-threatenedness" of the region increased when Ho Chi Minh gained control of government in North Vietnam. The Eisenhower Administration continued to regard the region as a threatened one throughout the 1950's.

[30] *Ibid.,* April 6, 1954, 4:2.
[31] *Ibid.,* April 8, 1954, 18:1.   [32] *Ibid.,* May 12, 1954, 6:2.
[33] Dwight D. Eisenhower, *Mandate for Change* (Garden City, N.Y.: Doubleday, 1963), p. 333.

APPEAL TO FORCE

This perception of mainland Southeast Asia did not change significantly when the Kennedy Administration took office in 1961. On one occasion, during a television interview, President Kennedy went so far as to say that he accepted the domino theory as applied to Southeast Asia.[34] As with President Eisenhower, this may have been an overstatement, but the Kennedy Administration did believe that a Communist government in South Vietnam would increase the probabilities of Communist governments in neighboring countries. As Arthur Schlesinger observed of the views of the major decision-makers in 1961, whether the domino theory had had any validity in 1954, it gained appropriateness as other nations of the region tied their security to South Vietnam and the United States.[35] As stated in the State Department publication of December 1961 *A Threat to the Peace,* a "Communist victor' ' in South Vietnam would "seal the fate of Laos" and subject Cambodia and Thailand to guerrilla tactics.[36]

The military intervention that began in South Vietnam in 1961 expanded to the neighboring countries of North Vietnam and Laos in 1965 and to Cambodia in 1970, just as the intervention in Korea had expanded. Again, as in Korea, the expansion seemed to violate the rules of intervention. Although the Johnson Administration may have perceived a threat of Communist government in Laos because there

---

[34] John F. Kennedy, NBC interview with Huntley-Brinkley, September 9, 1963, *Department of State Bulletin,* Vol. 49 (September 30, 1963), p. 499.

[35] Schlesinger, *op. cit.,* p. 538.

[36] U.S. Department of State, *A Threat to the Peace,* Part I, Far Eastern Series No. 110 (Washington: Government Printing Office, 1961), pp. 51–52. This document was intended for public consumption, but similar rhetoric appeared in important internal documents. Secretary McNamara, Under-Secretary of Defense Roswell Gilpatric, and the Joint Chiefs of Staff prefaced a memorandum of November 8, 1961, to the president, recommending the use of American combat troops in Vietnam with the following words: "The fall of South Vietnam to Communism would lead to the fairly rapid extension of Communist control, or complete accommodation to Communism, in the rest of Southeast Asia and in Indonesia." U.S. Congress. House. Committee on Armed Services, *United States–Vietnam Relations, 1945–1967,* a study prepared by the Department of Defense, Sec. V, Vol. 11 (12 vols.; Washington: Government Printing Office, 1971), p. 343. Similar language prefaces a recommendation to the president of November 11 from Rusk and McNamara: "The loss of South Viet-Nam would make pointless any further discussion about the importance of Southeast Asia to the free world: we would have to face the near certainty that the remainder of Southeast Asia and Indonesia would move to a complete accommodation with Communism, if not formal incorporation within the Communist bloc." *Ibid.,* p. 359. These statements had bargaining purposes; they are overdrawn and the reference to Indonesia was deleted from later public documents. Nevertheless, these words suggest the rhetorical climate in which decision was reached in November 1961.

had been a many-sided civil war there that included a significant Communist element, and although the Nixon Administration could have seen the risk of a Communist government in Cambodia, no such perception was possible for North Vietnam. North Vietnam already had a Communist government. Also, the bombing of Laos was for the most part not directly related to the Laotian civil war, which had been relatively quiet since the Geneva settlement of 1962. Instead, the bombing of Laos was primarily the bombing of the Ho Chi Minh Trail, a supply route from North to South Vietnam. The ground operation in Cambodia was also primarily directed against Viet Cong supply caches and a military command headquarters in regions of the country bordering South Vietnam. Such threat as there was to Cambodia itself was left largely to the Cambodians to contain. What the expansion of the intervention demonstrates is that, as in the case of North Korea, military action can sometimes be expanded within a region into countries where it would not begin.

THE DOMINICAN REPUBLIC

A factor crucial to the occurrence of United States military intervention in the Dominican Republic was the perception of major American leaders in 1965 of Latin America as a region of special interest to the United States, as President Johnson said in his State of the Union address, January 4, 1965:

> With the free Republics of Latin America I have always felt—and our country has always felt—very special ties of interest and affection. It will be the purpose of my administration to strengthen these ties. Together we share and shape the destiny of the new world.[37]

The president did not suggest in this speech that such "special ties" existed between the United States and any other major region of the world. Of Asia he merely said, "Our own security is tied to the peace of Asia." Of Europe he said, "[United States] European policy is not based on any abstract design. It is based on the realities of common interests and common values, common dangers and common expecta-

---

[37] President Lyndon B. Johnson, "The State of the Union," address to Congress, January 4, 1965, *Department of State Bulletin*, Vol. 52 (January 25, 1965), p. 96.

tions." The president did not speak of United States ties to Africa, nor did he even mention the Near East. Ambassador Ellsworth Bunker, not a major decision-maker but United States representative to the Council of the Organization of American States, presumably spoke for major decision-makers in a January 30, 1965, speech in which he quoted President Johnson and cited the deep historical roots of those "special ties of interest and affection." [38]

The "special ties" meant, among other things, that men in Washington viewed the possibility of another Communist government in the Western Hemisphere as radically unacceptable. President Johnson said so himself on May 2, 1965, although only after the fact of United States military intervention in the Dominican Republic:

> The American nations cannot, must not, and will not permit the establishment of another Communist government in the Western Hemisphere. This was the unanimous view of all the American nations when, in January 1962, they declared, and I quote: "The principles of communism are incompatible with the principles of the inter-American system."
>
> This is what our beloved President John F. Kennedy meant when, less than a week before his death, he told us: "We in this hemisphere must also use every resource at our command to prevent the establishment of another Cuba in this hemisphere . . . ." [39]

The attitude that another Communist government in Latin America was radically unacceptable has been called by some the "another Cuba" complex. Journalist-biographer Philip Geyelin, Senator J. William Fulbright, and Ambassador Philip Bonsal have agreed that this attitude existed among top United States political leaders in April 1965.[40]

[38] Ellsworth Bunker, "The United States and Latin America: 'Special Ties of Interest and Affection,' " address before the Pan American Liaison Committee of Women's Organizations, Washington, D.C., January 30, 1965, *Department of State Bulletin*, Vol. 52 (March 1, 1965), pp. 301–4.

[39] President Lyndon B. Johnson, statement of May 2 broadcast over radio and television, *Department of State Bulletin*, Vol. 52 (May 17, 1965), p. 746. President Johnson's earlier statements on the crisis did not emphasize a Communist threat. The explanation may be that each of the earlier statements was brief and devoted primarily to describing what the United States was doing. The statement of May 2 was the first extended explanation and justification for the intervention. See also President Lyndon B. Johnson, statement of April 28, statement of April 30 broadcast over radio and television, and statements of May 1, *Department of State Bulletin*, Vol. 52 (May 17, 1965), pp. 738–44.

[40] Philip Geyelin, *Lyndon B. Johnson and the World* (New York: Praeger, 1966), p. 254; Senator James W. Fulbright, *Congressional Record* (daily), Sen-

The Johnson Administration further perceived the possibility of a Communist government in the Dominican Republic after armed conflict erupted there on April 24, 1965, but two factors that existed before that date may have predisposed top American leaders to see this possibility. One was the belief that Cuba and Castro sought to export Communist revolution to other Latin American countries. Though expressed often, this belief was stated in especial detail by Under-Secretary of State George Ball in April 1964.[41] The second factor was the apparent and long-held conviction of United States policy-makers that the Dominican Republic was particularly susceptible to a Communist government.[42] Even President Kennedy had seemed to share the fear that non-Communist liberals in the Dominican Republic might not be strong enough to prevent such a government.[43] There were in fact four Communist parties in the Dominican Republic in January 1965: the Dominican Socialist Party (PSP), which changed its name to the Dominican Communist Party (PCD) in August 1965; the Popular Dominican Movement (MPD); the National Revolutionary Party (PNR); and the 14th of June political grouping. Of these, the 14th of June was the one the State Department's Bureau of Intelligence and Research reported had a "mass following." [44]

What was the perception of the situation in the Dominican Republic held by major decision-makers the evening of April 28, 1965, when overt military intervention was approved? They apparently perceived three intertwined, salient characteristics: general disorder and lack of government, a threat to the lives of United States citizens in the Dominican Republic, and the possibility of a Communist government in

ate, September 15, 1965, p. 23003; and Philip W. Bonsal, "Open Letter to an Author, The Dominican Republic: Days of Turmoil," letter from Philip Bonsal to John Bartlow Martin, *Foreign Service Journal*, Vol. 44 (February 1967), p. 41.

[41] George Ball, "Principles of Our Policy Toward Cuba," address before the Omicron Delta Kappa Society, Roanoke, Va., April 23, 1964, *Department of State Bulletin*, Vol. 50 (May 11, 1964), pp. 738–44. President Johnson's account of the Dominican intervention in his memoirs also alludes to the omnipresence of Castro in the Caribbean; but Johnson does not elaborate the point. Lyndon B. Johnson, *The Vantage Point: Perspectives of the Presidency, 1963–1969* (New York: Holt, Rinehart and Winston, 1971), p. 188.

[42] This theme recurs frequently in John Bartlow Martin's account of his ambassadorship, *Overtaken by Events* (Garden City, N.Y.: Doubleday, 1966), esp. p. 476.

[43] Schlesinger, *op. cit.*, p. 770.

[44] U.S. Department of State, Bureau of Intelligence and Research, *World Strength of the Communist Party Organizations*, 17th Annual Report (Washington: Department of State, 1965).

APPEAL TO FORCE

the Dominican Republic. Of the first perception the president himself said on May 2, 1965, that during the first days of revolt, "control and effective government dissolved in conflict and confusion." [45] Of the second perception President Johnson said that Ambassador Bennett's "critic" cable emphasized the danger to United States nationals.[46] Philip Geyelin, John Bartlow Martin, and the Center for Strategic Studies, none of whom were present at the time of decision but all of whom subsequently had access to major foreign affairs leaders and to important documents, agree that the top leaders perceived a threat to United States citizens in the Dominican Republic.[47] It is also agreed by both "insiders" and outside observers that the major decision-makers discerned the possibility of a Communist government in the Dominican Republic.[48] The president himself said as much in his May 2 speech:

> The revolutionary movement took a tragic turn. Communist leaders, many of them trained in Cuba, seeing a chance to increase disorder, to gain a foothold, joined the revolution. What had begun as a popular democratic revolution, committed to democracy and social justice, very shortly moved and was taken over and really seized and placed into the hands of a band of Communist conspirators.[49]

Under-Secretary of State Thomas Mann, however, has insisted that no decision was made on "whether the Communist elements in the rebel camp presented a clear and imminent peril to the freedom of the Dominican nation" until the next evening, April 29.[50] Nevertheless,

---

[45] President Lyndon B. Johnson, statement of May 2, 1965, broadcast over radio and television, *op. cit.*, p. 744.

[46] *Ibid.*

[47] Center for Strategic Studies, *Dominican Action—1965*, Special Report No. 2 (Washington: Center for Strategic Studies, Georgetown University, 1966), pp. viii–ix; Geyelin, *op. cit.*, p. 256; and Martin, *op. cit.*, p. 705.

[48] Center for Strategic Studies, *loc. cit.*; Geyelin, *loc. cit.*; Martin, *loc. cit.*; Fulbright, *op. cit.*, p. 23001; and Theodore Draper, "Dominican Crisis: A Case Study in American Policy," *Commentary*, Vol. 40 (December 1965), pp. 40–41. Although Draper allows that Washington saw a Communist threat in the Dominican Republic, he has also asserted that many policy-makers opposed the return of Juan Bosch to the Republic whether or not they saw a Communist threat through him. "The Dominican Intervention Reconsidered," *Political Science Quarterly*, Vol. 86 (March 1971), pp. 29–30.

[49] President Lyndon B. Johnson, statement of May 2, 1965, broadcast over radio and television, *op. cit.*, p. 745.

[50] Thomas Mann, "The Dominican Crisis: Correcting Some Misconceptions," address before the Inter-American Press Association, October 12, 1965, San Diego, Calif., *Department of State Bulletin*, Vol. 53 (November 8, 1965), p. 735.

PERCEPTIONS OF THREAT

Mann admitted that the major decision-makers were aware of, and concerned about, "the growth of Communist influence" when they decided, on April 28, to send the first troops. This fact would suggest that United States political leaders need not always verbally and formally make a decision that there is a great possibility of a Communist government for United States overt military intervention to occur. In some situations it may be enough that the policy-makers believe and tacitly agree that there is a significant possibility of such a government.

PERCEPTION AND MISPERCEPTION

Each time United States overt military intervention began in a region, decision-makers evidently perceived the possibility of a new Communist government. The interventions also seem to demonstrate other things about perceptions of threat. The Korean intervention indicates that political leaders may perceive threat in a situation and so intervene even when they do not expect they will. As Secretary Acheson's speech suggested, the Truman Administration did not expect to intervene in a Korean conflict. The Lebanese intervention suggests that perceptions of threat may be transient; the perception may change after intervention begins. The Dominican and Lebanese interventions may indicate the possibility of one kind of misperception—the perception of significant Communist threat where there is only the remote possibility of Communist government. The Vietnam intervention suggests the possibility of a different kind of misperception—the underestimation of threat and the misunderstanding of the nature of a threat. In the late 1950's decision-makers apparently assumed the major threat to South Vietnam to be the likelihood of North Vietnamese invasion; after 1960 they realized the major threat was from guerrillas inside South Vietnam, but they consistently underestimated the kind and amount of United States force required to subdue the insurgents.

All these "lessons" of the interventions dramatize the distance between reality and perception. If reality spawns perceptions, it does not rear them to consciousness. The opportunities for distortion are manifold. One source of distortion may be the dependence of policy-makers on reports. In each situation where American intervention occurred, decision-makers received reports describing the extent and nature of the danger of a Communist government. The reports may not always have mirrored reality with accuracy, and the decision-makers may not always have interpreted them correctly. Another possible source of distortion may be the inaccurate assumptions United States leaders hold of countries before crisis erupts. The Truman Administration seemingly assumed in early 1950 that it would not intervene in Korea, underestimating both its own inclinations and the blatancy with which South Korea might be threatened. For the Dominican Republic and for the Fertile Crescent, political leaders assumed a great danger of Communist governments when the real threat of communism may have been very small. And when acting in Vietnam, the Kennedy and Johnson administrations carried assumptions about the usefulness of modern military forces in containing guerrilla war and about the viability of the Saigon government that may have grossly overestimated the abilities of both America's forces and South Vietnam's government.

4

RESTRAINTS ON INTERVENTION

The theory of United States overt military intervention we are advancing maintains that the direct and open use of force occurs only in the absence of specific obstacles. One requirement is that major American decision-makers perceive the threat of a new Communist government. As we have seen, the four times intervention occurred after World War II, they did see such a threat. But the international system, top-level decision-making practices, and the operational code of major decision-makers raise additional barriers. If the theory is correct, none of America's postwar interventions should have violated even one of the restraints. The further requirements envisaged by the theory, as detailed in Chapter 1, can be condensed to the following five predictions about a decision to intervene: (1) intervention will not entail fighting the Soviet Union directly; (2) it will not require the use of nuclear weapons; (3) the president will not permit others a veto; (4) intervention will not have become unnecessary because of an early end to the threat, the assumption of the burden by another nation or international organization, or the containment of the threat by local actors with no more than limited American assistance; and (5) there will exist a request, armed conflict, and condemnable intervention by another nation sufficient to yield moral justification for United States action. If the system of restraints does determine the when and where of overt military intervention by the United States, all of these predictions will be correct for each of the four interventions.

APPEAL TO FORCE

FIGHTING THE SOVIET UNION

American forces did not meet Soviet troops in any of the four interventions. Objectively, then, American action in Korea, Lebanon, Vietnam, and the Dominican Republic did not require that the United States fight the Soviet Union. A subtler question is whether United States decision-makers *thought* that intervention would lead to war between the superpowers. This restraint must act through the minds of the men who make the decisions. There was no thought of global war when overt military intervention began in Vietnam and the Dominican Republic. By 1961 Vietnam had been in crisis long enough that Washington knew from intelligence reports that there were no Russian troops in the vicinity, and beginning close combat support was too little different from past actions to generate fear that the Soviet Union would retaliate. The Dominican Republic was far from Russian shores, and no Soviet combat troops were stationed anywhere in the Western Hemisphere in 1965. Nor did the Soviet Union have forces in Lebanon or Korea at the time of those decisions. None had been stationed in the Fertile Crescent at any time since World War II, and those in North Korea had been withdrawn in 1948. Nevertheless, the possibility of Russian counterintervention was discussed before the decisions were made in 1950 and 1958.

The question of Soviet reaction arose early in the discussions on Lebanon the morning of July 14, 1958. News of the coup in Iraq began the day. Allen Dulles, director of the Central Intelligence Agency, was among the first to hear; he called his brother, Secretary of State John Foster Dulles, by 7:00 A.M.[1] President Eisenhower was also informed as he entered his office. Secretary Dulles and the president conferred with one another by telephone; afterward they held independent discussions with advisers. General Nathan Twining, chairman of the Joint Chiefs of Staff, Deputy Secretary of Defense Donald Quarles, and Assistant Secretary of Defense for International Security Affairs Mansfield Sprague assembled at the secretary of state's office shortly after 9:00 A.M. (General Twining had already talked to the president.) Also attending Dulles's meeting were State Department personnel, including Counselor G. Frederick Reinhardt and Under-Secretaries Robert Murphy and Loy Henderson. Allen Dulles and Norman Paul of the CIA

[1] Fletcher Knebel, "Day of Decision," *Look*, Vol. 22 (September 16, 1958), p. 17.

arrived within the hour.[2] Those from the Defense Department were asked their judgment whether the Soviet Union would react should the United States intervene in the Fertile Crescent. Their replies substantially agreed: although there was a risk of Russian response, particularly against Turkey and Iran, the Soviet Union would be deterred by the threat of United States nuclear retaliation. The agenda of a National Security Council meeting that had been scheduled for that morning to discuss civil defense studies was changed to focus upon the situation in the Near East. Secretary Dulles, Mansfield Sprague, General Twining, and Allen Dulles arrived at 10:45 to meet Secretary of the Treasury Robert Anderson, Vice-President Nixon, President Eisenhower, and others already on hand.[3] Allen Dulles opened the discussion, presenting what intelligence was available, and adding at the end his judgment that, if the United States did intervene, the Soviet Union would not join the conflict. Secretary of State Dulles then outlined the results of his earlier meeting at the State Department. At the conclusion of his analysis the secretary was asked whether he thought the Soviet Union would intervene if America acted; he did not think it would.[4] The question of whether Russia would respond came up once again that afternoon when twenty-two members of Congress met at the White House to be briefed and consulted on the Near Eastern situation. The congressmen invited included the leadership and senior members of both parties. Congressman Carl Vinson, chairman of the House Armed Services Committee, reminded those present of the possibility of a Soviet response and asked whether the Administration was willing "to go the distance," risking Russian retaliation. The members of the Administration present at the meeting, including Secretary Dulles, Allen Dulles, General Twining, and the president, expressed willingness to run the risk. Tankers of the Strategic Air Command were deployed to forward positions that afternoon when the president ordered the Marines to land. Forward deployment of tankers placed the nuclear-armed bombers of the Strategic Air Command on higher alert and also signaled Russia that America was ready to retaliate.

The Eisenhower Administration, congressional leaders, and senior military officers demonstrated willingness to approve the open and di-

---

[2] Eleanor Lansing Dulles, *John Foster Dulles: The Last Year* (New York: Harcourt, Brace and World, 1963), p. 143.

[3] Robert Cutler, *No Time for Rest* (Boston: Little, Brown, 1966), p. 363.

[4] Dwight D. Eisenhower, *Waging Peace* (Garden City, N.Y.: Doubleday, 1965), p. 271.

rect use of military force in Lebanon even if doing so risked military response from the Soviet Union. But the senior foreign policy, intelligence, and military experts—John Foster Dulles, Allen Dulles, and General Twining respectively—each heavily discounted the probability of Russian counteraction. One does not know what they would have done had they thought direct response more likely.

The decision to intervene in Korea indicates more clearly how great a risk of direct confrontation will be accepted. The Truman Administration was much more uncertain about what the Soviet Union would do in Korea than the Eisenhower Administration was about Lebanon. From the very beginning of the Korean conflict on June 24, 1950, the extent of Moscow's participation in the invasion was a matter of major concern in Washington. Had the Soviet Union directed it? If so, what were its intentions? If Russia was not directly involved at the outset, would it intervene later? By the time of the first Blair House conference, the foreign affairs leaders—President Truman and top officials of the State Department and the Department of Defense—had answered some of their own questions. Among those present at this meeting the night of June 25, 1950, representing the State Department were Secretary of State Dean Acheson, Under-Secretary James E. Webb, Assistant Secretaries John D. Hickerson and Dean Rusk, and Ambassador-at-Large Philip C. Jessup. The large Department of Defense delegation included Secretary of Defense Louis Johnson, Secretary of the Army Frank Pace, Secretary of the Navy Francis P. Matthews, Secretary of the Air Force Thomas K. Finletter, Chairman of the Joint Chiefs of Staff General Omar Bradley, Army Chief of Staff General J. Lawton Collins, Navy Chief of Naval Operations Admiral Forrest P. Sherman, and Air Force Chief of Staff General Hoyt S. Vandenberg.[5] The group assumed that the invasion was Soviet-controlled, although there were no reports from United States intelligence in Korea of Russian troop units among the attacking forces. Still, they were puzzled about the Soviet Union's intentions. Was it planning to strike elsewhere, too? Was it knowingly risking direct confrontation with the United States and thus global war? President Truman ordered an immediate worldwide survey of United States intelligence to find some indications of the intentions behind the actions. On the possibility of direct Soviet intervention in the Far East, the president directed that the balance of United States-Soviet forces in the Far East be ana-

[5] Glenn Paige, *The Korean Decision, June 24–30, 1950* (New York: Free Press, 1968), p. 125.

RESTRAINTS ON INTERVENTION

lyzed. He also asked the Joint Chiefs of Staff to estimate what would be needed to neutralize Russian bases in that area.

American intelligence was reanalyzed during the next twenty-four hours. Available information suggested Korea was not the beginning of a global onslaught, but merely a local conflict. The evening of June 26 the president and his policy advisers again gathered at Blair House to consider the Korean crisis. Under-Secretary of State H. Freeman Matthews here substituted for Under-Secretary Webb, and Navy Secretary Francis P. Matthews arrived only after the meeting adjourned; with these exceptions the group was the same as had met the night before.[6] Consensus existed at this second Blair House meeting that should the United States act in Korea, Soviet counterintervention would be improbable, yet possible. The conferees assumed that the Soviet Union would be surprised by American intervention; they believed Russia expected South Korea to be an easy victory, and they doubted that it had prepared a contingency plan for dealing with United States action.

Nevertheless, the Truman Administration recognized the risk of Soviet intervention and took steps to deter it. When the conference approved American air operations in support of South Korea, it was agreed by all that those operations ought not to extend to North Korea. One argument presented for limiting air strikes to the South was that avoiding the North would minimize the chance of direct Russian or Chinese intervention. The next day, June 27, the United States ambassador to Moscow delivered a note to the Russian foreign minister asking the Soviet Union to disavow responsibility for the attack on South Korea and requesting the use of its influence to effect a withdrawal. Few expected the note to end the attack, but it served notice of American concern and offered the Kremlin an opportunity to avoid direct involvement. The National Security Council meeting of June 28 took a further step to reduce the risk of confrontation with the Soviet Union by instructing the United States Far East forces that, if they met Russian troops, they should fight only to withdraw. The council members felt that in the event of Soviet intervention, they would be required to make further decisions. The policy-makers limited but did not avoid the risked confrontation: They approved air strikes in South Korea on July 26, and on July 29 they approved air strikes in North Korea as well.

All the discussions of possible Soviet intervention were based upon

[6] *Ibid.*, pp. 161–62.

the most fragmentary information in the first days of the crisis. The Truman Administration was even unsure that Soviet forces were absent from Korea. There had been no United States intelligence report of Russian combat troops in the invading force, but some newspapers had reprinted statements by South Koreans asserting direct Soviet participation.[7] The president and his chief advisers discounted these newspaper reports, however. The greater concern was that the Soviet Union might become involved.

The decision of June 26, 1950, suggests important limits of the restraint on intervention when it might confront the forces of the Soviet Union. First, military intervention can be restrained if Soviet forces are directly involved, but it is not necessarily restrained if decision-makers merely think the Soviet Union will counterintervene. American political leaders are willing to run some risk of direct confrontation. The tacit bargain between the United States and Russia merely restrains American initiation of direct confrontation. Of course, if the tacit bargain is truly reciprocal, American military intervention will deter Soviet military intervention—Russian counteraction would make the Soviet Union the initiator of open conflict between the superpowers. Second, the decision to intervene in Korea in the face of uncertainty about Soviet presence suggests that American leaders will run some risk of initiating confrontation if they judge the risk to be a small one.

AVOIDING THE USE OF NUCLEAR WEAPONS

The second restraint of the international system is the tacit bargain between the United States and the Soviet Union not to use nuclear weapons. All conflicts risk the eventual use of nuclear weapons, but the tacit agreement restrains military action that must resort to them at the very outset of hostilities in order for the intervention to be successful. The need for nuclear weapons arises when conventional force is inadequate for a given task. One does not always know whether conventional force will suffice, but it is sometimes clear at the beginning of a conflict that nuclear weapons will be needed. Two types of circumstances may clearly require them. First, they can be required because the conflict is too large for the total existing conventional forces of the United States. Since the demobilization of United States armed forces

[7] *Ibid.*, p. 171.

at the end of World War II, the country has not possessed enough troops to fight an all-out war either in China or in Eastern Europe without using nuclear weapons. Intervention in either region would require them; hence it is restrained. Second, the disposition of United States forces, and limited transport, can occasionally prevent effective, rapid intervention without nuclear weapons. For each postwar intervention, the United States had enough conventional forces conveniently deployed, and sufficient transport, to enter the conflict. But conventional sufficiency has sometimes been the product of accident.

The size of the United States Air Force in the Far East and the number of United States combat forces in that area were larger in June 1950 than they might otherwise have been because of the United States's occupation of Japan. The five garrison divisions in Japan were understrength, as was the Far East Air Force. Nevertheless, these were not token forces, nor were they incapable of combat. Also, they were stationed in the immediate vicinity of Korea, near enough for ready transport.

American military intervention in Korea began with air operations, then expanded to include an army regimental combat team, later two army divisions, and finally many more divisions, more aircraft, and ships. At the beginning of the intervention, General MacArthur and the Joint Chiefs of Staff verified the ability of the Far East Air Force to undertake conventional bombing-strafing missions in Korea, and air operations were at first expected to bring success. When the two army divisions were deployed, President Truman was assured the United States had the ability to get them to Korea and maintain them; the two divisions were expected to save South Korea. In fact, American conventional forces were less sufficient than Washington believed. The fighting ability of the North Korean army was badly underestimated and that of the South Korean army overestimated. In July and early August 1950, United States and ROK forces were pushed back to the tip of the Korean peninsula until they held only a shallow perimeter around the port of Pusan. The defenders were forced to a strategy of inflicting as many casualties as possible on the North Korean army. They ran a race against time, trying to expand United States forces in Korea before those there were overrun. Only the behind-the-lines amphibious assault at Inchon relieved the pressure on Pusan. Before Inchon, total failure was a real possibility. Nevertheless, the Truman Administration believed United States conventional forces were adequate when they approved overt military intervention in June. There is no indication that the use of atomic weapons was then considered at the presidential level. Nuclear weapons were not perceived as necessary for effective intervention in Korea when the action began.

The ability of the United States to intervene in Lebanon in 1958 was also in part the product of circumstances. During the 1950's the United States's limited-war capability was small. Especially lacking was the ability to move large forces long distances on short notice. Several developments in United States forces in 1956–58, however, made intervention without nuclear weapons possible. In 1956 the Composite Air Strike Force was established under the Air Force Tactical Air Command. The Composite Air Strike Force was capable of collecting a balanced force of tactical fighters, bombers, and reconnaissance and troop-carrying craft and sending them to trouble spots halfway around the globe. Composite Air Strike Forces were dispatched to Lebanon in July 1958 and also to Taiwan in August during the offshore islands crisis. In 1957 the United States Army began to form the Strategic Army Corps, formally establishing it in May 1958. This force included four army divisions stationed in the United States. The divisions were not transportable by air, but they could be moved by sea to reinforce other more rapidly deployed units in a limited war. In 1957–58 United States Army forces in Europe were reorganized into "pentomic" (five-part) divisions, each of which included batteries of Honest John short-range, atomic-warhead–tipped missiles and air-transportable battle groups. In addition, the number of Marine battalion landing teams in the Mediterranean increased above normal in 1958. Usually the Sixth Fleet included but one battalion, but in May of 1958, when a fresh amphibious task force arrived to relieve the one on duty, both were kept in the Mediterranean. In June, when a third battalion arrived to replace the first, a slower than usual transfer meant that on July 14 all three were still in the region, although one was nearing Gibraltar on its return to home port. Also, days before the Iraq coup the chief of naval operations had fortuitously sent two landing teams and their vessels to the eastern end of the Mediterranean. All these developments plus the preparation in May 1958 of the military contingency plan code-named BLUEBAT, mapping the complex logistics procedures necessary to the deployment of troops, gave ready conventional capability for intervention in Lebanon on July 14, 1958. So, when President Eisenhower asked General Twining on the morning of July 14 whether the United States could intervene, the general was able to assure him that it could.

For Vietnam and the Dominican Republic there existed unquestioned conventional warfare capability. Military intervention began in South Vietnam on a very limited scale—advisers at planning levels, Green Berets, and air force helicopters and crews in December 1961. The magnitude of the effort increased far more gradually than that in Korea, and between 1950 and 1961 American logistics had improved and the numbers of limited war forces had increased. Conventional intervention in the Dominican Republic was even easier. The Caribbean "ready group," an amphibious task force with a battalion of United States Marines aboard, had been sent to the vicinity of the Dominican Republic three days before intervention was approved. Also, stationed at Fort Bragg, North Carolina, within easy airlift distance of Santo Domingo, were two full-strength divisions of the Strategic Army Corps.

It is significant that none of the four interventions ever included the use of nuclear weapons, even after military operations expanded. Since such weapons would have been of no advantage in the Dominican Republic, the question of their use did not arise in that instance. But Washington did have to resist a temptation to use nuclear weapons in the three other interventions. Some American military officers favored bombing Manchuria and the bridges of the Yalu River with nuclear weapons after China entered the Korean War. Other officers urged the use of battlefield tactical nuclear weapons in Vietnam to increase American firepower. The "bomb" was not used in Korea; and although some units deployed to Vietnam had been trained to use tactical nuclear devices and some tactical nuclear weapons were briefly deployed in Vietnam during 1965, such weapons have not been used in Southeast Asia. United States decision-makers have held to the limit of "no nuclear weapons," although they have violated the agreement prohibiting chemical warfare by allowing the use of tear gas and tree-defoliating compounds in Vietnam. Before the nuclear era, chemical and biological agents were the horror weapons, and the combatants in World War II scrupulously avoided their use.

In order to avoid using nuclear weapons, American forces have had sometimes to engage in logistic contortions. The Marines that landed at Beirut on July 15, 1958, carried with them howitzers capable of firing both nuclear and conventional projectiles. The amphibious task force carried both kinds of ammunition for the howitzers. But when these big guns were taken ashore, only the conventional ammunition went with them, and the nuclear projectiles remained aboard the ships throughout the Lebanon operation. The army battle group sent to Lebanon a few days later also possessed nuclear weapons, but these,

APPEAL TO FORCE

too, were kept out of the country. The battle group's heavier equipment was shipped by sea after the combat troops were deployed by air. An Honest John rocket battery with atomic warheads was a normal part of the seaborne equipment. The battery was loaded aboard ship and sent to Lebanon, but it never arrived. The Honest John rockets were shipped back to Germany without landing in the Near East.[8] Washington did not want nuclear weapons to be in Lebanon, much less to be used.

PREVENTING A NONPRESIDENTIAL VETO

By definition, if intervention occurs, the president has not permitted another policy leader to veto it. Nevertheless, it is interesting to see whom each president included in the decision-making process, for one of the most effective ways to avoid dissension in a discussion is to exclude those people who might disagree. There are some notable differences among the groups who made the decisions for intervention. On the one hand, the Korean and Lebanese decisions were taken within large groups; on the other, the Dominican decision was made by a small group.

The June 26, 1950, decision to intervene in Korea was made at Blair House with most of President Truman's chief foreign affairs advisers there. But no members of Congress attended. Present that evening were the president, Secretary of State Dean Acheson, Assistant Secretary of State for Far Eastern Affairs Dean Rusk, Assistant Secretary for International Organization Affairs John Hickerson, Ambassador-at-Large Philip C. Jessup, Secretary of Defense Louis Johnson, Secretary of the Army Frank Pace, Secretary of the Air Force Thomas Finletter, and the entire Joint Chiefs of Staff—Generals Bradley, Collins, and Vandenberg and Admiral Sherman.[9] None of those present opposed intervention by air strikes in South Korea. Only after the decision to intervene was made were members of Congress consulted. The morning of June 27 Secretary Acheson and Vice-President Alben Barkley met fourteen Republican and Democratic legislators, among them Speaker of the House Sam Rayburn, House Majority Leader John McCormack, Senate Majority Leader Scott Lucas, Sena-

---

[8] Nathan F. Twining, *Neither Liberty nor Safety* (New York: Holt, Rinehart, and Winston, 1966), p. 65; and Maxwell D. Taylor, *The Uncertain Trumpet* (New York: Harper, 1959), pp. 9–10.

[9] Paige, *op. cit.*, pp. 161–62.

tors Tom Connally and Styles Bridges, and Congressmen Carl Vinson and Mike Mansfield. The vice-president and the secretary informed the legislators of the decisions made; they did not ask for judgments, and they did not request a resolution in support of the decisions taken. None of those present said they opposed the use of the air force in Korea.

Later decisions of that same week were also made in large executive conferences: to commit service troops, to expand air operations to North Korea, and to commit two full divisions of combat troops. An exception was the decision to commit a regimental combat team, which was approved early in the morning of June 30, only hours before the National Security Council approved the commitment of two divisions. President Truman, in this instance, acted alone in a telephone conversation with Secretary of the Army Pace after General MacArthur had requested both the regimental combat team and the two divisions. All the group decisions were unanimous, and no major decision-maker opposed President Truman's single unilateral action after it was taken. After all these decisions had been made, the president and thirty of his advisers and their aides again briefed congressmen, late in the morning of June 30. The congressional delegation of fifteen included most of those who had been invited to the first briefing. The only one to object was Senator Kenneth Wherry, Senate minority leader, who had not attended the first meeting. He did not oppose the substance of the decisions; he merely said he felt Congress should have been consulted before the decision to commit combat forces had been made.[10] The unanimity among the executive decision-makers meant the president overrode no objections in approving overt military intervention; he did not have to consider whether to permit a veto. Also, the support of leading members of Congress suggests that had they been included in the actual decisions, they would not have argued against intervention.

The decision to intervene in Lebanon was also made within a large group of presidential advisers; but before United States forces were ordered to move, the Administration briefed members of Congress and asked their opinion. Secretary Dulles's morning meeting at the State Department considered alternatives: acting through the United Nations; "wait and see"; a statement warning of possible American intervention; or direct American action.[11] The alternatives to direct action came to appear unattractive, in general because they were thought too slow. By 10:30 the group was agreed that overt military intervention

[10] *Ibid.*, pp. 262–63.   [11] Knebel, *op. cit.*, p. 17.

appeared the best course of action. Dulles's group moved to the White House, where the alternatives were again discussed, this time in a larger group. Most of the major executive decision-makers were at the White House meeting: the president and the vice-president, the secretary of the treasury, the two Dulles brothers, the deputy secretary of defense, the chairman of the Joint Chiefs of Staff, and others. Allen Dulles opened the meeting with a pessimistic intelligence briefing. After the briefing President Eisenhower very nearly omitted asking Secretary Dulles for his appraisal; he started to turn to General Twining. Robert Cutler, secretary of the National Security Council, later interpreted that near slight to mean the president had already made up his mind to approve overt military intervention.[12] The president, however, did not announce a decision at that point, whether or not he had already formed one. The secretary of state gave his presentation, outlining the advantages and disadvantages of the alternatives discussed at the earlier meeting, after which the alternatives were discussed by all. The meeting was still going on at noon, when it was suggested that congressional leaders be called immediately for a briefing, and the decision was made to ask them to meet at the White House at 2:30 P.M. Both President Eisenhower and Secretary Dulles said they thought it important not to present a formal decision to the assembled leaders, apparently believing that a final decision in advance of the meeting would diminish support for any action taken. Accordingly, General Twining was directed to alert the Marine landing teams with the Sixth Fleet, but not to order them to land.[13]

Twenty-two members of Congress met at the appointed hour, including Senators Mansfield, Fulbright, Knowland, and Bridges and Congressmen Rayburn and Vinson. The president, Secretary Dulles, Allen Dulles, and General Twining each took a part in describing the situation in the Near East and the possibilities for action. The Administration explained that military intervention in Lebanon with a simultaneous appeal to the United Nations was their tentative decision. President Eisenhower then asked the legislators for their observations; they expressed more disagreement here than they had at the time of the Korean decision. Congressman Rayburn asked whether the fighting in Lebanon was not strictly a civil war; Senator Fulbright doubted that the conflict was Communist-inspired. If the United Nations Observation Group could not clearly identify Syria as a supporter of the Lebanese opposition, the senator asked, how could the Administration be sure of its own data? Senator Fulbright felt that unless Syria was sup-

[12] Cutler, *op. cit.*, p. 363.   [13] Knebel, *op. cit.*, p. 18.

porting the opposition, the United States ought not to intervene. Both Senators Mansfield and Fulbright said they preferred United Nations action, but other congressmen, including Vinson and several of the Republicans, supported direct American action. Despite some dissatisfaction, the congressional leaders generally accepted the plan to intervene in Lebanon, and not even Rayburn, Fulbright, or Mansfield tried to alter it.[14] Yet few present gave strong and open support. President Eisenhower inferred from this that the congressional leaders would support no broader action in the Fertile Crescent than the discussed intervention in Lebanon.[15] The president anticipated that intervention in Jordan or Iraq would not receive congressional support. After the legislators left the White House at 4:30 P.M., discussion turned to the details of intervention. The BLUEBAT military contingency plan was accepted and modified to include United States Army units in Europe in place of the British forces on Cyprus as originally planned. The decision was made to land the nearest Marine landing team on the Beirut beach with the next daytime high tide—3:00 P.M. the next day, Beirut time. At 5:30 P.M., Washington time, President Eisenhower told General Twining to execute the plans. The order was for intervention in Lebanon only.

It cannot be said that a congressional veto alone prevented simultaneous intervention in Lebanon, Jordan, and Iraq: for one thing, there was no armed conflict in Jordan, nor in Iraq (there the coup was quick and decisive); for another, there was no expectation that the new Iraqi government would request United States presence. As it developed, the intervention did not expand to Jordan or Iraq. As the American expansions of the conflicts in South Korea and South Vietnam demonstrate, interventions once begun may be expanded to include countries in which the United States would not begin overt action in a region. It is possible that Eisenhower permitted congressional leaders to veto expansion to Jordan and Iraq after the troops landed in Lebanon. However, the evaporation of the perceived Communist threat to the region a few days after the Marines landed no doubt also contributed to the limiting of the conflict.

Little has been written about the decision to provide combat military assistance to South Vietnam in December 1961. Even the "Pentagon Papers," a study of the history of United States-Vietnamese relations prepared by the Department of Defense for use within the government but leaked to the public, provide little information on who

[14] Sherman Adams, *Firsthand Report* (New York: Harper, 1961), p. 291.
[15] Eisenhower, *op. cit.*, p. 272.

APPEAL TO FORCE

participated in the decisions or on the specifics of discussions. We do know that formal approval for the dispatch of helicopters and crews was given at a National Security Council meeting of November 15, 1961. But it is possible that the issue was settled by November 11 when Secretary of State Rusk and Secretary of Defense McNamara submitted a joint recommendation to President Kennedy that reversed an earlier position of McNamara's and proposed actions and language that were adopted without significant change at the National Security Council meeting.[16] Statute defines the members of the National Security Council, and it is likely that Secretaries Rusk and McNamara, Vice-President Lyndon Johnson, Director of the Office of Emergency Planning Frank B. Ellis, Special Assistant to the President for National Security Affairs McGeorge Bundy, as well as the executive secretary of the council, Bromley Smith, were all present with President Kennedy at the important November 15 meeting. That General Maxwell Taylor's key recommendation for the use of ground troops in Vietnam was contained only in telegrams for "the eyes only" of the president, secretary of state, and secretary of defense makes it probable that discussions were limited to key Administration policy-makers. Thus, congressional leaders were likely excluded, but one might guess the names of some of the others who may have taken part on or before November 15: General Taylor and Deputy Special Assistant for National Security Affairs Walt W. Rostow—the two who made the original recommendations that triggered the decision; Central Intelligence Agency Director John A. McCone; Assistant Secretary of State for Far Eastern Affairs W. Averell Harriman; Under-Secretary of Defense Roswell Gilpatrick; and the Joint Chiefs of Staff, especially the chairman, General Lyman L. Lemnitzer. Whether or not to send helicopters and crews for them was apparently never in dispute after Taylor and Rostow returned from Vietnam. So far as we know, no one sought to veto the action; therefore, the president did not have to consider whether to permit it to be vetoed. Indeed, General Taylor, and, initially, Secretary McNamara, Under-Secretary of Defense Gilpatrick, and the Joint Chiefs of Staff, pressed President Kennedy to act more strongly and send combat troops.[17]

[16] U.S. Congress. House. Committee on Armed Services, *United States–Vietnam Relations, 1945–1967*, Sec. IV.B.1, Vol. 2 (12 vols.; Washington: Government Printing Office, 1971), p. 133.

[17] *Ibid.*, Sec. V, Vol. 11, p. 343; and Theodore Sorensen, *Kennedy* (New York: Harper & Row, 1965), pp. 653–55.

RESTRAINTS ON INTERVENTION

The decision to appeal to overt military force was thus made by a group that included the president and his key advisers. The circumstances thus resemble those for the decisions on Korea and Lebanon —choice made within a large group—but leaders of Congress were probably not consulted as they were before the final decision on Lebanon. They were probably not even briefed after the decision had been reached. The members of the National Security Council reportedly agreed not to publicize or emphasize the changes in policy approved on November 15.[18]

The circumstances of the decision to intervene in the Dominican Republic differed from those of the others. At 4:45 P.M., April 28, 1965, Secretary of State Rusk, Under-Secretary of State George Ball, and Secretary of Defense McNamara arrived at the White House to discuss the Vietnamese situation with President Johnson and his two special assistants, William Moyers and McGeorge Bundy.[19] At 5:30, during the discussion on Vietnam, the president received a cable from Ambassador Bennett describing the deteriorating situation in the Dominican Republic and recommending the intervention of American troops. President Johnson reportedly called Under-Secretary Thomas Mann at the State Department immediately.[20] Mann had been following closely the developments in the Dominican crisis. The president also called Senator Richard Russell at home to ask his opinion. Senator Russell inquired whether there was Communist influence among the Dominican revolutionaries, to which the president responded that there definitely was. Russell then recommended intervention to "avoid another Cuba."[21] Among the three advisers at the White House, none opposed military intervention. Rusk stated explicit support for military action. The decision to intervene was taken on the spot, without assembling a larger group of presidential advisers and without consulting any other members of Congress. By 6:00 P.M. the Defense Depart-

---

[18] *The New York Times,* November 17, 1961, 12:1.

[19] Lyndon B. Johnson, *The Vantage Point: Perspectives of the Presidency, 1963–1969* (New York: Holt, Rinehart, and Winston, 1971), p. 198; John Bartlow Martin. *Overtaken by Events* (Garden City, N.Y.: Doubleday, 1966), p. 656; and Rowland Evans and Robert Novak, *Lyndon B. Johnson: The Exercise of Power* (New York: New American Library, 1966), pp. 514–15.

[20] Philip Geyelin, *Lyndon B. Johnson and the World* (New York: Praeger, 1966), pp. 251–52.

[21] Senator Richard Russell, *Congressional Record,* Senate (daily), September 21, 1965; quoted in Theodore Draper, "Dominican Crisis: A Case Study in American Policy," *Commentary,* Vol. 40 (December 1965), p. 54.

ment was authorized to land up to 500 Marines. An hour later, as the Marines were landing, President Johnson informed congressional leaders of his decision.

The differences among the decisions indicates that there is room for "presidential style" in approving overt military intervention, as there is for other kinds of action. Truman used the large-group method to generate decisions, although he excluded members of Congress. Kennedy's practice was similar. Eisenhower also used large-group discussion, but he formally consulted members of Congress. Johnson relied only upon himself, those advisers who happened to be on hand, and a few more who could be reached by telephone. Johnson consulted but one member of Congress, albeit the single most influential member of the Senate. No president permitted another decision-maker a veto, but each avoided doing so in a different way. Johnson may have prevented objection by his choice of whom to consult. Eisenhower chose to override, in a sense, the objections of some legislators. And Truman was lucky—no one objected to intervention in Korea when it began.

INCREMENTAL DECISIONS

A striking similarity among the four interventions is that each was the product of a series of incremental choices. Military intervention was never the first action chosen to deal with crisis; some less extreme action was always tried first. Since decisions are made incrementally, there are three ways in which overt military intervention may become unnecessary before it is approved: an early step may solve the situation; another nation or the United Nations may intervene, assuming the burden for the United States; or the local actors may demonstrate that they can contain the situation with no more than limited American assistance. Each time the application of direct military force was approved—in Korea, Lebanon, Vietnam, and the Dominican Republic—American foreign affairs leaders perceived that overt military intervention was still necessary.

First steps solved none of the four crises. For Korea the first step was the June 25 request to the United Nations Security Council for a resolution condemning the invasion and demanding a cease-fire and withdrawal. The resolution was passed by the council the afternoon of June 25, but it brought no sudden change. That night a second step was approved—providing South Korea with more military equipment. Still the invaders gained ground. By the evening of June 26 General

RESTRAINTS ON INTERVENTION

MacArthur was reporting North Korean tanks entering the suburbs of Seoul. That evening the Blair House conferees approved overt military intervention.

American efforts in the Lebanese conflict began with an assurance of support to President Chamoun and the granting of military equipment. Both of these actions were taken in mid-May, and in June, Washington supported the sending of a United Nations investigating committee. But none of these early actions ended the conflict. By July the Lebanese opposition controlled more territory than it had in May. President Chamoun claimed on June 24 that United Arab Republic intervention was not declining, but increasing.[22] Foreign Minister Charles Malik said the same thing before the United Nations Security Council on July 8. Iraq charged in July that Communists were openly entering Lebanon through Syria.[23] And on July 14, when news of the Iraq coup reached Beirut, people rushed out of the opposition-held sections of the city to celebrate in the streets. The Lebanese conflict appeared even more serious after the first American efforts.

To South Vietnam the United States provided more than $2 billion in economic and military assistance between 1954 and 1961. An army was built, Americans trained the men who would train the army, and in May 1961 United States advisers were attached directly to ARVN units. The Viet Cong, however, were stronger and more effective by the winter of 1961 than they had been before. Limited military assistance had failed to solve the conflict.

Early in the Dominican conflict Washington permitted United States representatives to try to form a military junta. The eventual formation of a junta, April 28, did not end the conflict; so the anti-Boschist military were provided with walkie-talkies to permit their scattered forces to communicate with each other. These efforts were quickly judged failures, and overt military intervention was approved later the same day. Clearly, the preliminary steps in the four crises were different, but in each instance something less than overt military intervention was tried first, and the something less failed.

There was no other agent acceptable to Washington that was able to assume the burden in any of the four situations. In 1950 the only non-Communist forces of any size in the Far East were the American divisions in Japan and the Nationalist Chinese army on Taiwan. Chiang Kai-shek did offer 33,000 troops for use in Korea, but the

[22] U.S. Embassy–USIS Press, Beirut, *Lebanese Press Review*, June 25, 1958, p. 3.

[23] *Ibid.*, July 11, 1958, p. 2.

president rejected the offer, which was received in Washington the evening of June 29. Among the reasons for rejecting the offer were that the troops would have to be re-equipped in order to fight in Korea and that Truman and his advisers thought the troops ought to remain on Formosa to protect the island.[24] Another reason for rejection was fear that Nationalist Chinese participation would encourage Peking's direct intervention. Indeed, at the second Blair House meeting, the evening of June 26, it was decided to deploy elements of the Sixth Fleet in the Straits of Formosa to prevent Peking from attacking Taiwan and deter Chiang from attacking the mainland. The Truman Administration feared that Nationalist Chinese provocations would bring reprisals from Communist China and so create a larger conflict.[25] Thus, for several reasons, the only other force available for intervention in Korea was unacceptable to American decision-makers.

No other power could assume the burden of intervention in Lebanon, given the Eisenhower Administration's perception that an immediate presence was needed. The National Security Council explicitly rejected United Nations action as too slow. This had been the conclusion of Secretary Dulles's morning conference July 14, and the council agreed. Allen Dulles's observation that Lebanon could fall while the United Nations Security Council discussed the matter was widely approved at the meeting.[26] British or French intervention was also possible, although the widely condemned British-French-Israeli invasion of 1956 had made such action undesirable from an American point of view. President Chamoun had requested assistance of all three nations, not only of the United States. France, however, had no significant forces in the area, and its past occupation of Lebanon and Syria to 1946 under League of Nations mandate had made it most unpopular in the Fertile Crescent. The Eisenhower Administration and State Department careerists so opposed French intervention that when a French warship stationed itself off Beirut a few days after American intervention began, United States representatives persuaded the ship to withdraw. British intervention was a greater possibility, but its paratroops on Cyprus numbered only 3,000. The Cyprus contingent was so small that it had been thought necessary in the planning of May to combine it with American troops so that it would be of useful size. The afternoon of July 14 Eisenhower and the Joint Chiefs of Staff de-

[24] Paige, *op. cit.*, p. 249.
[25] Harry S. Truman, *Memoirs*, Vol. II (2 vols.; Garden City, N.Y.: Doubleday, 1956), p. 337; cited in Paige, *op. cit.*, pp. 167–68.
[26] Knebel, *op. cit.*, p. 18.

cided not even to include the British force in the Lebanese intervention. Some senior military officers felt there would be severe logistical problems supplying two dissimilar forces, and Eisenhower and his advisers decided to leave the paratroops on Cyprus as a reserve for possible expanded operations in the region.[27] Turkish, Iranian, or Israeli interventions were also possible, but none of these were viewed as desirable. Actions by any of these states could have created a larger conflict, and one function of American intervention was to deter action by other regional powers.

There were fewer alternatives for Vietnam in 1961 and the Dominican Republic in 1965. There was no prospect that the United Nations Security Council could send a force to South Vietnam. Given the Soviet Union's ties to North Vietnam, a resolution for such action would likely be vetoed. Besides, the United Nations was financially strained by its continuing operation in the Congo. France under de Gaulle had abandoned most of its ties to the Indochinese states, and Britain had just concluded a long and costly operation in Malaya and did not seem interested in South Vietnam. The major decision-makers of the Kennedy Administration chose a path of action that excluded all other nations. They chose to limit the extent of intervention by emphasizing highly technical services: helicopter transport, counterinsurgency training, and staff guidance. No other member of the Southeast Asia Treaty Organization was so well equipped to provide these services.

There were even fewer alternatives in the Dominican crisis. The Council of American States had never been swift to act. The United States had never encouraged United Nations operations in the Western Hemisphere, as the Soviet Union had never encouraged United Nations operations in Eastern Europe. On April 28, 1965, there was no one else to assume the burden when President Johnson concluded that military action was necessary.

The third way that overt military intervention can become unnecessary is if major decision-makers perceive that local actors can contain the threat of Communist government without direct American intervention. But this was not an obstacle to any of America's interventions. Each time the act was approved, the decision-makers believed that local non-Communist forces were weakening. The first meeting at Blair House, June 25, 1950, was hampered by lack of information about what was happening in Korea. The situation was ambiguous. North Korean troops had taken Kaisong the first day, but they were

[27] Eisenhower, *op. cit.*, p. 273.

being contained at other points on the border. Thus, in evaluating the situation, the conferees relied on past calculations of the strengths of North Korean and South Korean armies. In part because they overestimated ROK strength, they believed that South Korea could contain the threat itself—unless Pyongyang received extensive aid from China or the Soviet Union.[28] That evening the Blair House conference merely approved more military equipment for the defenders. By the next evening, when the group met again at Blair House, more information was available, most of it discouraging. General Bradley opened the meeting by reading an estimate of the situation sent by General MacArthur, in which MacArthur observed that North Korean tanks were penetrating the suburbs of Seoul, that ROK troops were unable to contain the attack for lack of tanks and air power, and that the South Korean army seemed to lack the will to fight. The message concluded that "a complete collapse is imminent." [29] President Truman and the others accepted MacArthur's estimate; they were convinced that without further American action South Korea would be overrun. Discussion turned to the actions the United States should take to prevent collapse. Deployment of ground troops was not suggested; instead, discussion focused on the use of United States air and naval power. At the meeting's end the Far East Air Force was authorized to attack North Korean units south of the 38th Parallel, the decision-makers believing that this form of American military intervention would suffice. That they believed air operations would suffice reflected both an overestimate of the value of air strikes and a continued, ill-founded faith in the fighting capability of the South Korean army. Three days later the estimates were revised and American combat troops were dispatched.

American perceptions of the strength of the Lebanese government followed a similar course. On May 13, 1958, when President Eisenhower and Secretary Dulles met to consider the question asked by President Chamoun of Ambassador Malik—"What would the United States do if Lebanon requested assistance?"—a Communist threat was already perceived. As Eisenhower later wrote: "Behind everything was our deep-seated conviction that the Communists were principally responsible for the trouble . . . ." [30] But Eisenhower and Dulles, believing that the Lebanese government could deal with the situation for the time being, extended an assurance of support if five conditions were met: (1) United States troops would not be sent to permit Chamoun a second term; (2) Lebanon's request for assistance must have the public concurrence of at least one other Arab state; (3) troops sent would

[28] Paige, *op. cit.*, p. 130.   [29] *Ibid.*, p. 162.   [30] Eisenhower, *op. cit.*, p. 266.

have the dual purpose of protecting American life and property and assisting the legal Lebanese government to preserve the integrity and independence of Lebanon; (4) Lebanon, not the United States, should lodge a complaint with the United Nations Security Council against United Arab Republic interference; and (5) Lebanon should first rely on its own resources to deal with the situation before appealing for United States assistance. Those five conditions were stated in State Department cable 4271 sent to Ambassador McClintock to be delivered to President Chamoun.[31] The last condition is instructive; Eisenhower and Dulles believed the Lebanese government possessed the means to protect itself, assuming that the Lebanese army would fight forcibly on behalf of the government. Accordingly, they merely approved an increase in United States military assistance to Lebanon. The assumption proved incorrect; the army under General Shehab took an impartial role, merely containing overt conflict. In part, this inaction could be attributed to the fact that the Lebanese army was not a vigorous fighting unit. Like many other armies of the region, it could be rent by political conflict; and General Shehab sought to keep the army intact. In part, the noncombatant role may also have stemmed from Shehab's own interest in gaining power.

The belief that the Lebanese government was strong enough to resist the Communist threat without American military intervention persisted until July 14. It even survived a crisis in mid-June when, over a tension-packed weekend, direct military action was seriously considered. On Saturday, June 14, opposition paramilitary forces broke out of the Basta in Beirut and threatened to overrun the presidential palace. The British embassy evacuated British nationals, including nonessential embassy personnel.[32] The United States embassy did not react so strongly, but it did evacuate the families of embassy staff.[33] That day both John Foster Dulles and Allen Dulles were attending a class reunion at Princeton. On learning that afternoon of the new crisis in Lebanon, they both flew back to Washington. Secretary Dulles spent the rest of the day and all of the next in intensive discussions on this single issue. Sunday afternoon a stream of advisers met the secretary of state at his home. The afternoon's planning and discussion climaxed

---

[31] *Ibid.*, p. 267; Robert McClintock, "The American Landing in Lebanon," *U.S. Naval Institute Proceedings*, Vol. 88 (October 1962), pp. 66–67; and Robert McClintock, *The Meaning of Limited War* (Boston: Houghton Mifflin, 1967), p. 102.

[32] Desmond Stewart, *Turmoil in Beirut* (London: Allan Wingate, 1958), p. 107.

[33] Charles W. Thayer, *Diplomat* (New York: Harper, 1959), p. 20.

with a 6:30 P.M. meeting at the White House. Secretary Dulles, Under-Secretary of State Christian Herter, Assistant Secretary of State for Near East and South Asian Affairs William Rountree, Under-Secretary of Defense Donald Quarles, and General Nathan Twining, chairman of the Joint Chiefs of Staff, met with President Eisenhower.[34] Direct action was considered but not taken.[35] The decision-makers decided to await further information. When that further information arrived in the following days, it indicated that the threat to Chamoun was not so serious as the reports of Saturday suggested.

Only after the Iraq coup of July 14 did the Eisenhower Administration decide that the Lebanese government could not contain the threat of communism. News of the Iraq coup seemed to have great psychological effect in both Beirut and Washington. The Lebanese opposition was elated. President Chamoun was distraught and immediately asked the British, French, and American ambassadors for assistance. President Eisenhower has reported that his first reaction on being briefed at 7:30 A.M. was that the coup completely changed the Fertile Crescent situation; he saw a real possibility of the "complete elimination of Western influence in the Middle East." [36] The suddenness and the unexpectedness of the blow in Iraq, especially since it occurred in the presumed stable core of the Baghdad Pact, seemed to raise doubts about the stability of all governments in the region. Most disturbing was that the coup appeared to have mob support. The psychological effect of the Iraq coup was immediate. The discussions among major American decision-makers began that morning with a shared assumption that action had to be taken. There was sudden and unanimous agreement among all members of the Administration that Lebanon could no longer protect itself.

Unlike its view of Chamoun's government, the United States's perception of the Diem government's strength did not change suddenly. Neither the Eisenhower nor Kennedy Administration believed the South Vietnamese government could survive without extensive outside support, although both hoped outside support might become unnecessary in the future. The question was what kind of assistance and how much of it South Vietnam required. In 1961 the new Kennedy Administration saw the Vietnamese situation as deteriorating. Secretary of State Rusk told a news conference on May 4, 1961, that the armed strength of the Viet Cong had grown from 3,000 men in 1954 to 12,-

[34] John Foster Dulles Papers, Princeton University Library, I.–H., Engagements, 1958–1959, Calendar for 1958, page insert for June 15, 1958.
[35] Eleanor Lansing Dulles, *op. cit.*, p. 132.   [36] Eisenhower, *op. cit.*, p. 269.

RESTRAINTS ON INTERVENTION

000 in early 1961.[37] Four days later the secretary told the NATO foreign ministers' meeting in Oslo that the Communist threat in Vietnam was potentially more serious than that in Laos.[38] Vice-President Johnson returned from his May mission to Vietnam with further information on the decline of Saigon's control and the growth of the Viet Cong's. On Johnson's return, the Administration agreed to increase the size of the military assistance group in the South and support an increase in the size of the South Vietnamese army. At the time, the Kennedy Administration, preoccupied with the situation in Laos, believed that these steps would suffice. The situation in Vietnam continued to deteriorate, however. A Special National Intelligence Estimate of October 5, 1961, produced by the several United States intelligence agencies, estimated the number of "armed, full-time Viet Cong" at 16,000.[39] The Taylor-Rostow mission confirmed the reports of a worsening situation. There was disagreement on what to do next, but it focused, not on whether the Diem government needed further assistance to survive, but on what kind of assistance it needed. The Taylor-Rostow mission returned with three sets of recommendations. The first was for reform of the Diem government. The second was for substantially increased military assistance in the form of more equipment, including helicopters, and advisers both to train the South Vietnamese in the use of the new equipment as well as to operate the equipment until the South Vietnamese were competent in its use. The third recommendation was for a United States ground force of 8,000 men. Walt Rostow also argued on behalf of contingency planning for bombing military targets in North Vietnam.[40] The recommendation for reform was readily accepted. The other recommendations, however, were the subject of extended discussion. Because of differing views of the needs of the Diem government, all of the mission's recommendations were not accepted. A National Security Council meeting of November 15 specifically approved further military assistance: training advisers and advisers in guerrilla warfare, logistics, communications, engineering,

---

[37] *The New York Times,* May 5, 1961, 10:1. The figure of 12,000 Viet Cong was also used within the government. It appeared in the National Intelligence Estimate "Prospects for North and South Vietnam" of August 15, 1961. U.S. Congress. House. Committee on Armed Services, *op. cit.,* Sec. V, Vol. 11, p. 246.

[38] *The New York Times,* May 9, 1961, 4:2.

[39] U.S. Congress. House. Committee on Armed Services, *op. cit.,* Sec. V, Vol. 11, p. 293.

[40] Roger Hilsman, *To Move a Nation* (Garden City, N.Y.: Doubleday, 1967), pp. 422–23.

and intelligence [41] who would provide staff services for the South Vietnamese army. The meeting also approved the deployment of United States helicopter teams, with the helicopters to be serviced and piloted by American personnel.[42] These helicopter teams were the first to engage in overt military intervention in South Vietnam. The recommendation to send combat troops was not approved. It was agreed that the provision of staff services and close combat support, coupled with reforms by the Diem government, would be enough. They were not, however.

The evening of April 28, 1965, when overt military intervention was approved for the Dominican Republic, President Johnson and his chief advisers also saw great weakness among non-Communist elements. The night of April 27 the Molina Urena government disintegrated as some of its key members, including Molina Urena, took asylum in foreign embassies. The anti-Boschist military offensive ground to a halt at the same time. There was no national government. Even Santo Domingo was without a government. Through cable and telephone Washington was more quickly informed of developments in Santo Domingo than is often the case in crises. Johnson, Rusk, McNamara, and Mann perceived disunity, confusion, even chaos in the Dominican political scene—and their perception was correct. They also believed that those non-Communists who had a degree of power in Santo Domingo—the junta members and the non-Communist revolutionaries—could not effectively control the situation. John Plank has summarized President Johnson's view: To the president, the "non-Communist elements were too weak, too lacking in political sophistication, and too little skilled in the arts of governance, to withstand Communist infiltration and subsequent control." [43] The order for the Marine landing was given.

The perceived strength of local actors, which indicates the need for military action, is a key to the timing of intervention. A belief that local actors are strong enough to contain the threat can postpone direct action until it becomes unnecessary as the situation is solved in other ways; but if the situation is worse than is thought, postponement may make later military intervention ineffective. A perception of weakness can result in timely action, but if that view is inaccurate, an unnecessary action may result. It is, therefore, distressing how often

---

[41] *The New York Times,* November 17, 1961, 1:6.

[42] Sorensen, *op. cit.,* pp. 654–55.

[43] John N. Plank, "The Caribbean: Intervention, When and How?" *Foreign Affairs,* Vol. 44 (October 1965), p. 41.

decision-makers' impressions have been wrong. The Truman Administration thought the South Korean army was stronger, and the North Korean army weaker, than was in fact the case. The Eisenhower Administration may have overestimated the weakness of the Lebanese government, judging by later events. The Kennedy Administration overestimated the ability of the Saigon regime to contain the Viet Cong with only limited American military intervention. President Johnson alone seems to have accurately assessed the strength of the Dominican government and military; he thought they had no unity and little strength. He was right, but he may have erred in his judgment that there was a threat of Communist government, which made strength necessary. The inadequacy and lateness of information, the lack of time, and the dependence on past judgments and past assumptions endemic to top-level decisions in large organizations all contribute to inaccuracy in leaders' images of events abroad.

THE BASES FOR MORAL JUSTIFICATION

The operational code of major American decision-makers seemingly requires three elements to legitimize overt military intervention: conflict which threatens a foreign government, a request, and the intervention of some other outsider that can be demonstrated and condemned. All four of the situations receiving American military intervention met all three of these tests. That there was conflict threatening government was unquestionable in each instance. North Korean forces were fighting South Korean troops in 1950. Lebanon was divided into armed camps, and if the overt conflict between them was minimal, the implicit threat to government in Lebanon was serious. As early as 1959 South Vietnam was clearly torn by insurgent guerrilla war; the toll among village leaders was frightful. By 1961 the scope of conflict had expanded; Saigon no longer controlled much of the countryside. The Dominican Republic, too, experienced grave conflict, beginning on April 25, 1965. Even if some of the reports of "blood running in the streets" exaggerated the extent of the conflict, the violence did force the collapse of the Reid government. The conflicts varied in magnitude, however. That in Korea proceeded at a rate killing hundreds of thousands of people a year, that in South Vietnam but tens of thousands in 1961, and the fighting in Lebanon and the Dominican Republic, although briefer, killed only a few thousand in their full course.

APPEAL TO FORCE

Each situation also provided a request decision-makers could show the American people and the world, although each request was different in form. The Republic of Korea's request was the most formal. The afternoon of June 26, hours before the second meeting at Blair House, Korea's ambassador, John M. Chang, delivered directly to President Truman an official, written request for assistance from the National Assembly of the Republic of Korea.[44] The appeal was vaguely worded, asking only for "increasing support" and "effective and timely aid." Ambassador Chang also delivered a personal appeal from President Syngman Rhee. The ambassador and President Truman talked at some length, but Chang did not specifically ask for the commitment of American troop units. Yet the appeal was so broadly worded as to include that request, and no decision-maker and no observer could presume that the government of South Korea would oppose American military intervention. On June 27 President Truman issued a public statement, in which he did not cite the South Korean request. In this, the first American intervention after World War II, the request was seemingly taken for granted. The White House statement emphasized the need to support the United Nations Security Council resolution of the preceding day asking for a cease-fire and North Korean withdrawal. Later presidential statements also failed to mention the request of the Republic of Korea.

The request of Lebanon's government was less formal because it was unwritten. On July 14, 1958, President Chamoun called the ambassadors of the United States, Britain, and France for individual audiences and orally requested of them immediate military intervention. Of Britain and France he asked intervention within twenty-four hours. Of United States Ambassador McClintock he asked intervention within forty-eight hours, in the mistaken belief that American forces could not get there sooner. McClintock transmitted Chamoun's verbal request to Washington in a cable that reached Secretary Dulles's desk between 8:45 and 9:00 A.M., more than an hour before the National Security Council meeting.[45] Not until August 6, three weeks after United States troops arrived, was anything put in writing, but this document was not truly a request. On July 31 McClintock deposited a note with the Lebanese government on behalf of the United States, which became part of a "status of forces" agreement when Foreign Minister Charles Malik deposited a responding note for Lebanon on August 6. The American note said that United States forces were stationed in Lebanon at the request of the Lebanese government. Leba-

[44] Paige, *op. cit.*, pp. 156–59.   [45] Knebel, *op. cit.*, p. 17.

non's note accepted the American one without reservation.[46] Nevertheless, President Eisenhower treated President Chamoun's oral communication as a request. When Eisenhower announced American troop landings to the American public July 15, 1958, he cited Lebanon's appeal for assistance.

An earlier episode in the Lebanese crisis demonstrated something else about requests—they do not by themselves precipitate intervention, even in those countries where intervention later occurs. The Eisenhower assurance of May 13 that the United States would honor a request for assistance from Lebanon had stated several conditions, most of which the Chamoun government had fulfilled early in the conflict. Lebanon lodged a formal complaint with the United Nations against United Arab Republic intervention on the first of June. The United Nations Security Council met beginning June 6. Lebanon asked that the council stop the interference, but no member gave full support to the demand. The council accepted the modest Swedish proposal for an observation group. That Lebanon appealed to the United Nations fulfilled one of the conditions of the May 13 assurance. Before appearing at the Security Council, the Lebanese government asked the Arab League to halt United Arab Republic aggression. The Chamoun government had earlier obtained the support of King Hussein of Jordan and King Faisal of Iraq for its demands. At the meeting of the Arab League, Jordan and Iraq made known their support, thus fulfilling another of the conditions of the May 13 assurance. The support of Jordan and Iraq was not enough to produce action from the Arab League, however. The third condition of the Eisenhower-Dulles assurance merely stated that United States troops would not be sent if Lebanon did not need them. The last two conditions of the assurance were really statements of what United States forces would do if they were deployed in Lebanon: they would not be used to keep Chamoun in office when his term expired, and they would have the dual purpose of protecting Lebanon and protecting American citizens. Chamoun could have publicly renounced any intention to stay in office beyond the constitutional limit earlier than he did; he did not make such a statement until the very end of June. Yet the conditions attached to the American assurance of May 13 had been substantially fulfilled by the middle of June. By mid-month the Lebanese cabinet had autho-

---

[46] U.S. Treaties, "Status of United States Forces in Lebanon, Agreement Between the United States of America and Lebanon Effected by Exchange of Notes Dated at Beirut July 31 and August 6, 1958," *Treaties and Other International Acts*, No. 4387 (Washington: Government Printing Office, 1958).

rized Chamoun to request United States intervention if he deemed it necessary.[47]

Then, in the latter part of June, Chamoun expressed interest in the immediate presence of American troops. On two occasions he reportedly contacted Ambassador McClintock, and both times the ambassador reportedly discouraged him. The first time, Chamoun sent an emissary to the United States embassy with what McClintock construed as a request for United States intervention. McClintock told the emissary that Chamoun himself would have to make the request. Chamoun did not do so. On the second occasion, Chamoun verbally suggested United States intervention to the American ambassador, but McClintock told him the request would have to be made in writing.[48] Chamoun did not act accordingly, but merely let the matter pass. It is striking that McClintock should demand in June that the request be in writing when he accepted a purely verbal request in July. Whether or not Washington had directed its ambassador to discourage any request from Chamoun, it permitted him to act so as to do so. Although the stated conditions for accepting a request had been fulfilled, the major decision-makers believed in June that the Lebanese government could effectively resist the Communist threat. On July 14, however, Washington no longer held such faith, and it accepted and acted upon a request.

The requests for intervention in South Vietnam and the Dominican Republic were in some ways more questionable. The Diem government in 1960 and early 1961 was apparently unenthusiastic about suggestions for the introduction of United States combat forces. By the time of the Taylor-Rostow mission in October 1961, however, Diem, although still ambivalent, was apparently more receptive. Whatever Diem's ambivalence about American combat troops, he did seek close combat support military assistance. The first week of November, shortly after the departure of Taylor and Rostow, Diem specifically pressed a demand for helicopters upon Ambassador Nolting; and on November 9 he specifically asked General Lionel McGarr, chief of the United States Military Assistance and Advisory Group in Vietnam, for American pilots to fly them.[49] Diem also made a public request for further assistance against the insurgents (without specifying the form of assistance) and pledged himself to reform, in an exchange of letters with President Kennedy published on December 15. The timing of the

---

[47] Interview with Ambassador McClintock.   [48] Thayer, *op. cit.*, pp. 24–25.
[49] U.S. Congress. House. Committee on Armed Services, *op. cit.*, Sec. IV.B.1, Vol. 2, p. 112.

public request and the beginning of American intervention were extremely close: United States helicopter teams began flying ARVN troops into combat that very week. The request was not a sudden one, however. A State Department telegram of November 14 instructing Ambassador Nolting to inform Diem that the United States was prepared to increase its assistance under certain conditions (including the condition of reform) also provided a draft letter for Diem with which to request increased aid! The ambassador was instructed to see Diem, and after determining that he was prepared to make reforms,

> inform him that we wish to provide our aid in response to his written request, to which we would plan to give wide publicity. This, combined with the Jordan Report, would serve as the public base for our support. Consequently, you may at a time you consider suitable offer him the proposed draft letter from him to President Kennedy the text of which is supplied in the immediately following telegram. When you give him the draft, you may indicate that we do not expect his letter to be a verbatim copy. In fact, we hope it will not be, but we think it wise from the standpoint of world opinion to include the substantive points mentioned therein.[50]

Although Diem's public request was widely publicized, the beginning of overt military intervention was not. Indeed, the United States maintained the fiction over the next few years that Americans were not directly involved in the conflict. The decision-makers attempted to minimize the change of role that began in late 1961. The Republican National Committee newsletter *Battle Line* charged on February 13, 1962, that the Administration was not being candid about the extent of United States activities. When asked about this charge at his news conference the next day, Kennedy managed to answer the question without saying more than that the United States had increased its assistance.[51] A month later, at a March 15 press conference, Secretary of Defense McNamara was asked to describe the extent of United States combat involvement in Vietnam. In response, he enunciated a most interesting euphemism, saying that the United States was undertaking training programs and that United States military men had, in the course of the program, engaged in "combat-type training missions."[52] Under-Secretary of State George Ball claimed in a speech

---

[50] *Ibid.*, Sec. V, Vol. 11, pp. 404–5.
[51] *The New York Times*, February 15, 1962, 14:2.
[52] *Ibid.*, March 16, 1962, 1:5.

on April 30, 1962, before the Economic Club of Detroit that the United States was doing no more than providing "material and training personnel." [53]

The reality belied the rhetoric. In December 1961, before any of the statements had been made, United States minesweepers began to help the South Vietnamese navy patrol the coast against seaborne infiltration of men and supplies. The minesweepers were replaced in February 1962 by larger destroyer escorts. By early February 1962 there were 4,000 United States military personnel in South Vietnam. The helicopters carrying South Vietnamese troops were by then carrying "protective gunners," American servicemen standing in the doorways manning machine guns.[54] Also, in February the United States Military Assistance Command for Vietnam and Thailand was formed, under General Paul Harkins, to coordinate the operational aspects of the American military effort, separating them from the aid and advisory activities.[55] All of these actions were more than mere "training" activities.

Diem's request was like that of the Korean National Assembly—vague but in writing. In neither of these two cases did Washington use the request to legitimize intervention before the American public or the world. In the case of Korea, this was seemingly because the request was taken for granted. In Vietnam, however, one reason the request was not dramatized was to avoid emphasizing the new actions being taken. Diem's request thus legitimized overt military intervention only before the Kennedy Administration itself and before history. Yet its very existence indicates that major United States decision-makers will demand a request even if it is only for themselves and for the future. The Diem request served another function, of course. It publicly pledged the president of South Vietnam to reform the army and government, reform which the Kennedy Administration had consistently demanded but which had not occurred. The timing of the South Vietnamese request is also enlightening. The decision to intervene was made before the request was made, although the intervention did not begin until after it was made. This timing emphasizes again that the request was important in legitimizing the intervention, and perhaps

---

[53] George W. Ball, *Viet-Nam: Free-World Challenge in Southeast Asia*, U.S. Department of State Far Eastern Series No. 113 (Washington: Government Printing Office, 1962), p. 14.

[54] *The New York Times*, February 5, 1962, 1:8.

[55] Robert Scigliano, *South Vietnam: Nation Under Stress* (Boston: Houghton Mifflin, 1963), p. 151.

important to the actual carrying out of the decisions made; but the request did not itself stir the decision to intervene.

The request to intervene in the Dominican Republic was even more questionable, as it was contrived by Americans rather than freely offered by the Dominican government. The Dominican case was more complex than the others for the seeming absence of government on April 28. Who could legitimately issue an appeal was a question. The Johnson Administration apparently felt the need for a request and went to considerable lengths to obtain one phrased in the language it desired. The American military attachés and other members of the country team, who had tried since April 25 to form a military junta in Santo Domingo, finally received one the morning of April 28. Ambassador Bennett talked by telephone to Colonel Benoit, head of the new junta, about noon on April 28. Benoit told the ambassador the military could no longer protect American lives.[56] He also said the anti-Boschist military was in dire straits. Bennett talked to Washington by telephone shortly thereafter, informing the State Department of the situation and of Benoit's observations. Shortly before 2:00 P.M. Benoit telephoned the United States embassy, requesting that 1,200 Marines be landed to "help restore peace." [57] The specificity of this request is revealing. The Sixth Marine Expeditionary Force with the Caribbean "ready group" included approximately 1,200 combat Marines. Since Benoit would not likely have known this from Dominican intelligence, it is probable that he was supplied "1,200" as an appropriate number by one of the United States military attachés or a member of the United States Military Assistance Group then at San Isidro. Bennett again communicated with Washington. Between 3:00 and 3:30 P.M. Benoit submitted a written request for United States military intervention to a member of the embassy staff at San Isidro. Bennett probably had asked Benoit to send this request, which, according to former Ambassador John Bartlow Martin, cited the danger of communism in the Dominican Republic but made no mention of a danger to the lives of United States citizens.[58] Thus a written request was on hand at 6:00 P.M. when Johnson and his advisers approved overt military intervention, although some members of the group were dissatisfied with its language. Between 6:00 and 6:30 P.M. Under-Secretary of State Thomas Mann telephoned Bennett. Among other things, the under-

[56] Martin, *op. cit.*, p. 655.
[57] Center for Strategic Studies, *op. cit.*, p. 33; Martin, *op. cit.*, p. 656; and Tompkins, *op. cit.*, p. 35.
[58] Martin, *op. cit.*, p. 656.

secretary asked Bennett to obtain a request from Benoit that specified a risk to the lives of American citizens. After talking to Mann, Bennett contacted the embassy air attaché who had gone to San Isidro in the late afternoon. The ambassador asked the air attaché to obtain a written request from Benoit, stating that the junta could not protect the lives of American citizens. Benoit signed the following statement:

> Regarding my earlier request, I wish to add that American lives are in danger and conditions are of such disorder that it is impossible to provide adequate protection. Therefore, I ask you for temporary intervention to restore public order in this country.[59]

The air attaché returned to the embassy with the request about midnight, and the text was cabled to the State Department early on the morning of April 29, 1965, hours after the Marines had landed.

The Johnson Administration was clearly greatly concerned that there be a request from the Dominican Republic were the United States to intervene. It accepted a request from a government that had been formed in great part through the efforts of American representatives and whose control extended little beyond the perimeter of the San Isidro air base where the junta was headquartered. The major American decision-makers also dictated the language of the request. This great concern would suggest that the president and his advisers sought the request to legitimize overt military intervention.

The questionableness of the Dominican request makes it different from the South Korean, Lebanese, and South Vietnamese requests. But the South Korean, Lebanese, and South Vietnamese requests also differed from each other, in timing and as to whether they were written or oral. Thus there is variety among the forms of requests for intervention when intervention occurs. All that appears common to the four situations is that there was a request before military intervention began and that the request came from a government in the host country that could claim some degree of *de facto* control.

The third element demanded for moral legitimation of overt American intervention is the intervention of other outsiders. Outside interference that American decision-makers could condemn existed in each of the four crises, although the degree of intervention by others varied. In Korea it was blatant—North Korea invaded South Korea, committing overt military intervention. The United Nations Security Council certified that North Korea had indeed invaded the South in a resolu-

---
[59] Center for Strategic Studies, *op. cit.*, p. 40.

tion of June 25, 1950, demanding a cease-fire and withdrawal. President Truman and Secretary Acheson referred to the act of aggression and to the United Nations Security Council resolution in each of their public statements during the week of June 25–30.

United Arab Republic intervention in Lebanon and North Vietnamese intervention in South Vietnam were less blatant. As early as May 1958, and perhaps before, Syria, then part of the United Arab Republic, provided money to elements of the Lebanese opposition. Also, some Syrians, including at least one high-ranking Syrian army officer, entered Lebanon to take up arms in the conflict. The amount of assistance provided by the United Arab Republic was limited; most of the opposition did not depend on Syrian men, supplies, and money. Still, the assistance was significant. Syrian intervention became more difficult to demonstrate after the preliminary report of the United Nations Observation Group in Lebanon. The group's report of July 3, 1958, said little evidence had been found to substantiate the Lebanese claim of outside interference. Therefore, American decision-makers themselves had to publicize Syrian intervention in order to legitimize American action. On July 16, the day after the first Marines landed, Under-Secretary of State Christian Herter, testifying at a closed joint session of the Senate Foreign Relations Committee and the House Foreign Affairs Committee, gave the committee members a written summary of American intelligence, in which he described a large number of specific instances of Egyptian-Syrian intervention in Lebanon from May to July 1958.[60] Most instances cited were border crossings of men or military equipment. The same intelligence was then given to members of the United Nations Security Council and also released to the press.

North Vietnamese intervention in South Vietnam was similar to Syria's intervention in Lebanon—it, too, was military assistance rather than overt military intervention. Sometime in 1958 a large number of former southerners, who had moved North in 1954 at the time of partition, returned to South Vietnam. Before their return they were trained in guerrilla warfare and agitation-propaganda tactics. Arthur Schlesinger has estimated that infiltrators numbered as many as 2,000 a year by 1960.[61] Secretary of State Rusk has offered a slightly higher estimate: 10,000 in the three years 1959 through 1961.[62] North Viet-

[60] *The New York Times,* July 17, 1958, 9:1.
[61] Schlesinger, *op. cit.,* p. 539.
[62] J. William Fulbright, ed., *The Vietnam Hearings* (New York: Random House, 1966), p. 238.

nam did more than train former southerners. In October 1961 the Republic of Vietnam presented a documented complaint to the International Control Commission against North Vietnamese direct intervention in the South. The complaint included photographs and other evidence of the infiltration of North Vietnamese regular army personnel.[63] Then, in mid-December the United States State Department released a "white paper," documenting North Vietnamese intervention in South Vietnam. The paper argued that North Vietnam directed the Viet Cong, had infiltrated military and civilian personnel into South Vietnam to join the indigenous insurgent forces, and supplied military and medical equipment to the Viet Cong.[64]

Outside intervention, other than America's own, was much more limited in the Dominican Republic than in Korea, Lebanon, or South Vietnam. Cuba was involved in the Dominican conflict, but not directly. Beginning in 1959, Cuba trained men who entered the Dominican Republic with the avowed aim of forming a Communist government. There was a blatant but small invasion on June 14, 1959. Most of the invaders were captured and imprisoned, but the date was adopted as the name for the largest Communist party in the Dominican Republic, the 14th of June Movement. When the United States intervened, President Johnson condemned Cuba for having trained many of the Communist party members involved in the Dominican conflict.[65] The President thus condemned Cuba for its "support" of one side in the crisis.

The intervention of others has varied in the four crises—from overt military intervention by North Korea in South Korea to mere Cuban support in the Dominican Republic. The intervention by others, however, was enough in each instance for American decision-makers to consider United States military action morally justified. South Korea was perceived as "just another country," which meant that overt military intervention by another country was required to legitimize direct action by the United States. The North Korean invasion provided that justification. South Vietnam and Lebanon were each perceived as part of "Communist-threatened" regions. Since threats in Communist-

[63] *The New York Times,* October 25, 1961, 1:4.

[64] U.S. Department of State, *A Threat to the Peace,* Parts I and II, Far Eastern Series No. 110 (Washington: Government Printing Office, 1961). This document is also called the "Jorden Report."

[65] Lyndon B. Johnson, statement of May 2, 1965, broadcast over radio and television, *Department of State Bulletin,* Vol. 52 (May 17, 1965), p. 745; and Lyndon B. Johnson, statement to members of Congress at the White House, May 4, 1965, *Department of State Bulletin,* Vol. 52 (May 24, 1965), p. 821.

threatened regions are higher on the decision-makers' scale of significance, mere military assistance from another nation is enough to legitimize American intervention. North Vietnam and Syria provided military assistance to insurgents in South Vietnam and Lebanon. The Dominican Republic, a "special interest" country, required only that some other country "support" combatants in conflict, and Cuba intervened to that minimal extent.

RESTRAINTS AND THE EXPANSION OF INTERVENTION

None of the several restraints were obstacles to the beginning of intervention in either South Korea, Lebanon, South Vietnam, or the Dominican Republic. Intervention did not require nuclear weapons nor hold the prospect of immediately confronting Soviet troops. The president did not grant opposing decision-makers a veto, and direct American military involvement did not become unnecessary during the decision-making process. Also, each situation provided the moral justification demanded by the operational code of the makers of American foreign policy. None of the four interventions violated even one of the restraints at its beginning.

The interventions in South Korea and South Vietnam, however, did not remain limited to one country. When they expanded—to North Korea in the first instance, and to North Vietnam, Laos, and Cambodia in the second—some restraints were breached. The prohibition against nuclear weapons and against fighting the Soviet Union remained inviolate. In no instance did the president permit opposing leaders a veto (despite the reported opposition of several key leaders to the April 1970 expansion to Cambodia). Expansion, however, has sometimes come too soon in the incremental process. Cambodia requested extensive United States military assistance before the American invasion, but this assistance was not granted before American intervention began, much less given an opportunity to fail. The expansion of air action in South Korea to North Korea also came very quickly; bombing of the North began only two days after the start of bombing in the South and preceded the arrival of American ground troops.

The rules for moral justification have also been less strictly observed in the expansion of intervention than in the beginning of it. Requests have not been considered essential. Although the government of Souvanna Phouma in Laos might willingly have made a public request for the start of United States air strikes in its country in 1965, Washington did not ask for one. Indeed, no effort was made to publicly justify the action at its beginning, and the American public did not become aware of it until several years later. The Lon Nol government of Cambodia, too, would probably have made a request for United States intervention, but the Nixon Administration did not even inform it of the plan to use United States ground forces to attack Viet Cong sanctuaries in Cambodia until after the intervention had begun. It goes without saying, of course, that neither North Korea nor North Vietnam requested United States presence; nevertheless, the United States intervened in those two countries as well. In the cases of Laos and Cambodia it was possible for Washington to point to conflict endangering government and condemn North Vietnam for overt military intervention in those conflicts. In North Korea and North Vietnam, however, there was no conflict until the United States intervened and started it, and no one to condemn for intervention but the United States itself.

In point of fact, the justifications that have been used to legitimize American expansions of interventions have been different from those offered on behalf of initial interventions. The justifications for the bombing of North Vietnam and the earlier actions against North Korea were simultaneously tactical and punitive. North Korea was the aggressor and, it was argued, only by striking at the supply lines on its side of the border could its army be defeated. The defense offered for the beginning of the bombing of North Vietnam was more elaborate but reflected the same standards. In August 1964 President Johnson publicly declared that North Vietnam had attacked two United States vessels—the *Maddox* and the *Turner Joy*—in the Gulf of Tonkin. United States planes attacked naval installations in North Vietnam in retaliation. The justification was again simultaneously tactical and punitive: United States forces in the area had to be protected, and America could not permit an attack on its ships to pass without response. Whether there ever was an attack on the *Maddox* and the *Turner Joy* is uncertain. The evidence of it is meager. Some have suggested that the Johnson Administration misled Congress and the public by asserting that there was a clear attack where the evidence was ambiguous.[66] This is not the most important issue here, however. More important is that this justification for the expansion of overt military intervention to North Vietnam was markedly different from the justifications normally given when the United States begins intervention in a region. Minor

[66] Joseph C. Goulden, *Truth Is the First Casualty: The Gulf of Tonkin Affair —Illusion and Reality* (Chicago: Rand McNally, 1969), pp. 13-14.

attacks on American planes, ships, and ground forces stationed on the borders of Communist states have occurred frequently since World War II. Normally, the response is no more than a protest, even when the attack is relatively large and blatant, as in 1967 when North Korea seized the United States intelligence vessel *Pueblo*. An affront to American honor has not usually been sufficient to permit United States military retaliation. What was different about North Vietnam was that the United States was already using military force in the region and that North Vietnam had been painted as the "aggressor" in South Vietnam's conflict. Another difference was that the bombing had long been advocated as a tactical measure by some American leaders, ever since Walt Rostow proposed it in 1961 to deter further North Vietnamese action and to arrest the flow of supplies to the Viet Cong.

The public justifications for expanding military operations to Laos and Cambodia were also unusual. It was said that Laos harbored a supply route, that Cambodia provided sanctuaries for North Vietnamese and Viet Cong troops and supplies, and that neither of these sanctuaries could be tolerated. The willingness to attack sanctuaries is unusual; Washington has been respectful of sanctuaries when it has not already started overt military intervention in the region. For example, it tolerated the Communist sanctuary in Yugoslavia during the Greek civil war of 1946–49, prior to President Tito's closing of the border in 1949, and would not permit Greek army units to attack it.

Evidently, the system of restraints is rigidly applied only to the initiation of United States military intervention in a region. Once the United States is militarily involved, the restraints are no longer consistently applied.

5

WHERE MILITARY INTERVENTION HAS NOT OCCURRED

The United States has entered upon overt military intervention only when armed conflict already threatened a foreign government. America did initiate the fighting that took place in North Korea and the bombing of North Vietnam, but it did so only after it had begun military action in South Korea and South Vietnam. Without armed conflict, intervention cannot be "morally" justified unless the United States is already openly engaged in the region. Military intervention was not even used in the Cuban missile crisis of October 1962. That crisis comes closest of any since World War II to the model situation of "true peril." The Kennedy Administration *could* have perceived in it an imminent threat to the United States, but the president feared the psychological effect of the missiles on Americans, Soviet leaders, and other countries far more than he feared an imminent attack.[1]

The morning of October 15, 1962, President Kennedy received the first "hard" evidence—photographs—that the Soviet Union was constructing intermediate-range ballistic missile sites in Cuba. His advisers gathered at the White House that morning. McGeorge Bundy, Dean Rusk, Robert McNamara, Robert Kennedy, General Maxwell Taylor, and Lyndon Johnson were all present. Although there was no fighting in Cuba, discussions concentrated on a proposal to destroy the sites by a "surgical" air strike.[2] An *ad hoc* executive committee was appointed to analyze the possible courses of action. It included those

[1] Theodore Sorensen, *Kennedy* (New York: Harper & Row, 1965), p. 683.
[2] Arthur M. Schlesinger, Jr., *A Thousand Days* (Boston: Houghton Mifflin, 1965), p. 803; and Elie Abel, *The Missile Crisis* (Philadelphia: J. B. Lippincott, 1966), pp. 63–69.

APPEAL TO FORCE

advisers at the White House on October 15 plus others, such as Ambassador to the United Nations Adlai Stevenson and Under-Secretary of State George Ball. The air strike proposal was the focus of discussions for the next several days within the executive committee, but it was not adopted. Instead, the president approved a blockade of Cuba and an ultimatum demanding the missiles be withdrawn. The major objections expressed about the air strike were two. First, an air strike could not be fully effective unless it was massive, involving at least 500 sorties.[3] This would cause widespread destruction and loss of life, and Russian technicians would be among those killed. Second, as Robert Kennedy told the group when it met at the State Department the morning of October 18, a surprise attack on a small country would be "immoral" and a denial of American tradition, a view that President Kennedy reportedly shared.[4] Contingency plans for an air strike and for a paratroop invasion of Cuba existed, but they were not used.

Military intervention has not been used against mere threats to "American honor" since World War II either. Neither the stoning of Vice-President Nixon in Caracas, Venezuela, in 1958, nor the seizure of the American communications ship *Pueblo* by North Korea in 1967 was followed by military intervention. This was so despite a "show of force" in the Venezuelan incident, when United States paratroops were staged to Puerto Rico and Guantanamo Bay, Cuba, in May 1958. Nor have the many incidents of demonstrations before American embassies, of the burning of United States Information Agency libraries, of the kidnapping of American ambassadors and military attachés, or of the shooting down of American planes produced, by themselves, military retaliation. Perhaps the only instance in which an affront to honor immediately preceded military action occurred in August 1964, when North Vietnamese torpedo boats allegedly attacked the United States vessels *Maddox* and *Turner Joy* in Vietnam's Gulf of Tonkin. United States planes immediately attacked North Vietnamese military installations in announced retaliation. As pointed out in the previous chapter, however, this was not an isolated event, since the United States was already engaged in overt military intervention in South Vietnam.

There have been many other situations of interest to the United States since World War II that have lacked armed conflict threatening a government. There have been threats of attack by one country on

---

[3] Graham T. Allison, *Essence of Decision: Explaining the Cuban Missile Crisis* (Boston: Little, Brown, 1971), p. 60.

[4] Schlesinger, *op. cit.*, pp. 806–7; and Robert F. Kennedy, *Thirteen Days* (New York: W. W. Norton, 1969), pp. 38 and 49.

NO MILITARY INTERVENTION

another—by East Germany on Berlin in 1948, 1958, and 1962, and by Russia on Turkey in 1946–47. There have been times when American leaders feared that a Communist government would come to power by peaceful means and a few occasions when a Communist government did take over with little or no bloodshed; for example, Czechoslovakia in 1948, Syria in 1956–58, Ghana in 1960–66, Guinea after 1958, British Guiana in 1961, Brazil in 1963–64, and Chile in 1971. There have also been bloodless coups d'état, as that in El Salvador in 1960, where United States decision-makers feared a Communist party had an important role in the new government. Even Cuba in 1960–61, before the Bay of Pigs invasion, lacked armed conflict threatening the Cuban government. In addition, there was the French political crisis of 1958; conflict existed in Algeria, technically a part of France, but not in continental France. In none of these situations, despite their seeming significance, did the United States intervene with military force. Nor has intervention been undertaken when armed conflict began on a serious scale but was immediately suppressed, as in the army barracks revolt in Honduras of August 1956, the navy and air force mutiny in Brasília, Brazil, in September 1963, the abortive navy coup in Thailand in 1951, or the attempted army coup in the Brazzaville Congo in March 1971.

When no armed conflict has threatened a foreign government, overt military intervention has been restrained. Without such conflict there is insufficient moral legitimation for overt action, unless true peril is perceived, or unless the United States is already fighting in the region. But in many situations where there has been armed conflict, military intervention has failed to occur, even when the threat of a new Communist government has been perceived. In these conflicts direct military action has been obstructed by the other restraints of the international system, top-level decision-making practices, and the operational code. The postwar conflicts threatening government that did not elicit United States overt military intervention can be analyzed to reveal the operation of the several restraints. Appendix A provides a list of such conflicts, classified by the threat American leaders saw in each.

THREATS OF COMMUNIST GOVERNMENT IN "SPECIAL INTEREST COUNTRIES"

There have been several conflicts since World War II in which the president and his advisers believed that a Communist government could be established in a country of special interest to the United States. The conflict in the Dominican Republic in 1965 was the only one in which United States overt military intervention occurred. Appendix A-1 lists thirty-one situations of this type in which overt military intervention did not occur. In each of the latter, except one, one or more restraints on overt military intervention appeared to operate. Among them are such well-known conflicts as the Greek civil war of 1946–49, the Huk rebellion in the Philippines, 1946–54, the Castillo Armas exile invasion of Guatemala in 1954, the anti-Batista conflict in Cuba of 1956–59, and the Chinese civil war, which ended in 1949. In one less well-known conflict, the Paraguayan civil war of 1947, no restraints appear to have operated.

Greece, 1946–49

In the Greek civil war the United States provided military equipment and economic assistance to the government, and eventually provided staff assistance through military advisers at the division level of the Greek army. The United States did not provide close combat support nor send combat troops. The Greek conflict should be divided into two segments: the period from 1946 to spring 1947, and the period from spring 1947 through 1949, when conflict ended. British forces occupied Greece immediately after the war, and they remained there until 1947. President Truman has indicated he perceived the possibility of a Communist government in Greece as early as fall 1945.[5] He has also indicated that Great Britain requested United States "assistance" in Greece that same fall.[6] The president, however, agreed to provide economic assistance only. Large-scale conflict between the Greek army and Communist-led guerrillas broke out in September 1946 after a plebiscite voted to return King George, exiled during World War II. The British army engaged in little active fighting in Greece. Nevertheless, United States overt military intervention was restrained because it became unnecessary in the incremental decision-making process to approve such drastic action. It was most obviously unnecessary because Great Britain assumed the burden of military intervention in Greece, even if it did little fighting. It was also unnecessary because the major decision-makers did not believe lesser actions had yet failed to deter the threat of a Communist government. This latter perception assumed

[5] Harry S. Truman, *Memoirs*, Vol. I (2 vols.; Garden City, N.Y.: Doubleday, 1956), p. 522.
[6] *Ibid.*, p. 99.

NO MILITARY INTERVENTION

more importance after Great Britain withdrew its troops, restraining United States overt military intervention in the second segment of the conflict.

In February 1947 Great Britain informed President Truman that it planned to withdraw its forces by the first of April. The Truman Administration decided to provide the Greek government with large amounts of military and economic assistance, requesting authorization and appropriations from Congress for such assistance under what came to be called the Truman Doctrine; Congress approved. Nevertheless, the president perceived that the situation was turning for the worse in June 1947,[7] and, consequently, several further actions were taken. Britain left a military assistance group in Greece to train the Greek army, and Truman authorized a major show of force by the Mediterranean fleet. Later that year the United States military advisory group was expanded to provide assistance in planning (at the division level), but Great Britain continued to provide most of the assistance in training the army.

It can be asked why the major decision-makers did not go further and approve overt military intervention in the latter part of 1947, when the situation seemed to become more serious. There was evidence that Yugoslavia, Bulgaria, and Albania were supporting the guerrillas, an activity the United Nations Balkan Investigating Commission formally confirmed in a May 1947 resolution. The Greek government in June 1947 requested more United States military equipment; if encouraged, it presumably could have formally requested United States overt military intervention. What appears to have restrained such intervention was President Truman's conviction that lesser actions had not failed and that military assistance would be enough. Thus he considered that overt military intervention was still unnecessary, and he may have been supported in this view by the optimism of some senior United States military officers. Truman has indicated his belief that the Greek government's difficulty stemmed as much from lack of wide popular support, because of its composition and its policies, as from the actions of the guerrillas.[8] And as early as January 1948, Hanson Baldwin, who has long expressed the views of some senior United States military officers, wrote optimistically of the chance of Greek army success against the guerrillas.[9] In 1949 the guerrillas were defeated without United States overt military interven-

---

[7] *Ibid.*, pp. 108–9.   [8] *Ibid.*, p. 109.
[9] *The New York Times,* January 12, 1948, 4:4.

tion, in part because Yugoslavia closed her borders, ending their sanctuary. In October 1949 the guerrilla leadership announced it would no longer carry on military operations.

The Philippines, 1946–54

The Philippine war of 1946–54 is another conflict in which United States overt military intervention might have occurred had lesser actions failed. This conflict, as that in Greece, can be divided into two segments: 1946–49 and 1950–54. As Westerfield suggests, only in 1950 did major United States and Philippine decision-makers begin to take the Huk insurgency seriously.[10] The Philippines gained its independence in 1946. Under a May 1945 agreement between President Truman and President Osmeña, the United States continued to maintain bases in the islands, notably Subic Bay naval station and Clark air base. The conflict's roots also preceded independence. At the end of World War II one of the anti-Japanese guerrilla groups, the Huks, refused to disband, seized land in central Luzon, and established their own local governments. Intermittent armed clashes between Huk and government forces preceded independence and continued on a larger scale thereafter. United States combat forces stationed at bases in the Philippines, however, did not enter the conflict. It was soon apparent that many of the Huk leaders, including Louis Taruc, the preeminent leader, could be adjudged Communists. Despite this evidence, the United States from 1946 to 1950 did little more than provide a small military assistance program for the Philippine army. In 1950 the Huks substantially increased their activities, entering new provinces and setting up Communist governments in areas previously free of Huk action. In consequence, the United States increased both its economic and military assistance and expanded the military advisory group to provide further aid to the Philippine military. In 1950 United States decision-makers were reportedly considering overt military intervention to prevent the collapse of President Quirino's government.[11]

Why was overt military intervention rejected? More restraints operated in the Philippine situation than had in Greece. It would presumably have been possible to establish that the Huks were receiving support from other Communist countries, at least enough to give moral legitimacy to intervention in a special interest country. There

[10] H. Bradford Westerfield, *The Instruments of America's Foreign Policy* (New York: Crowell, 1963), p. 408.
[11] *The New York Times,* June 8, 1950, 17:2.

NO MILITARY INTERVENTION

was, however, some question as to whether the United States could have elicited a request for intervention from the Quirino government: President Quirino openly rejected the possibility of intervention in June 1950.[12] The Truman Administration also considered it unnecessary to approve overt military intervention. It is true that top policy-makers had little confidence in the leadership of the Quirino government.[13] Yet they reportedly believed the "Communists" lacked popular leaders, too.[14] Therefore, the Truman Administration considered Philippine anti-Communists strong enough to contain the threat if given extensive noncombat military assistance.

Instead of overt military intervention, the major decision-makers approved a covert political operation to elevate Ramon Magsaysay to power.[15] At the end of August 1950 Magsaysay was appointed Philippine national defense secretary. In November 1953, with the help of United States military officers, he was elected president. As Magsaysay rose in power, the Philippine army's power against the Huks also increased. With Magsaysay a member of the Philippine cabinet, it might have been possible to elicit a request for United States overt military intervention, but overt military intervention came to appear increasingly unnecessary. By September 1952 Magsaysay claimed the Huk military effort was broken. In May 1954 the Huk leader Louis Taruc surrendered.

Guatemala, 1954

The situation in Guatemala in 1954 was very different from that in the Philippines. The Central American nation was without armed conflict until June 18, 1954, when an army supplied and trained by the United States invaded from Honduras. President Eisenhower and Secretary Dulles had earlier concluded that Jacobo Arbenz Guzman's government, the established government, might well come under the domination of a Communist party.[16] In May Czechoslovakia sent a large shipment of arms to the Arbenz government, an act that could have been attacked as external support. Yet, despite the arms, without armed conflict posing an evident threat to the Guatemalan government, there was not the moral legitimacy that United States decision-

---

[12] *Ibid.*   [13] Westerfield, *op. cit.*, pp. 409–10.
[14] *The New York Times*, June 8, 1950, 17:3.
[15] Westerfield, *op. cit.*, pp. 408–9.
[16] Dwight D. Eisenhower, *Mandate for Change* (Garden City, N.Y.: Doubleday, 1963), pp. 3 and 83.

APPEAL TO FORCE

makers seem to require for overt military action. Instead, the Eisenhower Administration gave covert support to Colonel Castillo Armas's planned invasion, airlifting shipments of arms to Armas's exile forces in Honduras in May.[17] There were also reports of Central Intelligence Agency activity around the Armas camp. On June 18 the Armas forces entered Guatemala, and by doing so, the exiles created a situation of armed conflict. It may, therefore, be asked why the major decision-makers did not approve United States overt military intervention to support the exiles *after* the conflict had begun. After all, the success of the operation was most uncertain. Allen Dulles told President Eisenhower on June 22, four days after the invasion had begun, that he thought the operation still had no better than a 20 percent chance of success.[18]

Even after the conflict had begun, the situation lacked moral legitimation for United States overt military intervention. There was no government that would request it. Armas had not yet established a government; even if he had, before June 27 he could not have claimed any degree of *de facto* control. Arbenz, one might assume, would not request United States intervention. United States policy leaders took lesser actions to support the invasion after it was under way, for one, by providing two P-51 fighter-bombers in an indirect transaction. They also acted in the Organization of American States in a manner to prevent other countries, the OAS, or the UN from coming to Arbenz's assistance.[19] Then, on June 27, the Guatemalan army forced Arbenz to resign in favor of a military junta under Colonel Carlos Enrique Diaz. Armas's forces moved into Guatemala City, and on June 29 Diaz's junta was replaced in a bloodless operation by one in full agreement with Armas.

Cuba, 1956–59

The Cuban conflict of 1956–59 against dictator Fulgencio Batista was again a different kind of situation from those of the Philippines and Guatemala. The major decision-makers of the Eisenhower Administration apparently did not perceive the possibility of a Communist government in Cuba until after Fidel Castro came to power in 1959 and the conflict had ended.[20] There had been reports of Castro's ties to

[17] Jerome Slater, *The OAS and United States Foreign Policy* (Columbus: Ohio State University Press, 1967), p. 122.
[18] Eisenhower, *op. cit.,* p. 425. [19] Slater, *op. cit.,* pp. 122–23.
[20] Dwight D. Eisenhower, *Waging Peace* (Garden City, N.Y.: Doubleday, 1965), pp. 521–24.

NO MILITARY INTERVENTION

the Communist party, presumably including reports from United States Ambassador E. E. T. Smith. As President Eisenhower observed, however, these reports "were suspect because they originated with people who favored Batista." [21] It is indicative of major foreign affairs leaders' perceptions that the United States stopped permitting the sale of arms to Batista in April 1958. The anti-Batista elements captured Havana, and the country itself, on January 1, 1959. Within a year Eisenhower and his advisers realized that a Communist government had been established in Cuba. Even if major United States decision-makers had perceived the possibility of a Communist government in Cuba in 1958, however, and even if they had not perceived the non-Communists among the revolutionaries to be stronger than the Communists, United States overt military intervention might still have been restrained. It would have been difficult to demonstrate that either Fidel Castro or Raoul Castro was receiving support from other countries the United States could condemn for their intervention.

China, 1945–49

The Chinese civil war began in the late 1920's, but it was partially suspended during the 1930's and throughout World War II after Japanese troops invaded the country. It began anew in late 1945 and became one of the most significant postwar conflicts. One is uncertain how important the Truman Administration judged China to be. President Truman and his advisers may have regarded it as a special interest country, or they may have considered it just another country. They made conflicting statements about it, suggesting both that there was disagreement among advisers and that the key leaders were ambivalent. Because intervention is less easily restrained in special interest countries (thus making its absence more difficult for the theory to explain), China in 1945–49 is classified as a special interest country. Enough ties of "interest and affection" existed between the United States and China to make this classification plausible.

The civil war finally ended in 1949 with a Communist government under Mao Tse-tung in control of the most populous country in the world. The Nationalist government, its leader Chiang Kai-shek, and the Nationalist (or Kuomintang) army retreated to the island of Formosa. Many Americans were puzzled as to why President Truman did not intervene to prevent China's "fall." Some conservative Republicans charged that his Administration had either been infiltrated by

[21] *Ibid.*, p. 521.

APPEAL TO FORCE

"Communists" and duped by them or had sacrificed China because the president lacked moral fiber. Neither allegation explains the lack of intervention; these were mere political attacks. Intervention was simply prevented by one of the restraints of the international system.

Some American servicemen were stationed in China after World War II. Units were deployed to the country to accept the Japanese surrender in 1945, and some remained after the surrender. Many of those who remained helped administer the United States military assistance program for Chiang Kai-shek's army. But there were also a few Marine combat units, whose numbers steadily declined until the last were withdrawn in 1949. These units, however, were not "combat ready"—they were not authorized to move against defended objectives. Instead, they guarded supply dumps and rail lines already under Chinese Nationalist control; as the Chinese Communists approached a facility defended by United States troops, the Marines withdrew to still-controlled regions.[22] Thus the United States did not engage in even small-scale overt military intervention, although it might have done so. It was well known that a victory by Mao Tse-tung would bring a Communist government to China; Mao said so himself. Soviet forces did not directly participate; thus to intervene would not necessarily entail fighting the Russians. Yet the Soviet Union gave Mao Tse-tung's government at Yenan enough material aid to permit moral legitimation of United States action in China. Chiang Kai-shek was more than willing to request United States forces. Two restraints obstructed the action until 1947; after that, one alone prevented it. Until 1947 the Truman Administration reportedly believed that with military equipment and advisers the Nationalist government could prevent a total Communist victory and effect some sort of coalition or partition arrangement with Mao Tse-tung.[23] But after General Marshall's year-long efforts to bring about such an arrangement, and after General Wedemeyer's studied assessment of the military prospects for the Nationalist army in 1947, they were probably not so convinced. Thereafter, intervention was restrained simply because the United States could not undertake effective action without resort to nuclear weapons. After the demobilization of the United States Army and Marine Corps at the end of World War II, the United States did not have

---

[22] Henry I. Shaw, Jr., *The United States Marines in North China, 1945–1949*, reprinted (Washington: U.S. Marine Corps Headquarters, G-3 Division, Historical Branch, 1968).

[23] Dean G. Acheson, *Present at the Creation* (New York: W. W. Norton, 1969), p. 140.

the conventional capability to undertake large-scale ground action in the region.[24]

Paraguay, 1947

The Paraguayan civil war of 1947 did not receive the extensive press coverage in the United States that the Chinese conflict did. Nor did President Truman mention it in his memoirs. Yet it is possible that the major decision-makers perceived in the Paraguayan situation the possibility of a Communist government. President Higinio Morínigo, leader of the Colorado party, had ruled since 1940. There were occasional revolts against his rule before March 1947; but early in March a major revolt, joined by army elements, the opposition Febrista party, and the Communist party, occurred in the city of Concepción and the capital, Asunción. The Morínigo government immediately charged that the revolt was led by the Communists. There were reports that Bolivian Communists were aiding the revolutionaries.[25] The revolutionaries gained early success, capturing Concepción and seriously threatening Asunción. The conflict lasted several months. The United States offered mediation, which the Morínigo government rejected, but is reported not to have considered military force.[26] Eventually, in late August, the revolt was quelled, but before being defeated, the revolutionaries had carried their fight into the very streets of the capital city.

Given the conditions of this conflict, United States overt military intervention might have occurred. Bolivian Communist support could have been condemned; the Paraguayan president might have made a request. If the major United States decision-makers perceived the possibility of a Communist government, if they did not perceive it yet unnecessary to approve intervention (although the only "lesser act" they had taken was to offer mediation, which the government itself rejected), overt military intervention might have been expected. It is possible that President Truman discounted Morínigo's claim that a Communist threat existed, since right-wing dictators were then in the habit of making such charges freely. But uncertainty over the decision-makers' perceptions suggests that the pattern that appears to apply to other postwar situations applied imperfectly to this one. Per-

---

[24] Tang Tsou, *America's Failure in China, 1941–50* (Chicago: University of Chicago Press, 1963), pp. 365–67, discusses the very limited nature of American conventional military capability in the late 1940's.

[25] *The New York Times*, March 13, 1947, 20:4.   [26] *Ibid.*, August 15, 1947, 6:5.

haps the "containment" pattern of perception, under which overt military intervention would have been expected, was not yet rigidly applied in 1947.

Other postwar conflicts in Latin America appear to have met one or another restraint. In the Dominican Republic in 1961 there was little armed deadly conflict. When disorders occurred in November, a United States show of force was followed by both the flight of Ramfis Trujillo and an end to the disorders. In Bolivia in 1952, in Haiti in 1957, and in Peru in 1948, there was no apparent outside support that United States decision-makers could condemn. In the Colombian civil war of 1948–53 and the anti-Perón war of August 1955 in Argentina, major United States decision-makers did not seem to perceive a significant possibility of a Communist government.

THREATS OF COMMUNIST GOVERNMENT IN "COMMUNIST-THREATENED REGIONS"

Since World War II many situations have occurred in Communist-threatened regions in which major United States decision-makers perceived the possibility of a Communist government. The difference between situations in threatened regions and those in special interest countries is that in the former, United States decision-makers seem to require more extensive intervention by other outsiders they can condemn in order to lend moral justification to United States overt military intervention. In threatened regions American political leaders appear to require that there be documentable military assistance coming from another country, not mere "support." Those regions, outside the Western Hemisphere, that appear to have been viewed as Communist-threatened regions since World War II are mainland Southeast Asia and the Fertile Crescent plus Iran; sub-Sahara Africa was similarly perceived after 1960. Appendix A-2 lists thirty-five situations of armed conflict in those regions in which United States decision-makers seem to have perceived the possibility of the formation of a Communist government, but where United States overt military intervention did not occur. In each, one or more restraints appeared to have operated. Among them are six particularly interesting situations: the Burmese "civil war" of 1948–58; the Russian-Iranian crisis of 1946; the shah-Mossadegh conflict in Iran in 1951–53; the Congo conflict of 1960–64; Indochina in 1954; and the Laotian civil war of 1959–62.

NO MILITARY INTERVENTION

Burma, 1948–58

The Burmese civil war, characterized by intermittent rather than constant warfare, was one of the most complicated of the postwar conflicts. It can be divided into three parts: 1948–49, before Chinese Nationalist military intervention and before Chinese Communist military assistance; 1950–53, the period when Chinese Nationalist troops were in the country; and 1953–58, after the Kuomintang troops were withdrawn. It is assumed that the major decision-makers perceived the possibility of a Communist government in Burma during all three periods, although neither President Truman nor Eisenhower has explicitly said he did. Yet the threat was sufficiently obvious that knowledge of it may be assumed.

Burma gained full independence from Great Britain in January 1948 and formed a government with Thakin Nu as prime minister. Conflict erupted shortly after, the attacks on the government coming from more than one direction. On the left were the avowedly Communist "White Flags" and "Red Flags," which in the beginning warred with one another as well, and the "White Band," a non-Communist organization that joined the "Flags." On the right were the Karens, anti-Communist but opposed to Thakin Nu's government as well. During 1948 and 1949 the Communist organizations gained effective control over large sections of central Burma. There were, however, restraints on United States overt military intervention during this period. First, the Burmese national government was fiercely independent; that it would request military intervention by either Great Britain or the United States was unlikely. And there was no other government, save the Communist organizations in central Burma, that could claim any degree of *de facto* control and make a request—unless United States decision-makers chose to stretch the concept of government to the breaking point and recognize the Karen organization. Also, until mid-1949, there was little evidence that the Communist groups were receiving military assistance from another country. Then, in May 1949, it was reported that the Chinese Communists had pledged assistance to the Burmese Communists.[27]

The second period of the conflict, 1950–53, saw continued multisided warfare. The Communist forces were presumably receiving military assistance from the Peking government, but another new element was introduced. When Chiang Kai-shek removed to Formosa in 1949,

[27] *Ibid.*, May 6, 1949, 7:4.

all of his troops did not go with him; some moved into northern Burma. It was later charged, as John Montgomery has noted, that United States military equipment was finding its way into the hands of these Kuomintang troops,[28] which they were using to fight the Burmese Communists. How much the United States aided the Chinese Nationalists in fighting the Burmese Communists is not clear. But that United States decision-makers should resort to this covert technique may be understandable; the situation lacked the moral legitimacy seemingly required for United States overt military intervention. There was conflict; after 1949 Peking presumably provided military assistance. Yet the likelihood that Thakin Nu would request United States overt military intervention was slight.

In 1953 the role of the Chinese Nationalist troops became obvious. Burma made a formal complaint to the United Nations against Chinese Nationalist "aggression," demanding that the troops withdraw. Simultaneously with the complaint, Thakin Nu terminated the United States economic assistance program. The United States helped evacuate the Chinese Nationalist troops, but the chance of a Burmese request for intervention declined further.

In the third period, 1953–58, there was an undercurrent of optimism among some lesser decision-makers. Hanson Baldwin had written as early as August 1952, expressing the view of senior United States military officers, that the central government was gaining against the Communists.[29] United States Ambassador Chester Bowles repeated the view in September of that year,[30] and reiterated it in a 1954 article in *The New York Times*.[31] It is not likely that Bowles's view was fully shared by the major United States decision-makers. Nevertheless, armed conflict apparently declined between 1953 and 1956, and in 1954 the Karens were given a separate state.

Then, in July 1956, Chinese Communist troops moved into northern Burma, but did not proceed far south. Thakin Nu gave no indication he would accept United States intervention. Nevertheless, in February 1957 he requested a resumption of United States economic assistance, which was granted. In 1958 revolutionaries began surrendering in large groups. President Eisenhower was apparently concerned that this meant a compromise had been effected that would cre-

---

[28] John D. Montgomery, *The Politics of Foreign Aid* (New York: Praeger, for the Council on Foreign Relations, 1962), pp. 32–33.
[29] *The New York Times,* August 22, 1952, 3:3.
[30] *Ibid.,* September 7, 1952, 3:4. [31] *Ibid.,* June 13, 1954, VI, p. 14.

ate a Communist party government in Burma.[32] Still there was no apparent likelihood that Thakin Nu's government would request United States intervention. In September 1958 General Ne Win overthrew the Nu government in a bloodless coup. The new government was strongly anti-Communist.[33] Armed conflict, which had already declined with the surrender of revolutionaries, virtually ended.

United States overt military intervention before 1950 was apparently restrained by the absence of a request and the lack of condemnable military assistance from other countries. In 1950 and after, although there were several points at which major United States decision-makers may have perceived a significant possibility of a Communist government, overt military intervention was apparently restrained by the lack of a request.

Iran, 1946

Iran in 1946 posed a unique situation. British, United States, and Russian troops had entered the country during World War II. After the war ended, Russian troops remained in northern Iran, while Great Britain and the United States removed nearly all of their forces. There was armed conflict, although it did not directly involve the Soviets. The shah's army was fighting dissident Kurdish tribes, which were demanding independence; the Soviet Union may have been supplying the Kurds with military equipment. In March 1946 President Truman received intelligence reports that Russian troops were moving south and west; one large unit was reportedly moving toward Teheran.[34] The president directed Secretary of State Byrnes to send a "blunt message" to Premier Stalin. On March 24, 1946, a few days after the note was received in Moscow, the Soviet Union announced that it would withdraw its forces. That Truman believed the blunt message would be enough to cause Soviet withdrawal is unlikely, although the president was undoubtedly relieved that it was enough. Given reports that Russian troops were moving toward Teheran, it is perhaps surprising that he did not authorize United States overt military intervention instead of relying on the blunt message. In that situation all other restraints seemed avoidable—but intervention would have meant fighting Soviet forces. It may also be that the "containment" pattern of perceiving a great threat in the possibility of a new Communist government any-

[32] Eisenhower, *Waging Peace*, p. 266.
[33] *The New York Times*, September 27, 1958, 1:6. [34] Truman, *op. cit.*, p. 95.

APPEAL TO FORCE

where was just being formed in 1946–47 and was not then fully established. This, too, could explain the absence of overt military intervention in Iran.

Iran, 1951–53

The second time after World War II that Washington feared the creation of a Communist government in Iran was in 1951–53. This time the threat did not involve the presence of Russian troops in the country. And unlike the extended conflict in Burma, there was no continuing armed conflict until the anti-Mossadegh coup of August 1953. The Iranian situation in 1951–53 can be divided into two periods. The first, 1951–52, had occasional armed conflict threatening the government. The second, from mid-January to August 19, 1953, did not. Isolated clashes were reported in 1951 and 1952, and in December 1951 a mock battle was fought in Teheran between 5,000 Communist-led troops and troops loyal to the government, which resulted in the deaths of only five persons.[35] Isolated conflicts between Communists and others occurred in northern Iran in 1951 and 1952. And there were occasional large riots in Teheran, as that in March 1952, as well as instances of tribal warfare. Yet by 1953 even the reports of isolated deadly conflict declined. The most significant behavior in 1953, before the August coup, appeared to be mob demonstrations, usually resulting in no deaths.

Major United States decision-makers of both the Truman and Eisenhower Administrations were apparently concerned about the possibility of a Communist government in Iran. At the end of April 1951 Mossadegh, leftist and extremely nationalistic, became premier of the Iranian government. He nationalized the foreign-owned Iranian oil companies on May 2, 1951. President Eisenhower, on taking office in 1953, apparently saw the possibility of a Communist government being established through Mossadegh, not because Mossadegh was himself a Communist party member, but because he sought an alliance with the Communist Tudeh party; President Eisenhower believed the Tudeh party, not Mossadegh, would control Iran.[36]

The major decision-makers of the Truman Administration in 1951–52, however, believed that the greatest possibility for a Communist government was through direct action by the Soviet Union. There

[35] *The New York Times,* December 7, 1951, 1:2.
[36] Eisenhower, *Mandate for Change,* pp. 3, 162–63.

NO MILITARY INTERVENTION

were reports that some in Washington feared a Communist coup in 1952.[37] Yet President Truman and Secretary Acheson seemed preoccupied with the possibility that the Soviets would create a minor incident in Iran as an excuse for overt intervention.[38] In June 1951 Secretary Acheson publicly warned the Soviet Union against taking such action. Since Soviet action was the main concern, it was in 1951–52 yet unnecessary in the incremental decision-making process to approve United States overt military intervention. Warnings had seemingly deterred Soviet military intervention. Even in November 1952, when Secretary Acheson briefed President-elect Eisenhower on foreign policy matters, the secretary's advice was to watch the Iranian situation for the problems that *might* arise.[39] Truman does not report that Acheson advised Eisenhower that there was an imminent threat of a Communist government from within Iran itself.

In 1951 and 1952 the United States joined in the boycott of Iranian oil, after the oil facilities were nationalized, but took no other overt action. The occasional conflict that occurred might have been used as moral justification for overt military intervention. The decision-makers might have elicited a request for intervention from the shah. It might have been possible to document Soviet military assistance to groups engaged in violence in northern Iran in 1951–52. The major decision-makers, however, apparently believed that warnings to the Soviet Union had succeeded and that the non-Communists in Iran, if Soviet action were restrained, would be strong enough to resist a Communist government, given the low level of conflict in the country at that time.

The situation changed in 1953. Mossadegh had obtained special ruling powers from the Majlis, Iran's lower house, in 1952, and the Majlis extended those powers for another year in January 1953. In April 1953 Mossadegh demanded that the shah's powers be reduced, that the shah no longer lead the army, and that he be made a constitutional monarch. These demands were not immediately fulfilled. At the beginning of August, however, Mossadegh received overwhelming support for his policies in a national plebiscite, convincing President Eisenhower that a Communist government in Iran was imminent.[40]

The Eisenhower Administration no longer perceived overt military intervention as unnecessary, but the situation did not provide moral legitimacy for such an action. The United States might have obtained a

[37] *The New York Times,* August 10, 1952, 5:1.
[38] Truman, *op. cit.,* pp. 343, 420–21.   [39] *Ibid.*
[40] Eisenhower, *Mandate for Change,* pp. 162–63.

APPEAL TO FORCE

request from the shah, although the shah had fled the country after attempting to remove Mossadegh on August 16.[41] Yet the other conditions for moral legitimation were lacking in 1953. Armed conflict threatening government was nearly nonexistent. Even if the major United States decision-makers had chosen to emphasize Tudeh party demonstrations in Teheran, bloodless as they usually were, as evidence of armed conflict, it is doubtful they could have documented a charge that the Soviet Union was giving more than mere encouragement to the demonstrations. Instead, Eisenhower and Dulles chose to give covert assistance to forces loyal to the shah.[42]

On August 19, 1953, army troops loyal to the shah, with anti-Mossadegh civilians, seized control of Teheran. Three hundred persons were reported killed within nine hours.[43] The coup was an immediate success; it succeeded too quickly to provide the occasion for United States overt military intervention. Mossadegh surrendered on August 20 and the shah returned.

The Congo, 1960–64

The Congo conflict of 1960–64 is another of the important conflicts in threatened regions. Unlike Iran in 1953, but like Burma, it had obvious armed conflict. The Congo gained formal independence from Belgium on July 1, 1960, with Joseph Kasavubu as president and Patrice Lumumba as premier of the new government. Within days after independence the Congo was torn by armed conflict. Native troops in the Force Publique mutinied. Belgium sent troops. On July 11 Moise Tshombe declared an independent (rightist) state in Katanga Province. That same day Patrice Lumumba reportedly approached United States Ambassador-designate Clair Timberlake; Ambassador Timberlake advised Lumumba to request United Nations assistance,[44] which Lumumba did that very day. The next day the Congo cabinet, without Lumumba's presence, directly requested United States intervention, but President Eisenhower advised the government to appeal to the United Nations.

Why didn't Eisenhower approve overt military intervention when it was requested in these first days of the crisis? He and his advisers

[41] *The New York Times*, August 17, 1953, 1:4.
[42] Eisenhower, *Mandate for Change*, pp. 163–64.
[43] *The New York Times*, August 20, 1953, 1:8.
[44] Ernest W. Lefever, *Crisis in the Congo* (Washington: Brookings Institution, 1965), p. 13; and Alan P. Merriam, *Congo: Background to Conflict* (Evanston, Ill.: Northwestern University Press, 1961), p. 212.

NO MILITARY INTERVENTION

were suspicious of Lumumba, soon regarding him as a "Soviet tool."[45] Thus they may have perceived the possibility of a Communist government in the first days of the conflict. But there were seemingly two restraints. In the first days the conflict lacked external military assistance the United States could condemn; it would have been difficult for the Eisenhower Administration to condemn Belgium's dispatch of troops and use that as justification for its own military intervention. The Soviet Union was not yet providing military assistance. Also, intervention proved unnecessary in the incremental decision-making process. United States decision-makers always seem to take at least one lesser action before approving overt military intervention. With Belgian troops in the country to prevent sudden coups, the first action the decision-makers took was to propose United Nations action. The United Nations Security Council moved with unusual speed to approve a United Nations peace-keeping force for the Congo early on the morning of July 14. As Lefever has noted, the peace-keeping proposal was adopted only because the Soviet Union would at that time agree.[46] The United States promptly provided an airlift, as well as money, to move United Nations troops to the Congo, but contributed no combat forces.

After July 14 overt military intervention on the part of the United States was unnecessary. The United Nations was assuming the burden. Yet the possibility of a Communist government in the Congo became more evident, as the Soviet Union began supplying military equipment and advisers to the Lumumba government. In September President Kasavubu dismissed Lumumba as premier and appointed Joseph Ileo in his place. The conflict became three-sided. The Kasavubu government was in Léopoldville (where most of the United Nations forces were stationed), Moise Tshombe's government was in Katanga, and Patrice Lumumba and Antoine Gizenga had forces in Stanleyville. Washington took the step of stationing a United States aircraft carrier at the mouth of the Congo River. Lumumba was killed in 1962, and in late February 1963 the Katanga secession ended. However, the conflict did not end, for the Stanleyville forces still remained a problem. United Nations forces withdrew, but in 1963 the Léopoldville government, now under Cyrille Adoula, requested the assistance of Belgian troops, which United States decision-makers supported. Belgium assumed the burden of military intervention. Still, the United States provided covert combat assistance and overt noncombat military assistance against the Stanleyville forces. In June 1964 pilots recruited

[45] Eisenhower, *Waging Peace*, p. 574.   [46] Lefever, *op. cit.*, p. 17.

by the Central Intelligence Agency reportedly began flying planes against the Stanleyville forces,[47] and in November of that year United States military aircraft openly flew Belgian paratroops into Stanleyville airport, which by November was outside the battle zone. The Belgian troops attacked and dispersed the Stanleyville forces. Thereafter, the Congo enjoyed relative calm until 1967, when new violence erupted. This renewed violence was quickly suppressed after the United States supplied a few transport aircraft. Thus United States overt military intervention never became necessary in the Congo.

Indochina, 1954

Indochina in 1954 was in serious conflict. It is perhaps surprising the United States did not intervene overtly, for Indochina was considered in Washington to be even more important than Burma. The explanation is that military intervention was restrained by a veto the president permitted other decision-makers. By 1954 the French were in a precarious position in Indochina; the Viet Minh were becoming stronger, and, should they win, a Communist government was a certainty. The United States increased its military assistance to the effort to defeat the Viet Minh. It supplied more funds and in early 1954 supplied B-26 light bombers to be flown by French crews, as well as American military technicians to service the planes and train the crews. But the Laniel government in France was becoming disheartened and discouraged in the effort. In mid-March the Laniel government decided to send General Paul Ely, chief of staff of the French army, to Washington, reportedly to obtain assurances of United States air retaliation if Chinese planes became involved in the conflict, and to find out what the United States would do if China sent "volunteers."[48] Another reported function of Ely's mission was to inform Washington how poorly the war was going and to obtain increased American assistance in building a larger "native" army to fight the Viet Minh.[49] However, by March 20, when Ely arrived in Washington, the Viet Minh had begun a ferocious attack on the French garrison at Dienbienphu, so

---
[47] *Ibid.,* p. 131.
[48] General Paul Ely, *Memoires, Vol. I, L'Indochine dans la Tourmente* (Paris: Plon, 1964), pp. 59–60; quoted in Geoffrey Warner, "Escalation in Vietnam: The Precedents of 1954," *International Affairs* (London), Vol. 41 (April 1965), p. 269.
[49] Melvin Gurtov, *The First Vietnam Crisis* (New York: Columbia University Press, 1967), p. 79; and Phillippe Devillers and Jean Lacouture, *End of a War* (New York: Praeger, 1969), pp. 72–75.

NO MILITARY INTERVENTION

effective that it substantially increased Washington's concern over the trend of events in Indochina.

The key foreign affairs leaders assured General Ely that the United States would retaliate if Chinese planes entered the conflict. Admiral Arthur Radford, chairman of the Joint Chiefs of Staff, reportedly signed an agreement on March 25 that United States planes would join in the conflict if Chinese planes intervened.[50] Ely's visit and the attack on Dienbienphu also brought forth plans for United States overt military intervention even if China did not intervene. At a March 26, 1954, meeting with Ely, Radford proposed that sixty B-29's based in the Philippines bomb around Dienbienphu. This plan, Operation Vulture, had been prepared by United States-French military staffs in Vietnam.

Were United States overt military intervention to occur in Indochina, it could, of course, take any of several forms, an aerial bombing mission around Dienbienphu being but one possibility. The deployment of United States combat ground troops was another possibility. The Eisenhower Administration, however, seemed less enthusiastic about the prospect of sending ground forces than dropping bombs. President Eisenhower told his advisers in January 1954 that he considered it not worthwhile to put United States ground forces in Indochina, that there were enough ground forces there already.[51] General Matthew Ridgway, army chief of staff, was among those who believed that in order for military intervention to be effective it would have to include ground troops.[52] He directed a survey to be made of what problems would be involved if the United States were to intervene on the ground in Indochina. The report considered the introduction of eight combat divisions plus thirty-five engineer battalions in the Red River Delta around Hanoi.[53] The report concluded that the area was "practically devoid of those facilities which modern forces such as ours find essential to the winning of war."[54] General Ridgway concluded that the United States was capable of intervention in Indochina (presumably without nuclear weapons), but that it would have to include ground forces and that the cost would be at least as great as that of Korea. The general transmitted his conclusions to President Eisenhower, presumably before the fall of Dienbienphu on May 7, 1954.

[50] *Ibid.*   [51] Eisenhower, *Mandate for Change*, p. 341.
[52] Matthew Ridgway, *Soldier* (New York: Harper, 1956), p. 276.
[53] James Gavin in *The Vietnam Hearings*, ed. James W. Fulbright (New York: Random House, 1966), pp. 67–69.
[54] Ridgway, *op. cit.*, p. 276.

APPEAL TO FORCE

Yet another possibility was a nuclear air strike around Dienbienphu. General Curtis LeMay, commander of the Strategic Air Command, reportedly prepared a plan for such a bombing.[55] This plan seems never to have surfaced in discussions among the major decision-makers.[56] For one thing, the strike would have been so effective it would probably have destroyed the Dienbienphu garrison along with its assailants. Not surprisingly, General Ely opposed the plan.

Operation Vulture or United States ground action—taken together, taken one following the other if the first failed, or either taken alone—seemed possible forms of overt military intervention in Indochina. The question was, under what conditions would the major leaders approve either or both actions? Eisenhower has said that one of the requirements in his mind was a "request of the French government, which request would have to reflect, without question, the desire of the local governments." [57] On April 4 the Laniel cabinet's "war committee" approved a request for United States intervention and gave it to United States Ambassador Dillon on April 5. If wanted, this request could have been construed as reflecting the "desire" of the governments of the Associated States of Indochina. If military assistance from an outside country that major decision-makers can condemn is required for United States overt military intervention in Communist-threatened regions, Secretary Dulles perceived that condition met. The secretary described the Chinese training and equipping of the Viet Minh in a speech to the Overseas Press Club on March 29. He also said Chinese military personnel were assisting the Viet Minh directly, providing staff services as well as assistance in communications, engineering, artillery, and logistics. Dulles repeated this last charge before the House Foreign Affairs Committee when he discussed the Mutual Security Program on April 5. Major United States decision-makers also seemed to believe the time had come for more drastic action, assuming that unless something more was done, North Vietnam would fall to the Viet Minh.[58] They were, of course, correct.

What appeared to restrain United States overt military intervention,

---

[55] Robert McClintock, *The Meaning of Limited War* (Boston: Houghton Mifflin, 1957), p. 167.

[56] However, Gurtov mentions that Admiral Radford spoke of the nuclear weapons aboard United States aircraft carriers in the South China Sea, targeted for points in China, during an April 4, 1954, meeting with leaders of Congress. Gurtov, *op. cit.*, p. 95.

[57] Eisenhower, *Mandate for Change*, p. 340.

[58] See, for example, Eisenhower's account of Dulles's reports during the secretary's visit to London in mid-April in *ibid.*, p. 348.

NO MILITARY INTERVENTION

in the form of Operation Vulture and the deployment of combat forces, was that President Eisenhower in effect permitted leaders of Congress to participate in the group of major decision-makers and to veto the action. By the beginning of April executive leaders had not decided whether American action, were they to approve it, would be unilateral or taken in concert with other nations. There may have been a preference for multilateral action. Secretary Dulles's speech of March 29 included a plea for "united action" in Indochina by non-Communist nations. The morning of April 3, just a few days after General Ely left Washington, Eisenhower arranged a secret meeting with leaders of Congress. The president apparently was not present, but Secretary Dulles, Admiral Radford, and Deputy Secretary of Defense Roger Keyes met eight congressional leaders of both parties. The members of Congress who attended were Senate Majority Leader William Knowland, Senator Eugene Milliken, Senate Minority Leader Lyndon Johnson, Senator Richard Russell, Senator Earle Clements, House Speaker Joseph Martin, Congressman John W. McCormack, and Congressman J. Percy Priest.[59] Dulles briefed the group and said that the president wished Congress to consider passing a joint resolution to authorize the use of air and naval forces in Indochina. Chalmers Roberts has said the secretary may have carried a draft of the resolution in his pocket. If so, he did not show the draft to the congressional leaders, who were not supportive. Senator Knowland was briefly enthusiastic, then became quiet as others asked questions. Admiral Radford revealed that if the first air strike were not successful, others would follow. Would United States ground troops be used? Admiral Radford would give no definite answer. Senator Clements asked the admiral whether the other members of the Joint Chiefs recommended intervention. Admiral Radford admitted that he alone among the chiefs favored the action. Senator Johnson asked whether United States allies had been consulted. Secretary Dulles revealed that they had not, yet. The meeting adjourned.

According to the president, Dulles concluded from the comments of the congressional leaders that "it would be impossible to get Congressional authorization for the United States to act alone." [60] At an April 4 meeting with his advisers President Eisenhower concluded that con-

---

[59] *Ibid.*, p. 347; Chalmers M. Roberts, "The Day We Didn't Go to War," *The Reporter*, Vol. 11 (September 14, 1954), p. 31; and Robert F. Randle, *Geneva 1954: The Settlement of the Indochinese War* (Princeton, N.J.: Princeton University Press, 1969), pp. 63–65.

[60] Eisenhower, *Mandate for Change*, p. 347.

gressional support for United States military intervention could be gained only by meeting certain conditions, the first among these being that intervention be undertaken in concert with other "free nations." Eisenhower apparently felt he needed congressional approval. As Gurtov has written in his account of this episode, "Congressional support was absolutely vital, in the President's mind, if the United States was to be party to war." [61] The only way to obtain that approval now was to persuade other countries to participate. Secretary Dulles began a search into ways to gain British and French support for some variety of joint operation in Indochina, but was unable to organize any "united action." The Churchill government was never enthusiastic about British intervention in Indochina. In the end it refused to approve even a joint declaration asserting opposition to communism in Southeast Asia and authorizing the use of military force. The Laniel government, too, was ambivalent. It was French pressure at the February 1954 Berlin conference of NATO ministers that initiated the call for a Geneva conference on Korea and Indochina. After Dienbienphu fell on May 7, the Laniel government offered the partition of Indochina in a seeming attempt to withdraw its forces as soon as possible.

In mid-April the Eisenhower Administration had explored once more the possibility of unilateral intervention but had dropped it. Vice-President Nixon was permitted, on April 16, to launch a "trial balloon" to again test public and congressional opinion. He did so in a "not for attribution" statement during a speech to the American Society of Newspaper Editors, indicating that United States intervention was still being considered. Reaction to the speech was highly critical, which the Administration reportedly interpreted as the expression of continued opposition to unilateral intervention.[62] Overt military intervention did not occur.

Laos, 1959–62

United States overt military intervention might well have occurred in Laos in 1961 or 1962, too, but it did not. The Laotian civil war during the period 1959–62 was a peculiarly complicated conflict. Not two but several Laotian factions vied for leadership of the country, and each suggested a different relationship between Laos and the United States. Nor were United States representatives united. The

[61] Gurtov, *op. cit.*, p. 94.
[62] James Reston, *The New York Times,* April 20, 1954, 11:3; and Robert J. Donovan, *Eisenhower: The Inside Story* (New York: Harper, 1956), p. 267.

NO MILITARY INTERVENTION

Central Intelligence Agency, the Agency for International Development, the Department of Defense, and the State Department each had representatives in the country, and the representatives of each sometimes supported a different Laotian politician and a different United States-Laotian relationship.

In 1954, when Indochina was divided, Souvanna Phouma became prime minister of Laos. Souvanna was a moderate who came to advocate a coalition government and international neutrality for Laos. In the mid-1950's the State Department successfully urged that the United States build a Laotian army. On United States insistence a Royal Lao Army of 25,000 men was created. It was at first trained by the French; after 1959 training responsibility was assumed by United States military advisers wearing civilian clothes and assigned to the United States Operations Mission, the economic aid mission.[63] The United States supplied it with equipment suitable for fighting conventional war, and the troops were paid from the proceeds of the sale of commodities supplied by the United States. No major Laotian political leader fully controlled the army, although General Phoumi Nosovan, who advocated alliance with the United States, was more successful than others; and by 1959 he rose to the position of minister of defense. The army was not united. It was not a fighting force, and throughout the conflict it declined to engage in potentially bloody battle. Nor did it control the country's land. A Communist guerrilla group, the Pathet Lao, under the titular leadership of Prince Souphanouvong, held safe areas in the mountains. The Pathet Lao guerrilla force had been organized about North Vietnamese regular army cadres.[64]

Government followed government in the late 1950's. In 1957 Souvanna Phouma reached an agreement with Prince Souphanouvong to form a coalition government pursuing a neutral foreign policy and to hold new parliamentary elections. Communist party candidates won several seats in those elections of May 1958. The United States withheld commodity imports, thus producing an internal crisis, since the commodity imports financed the army. Parliament then defeated the Souvanna Phouma government on a vote of no confidence, and Phoui Sananikone formed a new government without Communist participation. In December 1959 Phoumi Nosovan and other Royal Lao Army

---

[63] Bernard Fall, *Street Without Joy* (Harrisburg, Pa.: Stackpole, 1963), p. 324.
[64] Hilsman, *op. cit.*, p. 127; Bernard Fall, *Anatomy of a Crisis: The Laotian Crisis of 1960–61,* ed. Roger M. Smith (Garden City, N.Y.: Doubleday, 1969), pp. 112–18.

APPEAL TO FORCE

officers deposed Phoui in a bloodless coup. After blatantly rigged elections reportedly assisted by CIA agents,[65] Phoumi formed a pro-American government. But in August 1960 a Royal Lao Army battalion, under the command of one Kong Le, seized control of the government seat, Vientiane, and Phoumi fled to Savannakhet. Souvanna Phouma, then ambassador to France, was chosen by the king of Laos to form a new coalition government to include Phoumi. Phoumi's government resigned. The Soviet Union recognized Souvanna Phouma's as yet unorganized government. Phoumi, however, did not join this government, but formed his own under Prince Boun Oum. In September United States civilian airline transports began moving supplies to Phoumi at Savannakhet. In November the Soviet Union began airlifting supplies to the Pathet Lao. Then, in December, Phoumi moved his forces toward and into Vientiane. Souvanna Phouma fled to Cambodia; Kong Le and his battalion fled north and joined the Pathet Lao. Parliament recognized the Boun Oum government, as did the United States, but not the Soviet Union; the latter continued to recognize Souvanna Phouma, who, although in Cambodia, did not resign as prime minister.

By late December 1960 the situation was not merely confusing but also threatening. The Soviet Union was said to be supplying forty-five tons of arms and ammunition a day to the Pathet Lao and to Kong Le.[66] There were reports that North Vietnamese troops had entered Laos. President Eisenhower agreed to move elements of the Seventh Fleet toward North Vietnam and to inform the Soviet Union of the action.[67] At the same time United States "White Star" teams, combat-joining military advisers in civilian dress, were attached to Phoumi's battalions.[68] Still the Royal Lao Army failed to fight effectively. In January 1961 the Pathet Lao gained control of the Plain of Jars. By March they controlled much of the north-south road along the Mekong lowlands between Laos's two major cities, Luang Prabang and Vientiane. Phoumi Nosovan claimed that there were 60,000 North Vietnamese arrayed against him and asked for more United States aid.[69] Although Phoumi exaggerated, there may have been as many as 10,000 North Vietnamese troops assisting the estimated 15,000 Pathet Lao

[65] Arthur J. Dommen, *Conflict in Laos* (New York: Praeger, 1964), p. 133.
[66] Theodore Sorensen, *Kennedy* (New York: Harper & Row, 1965), p. 640.
[67] Eisenhower, *Waging Peace*, pp. 609–10.   [68] Hilsman, *op. cit.*, p. 127.
[69] Hugh Toye, *Laos: Buffer State or Battleground?* (London: Oxford University Press, 1968), p. 168.

NO MILITARY INTERVENTION

and 5,000 men under Kong Le's control.[70] The Royal Lao Army under Phoumi now consisted of 50,000 men, but they were widely dispersed and no match for the experienced fighters opposing them. The seriousness of the situation was obvious. As Sorensen later wrote of that moment in the spring of 1961, "A Communist conquest of almost every key city in the entire kingdom was an imminent danger." [71]

The opportunity for United States overt military intervention existed, and most of the restraints were inoperative. Although the Soviet Union was supplying the Pathet Lao, and although American military intervention risked Soviet counterresponse, Russian combat forces were not involved. A contingency plan, which did not require nuclear weapons, had existed for some time to deploy 60,000 United States combat troops in southern Laos, although its execution would severely tax America's limited war capability. Conflict threatened the several governments of Laos. Phoumi Nosovan had requested more aid, and he could be induced to specifically request United States troops. And the Soviet Union could be condemned for its role. What seemingly restrained overt military intervention was the incremental decision-making process. The Kennedy Administration had decided to try to form a coalition government and events made overt military intervention unnecessary. It was apparent that Phoumi Nosovan could not defeat the Pathet Lao completely. It was also apparent that SEATO allies would not assume the burden of military intervention. Yet major United States decision-makers apparently believed that Phoumi and other non-Communist Laotians were strong enough to prevent a total Pathet Lao victory before a coalition government could be formed, given United States military assistance and the low level of violence.

Decision-makers simultaneously explored the possibilities of a coalition government and United States overt military intervention. On February 19 the king of Laos had delivered a State Department-prepared speech declaring a policy of nonalignment and asking Burma, Cambodia, and Malaya to guarantee its neutrality. But the Soviet Union, China, and Prince Souphanouvong, speaking for the Pathet Lao, immediately attacked the speech. Nevertheless, Souvanna Phouma continued a world tour already begun, seeking support for an international conference to discuss Laos and to bring about a neutral regime. In the same period, President Kennedy and his advisers discussed military plans. At a March 9 meeting the president was pre-

[70] Dennis Warner, *The Last Confucian* (New York: Macmillan, 1963), p. 215.
[71] Sorensen, *op. cit.*, p. 640.

APPEAL TO FORCE

sented with a seventeen-step plan for gradual, stepped increases in United States military involvement. The group approved the first step —for United States military advisers to don their uniforms.[72] This step, however, was not put into effect until April.[73] No further actions were approved on March 9. Later in March, as the Pathet Lao "offensive" continued, the major decision-makers approved further military actions. After a series of meetings on March 20 and 21 the president authorized the return of Seventh Fleet units to the South China Sea.[74] He also approved the construction of a helicopter repair base at Udorn airfield in Thailand, near Laos, and the dispatch of 500 Marines to build it, plus helicopters. Kennedy announced these actions in a televised news conference on March 23. The manner of the announcement made the actions a "show of force."

At the same time the Kennedy Administration communicated with Soviet leaders, the president speaking personally to Soviet Ambassador Andrei Gromyko at the White House, and Secretary Rusk talking to him on other occasions. Kennedy and Rusk sought Moscow's support for a cease-fire and international conference on Laos.[75] Great Britain had suggested the revival of the International Control Commission for Laos and the holding of another Geneva conference. President Kennedy expressed public interest in this proposal and arranged to meet Prime Minister Macmillan March 26 at Key West, Florida, during the latter's visit to the Caribbean. Also, in a public statement the president asked India's Prime Minister Nehru to support a cease-fire in Laos. Nehru agreed. At Key West, Macmillan agreed to support military intervention in Laos if needed, but the closing communiqué called for a cease-fire and another Geneva conference.

The situation throughout late March and April was unpredictable. United States leaders implied in public that American military action would follow if the threat of Communist government could not otherwise be contained. But the prospect of military intervention was not pleasant, and it was uncertain whether and when they would resort to direct action. As Sorensen later said of President Kennedy: " [He] did not alter his posture (which combined bluff with real determination in proportions he made known to *no one*) that the United States would have to intervene in Laos if it could not otherwise be saved."[76] But signs of hope kept appearing, which postponed a decision to intervene. On April 1 Premier Khrushchev indicated that he was agreeable in

[72] *Ibid.*, p. 643.   [73] Hilsman, *op. cit.*, p. 134.
[74] Schlesinger, *op. cit.*, pp. 332–34.   [75] Dommen, *op. cit.*, pp. 191–92.
[76] Sorensen, *op. cit.*, p. 646.

principle to the proposal for a cease-fire and conference on Laos. On April 4 Russia suggested a cease-fire and conference to Hanoi in a Vietnamese-language radio broadcast.[77] On May 1 the Laotian factions negotiated a cease-fire, and on May 11 the revived International Control Commission reported a reduction in conflict. The Geneva conference began on May 16. Later in May the annual monsoon rains arrived, ending most military operations. On June 3 and 4 Khrushchev and Kennedy met in Vienna, where they agreed to use their influence toward a neutral coalition government.

The beginning of a conference at Geneva did not solve the Laotian crisis; but, coupled with a cease-fire, it did offer prospects of a settlement and prolonged the life of the anti-Communist factions. W. Averell Harriman assumed responsibility for conducting the negotiations, and it took him a year to reach a formal settlement. In the meantime crisis flared again. In November 1961 the United States provided Phoumi with twenty helicopters to be used in combat and to be flown by pilots of Air America, a private firm whose services the United States government has often employed for covert operations in Southeast Asia.[78] Thereafter, Phoumi strongly resisted pressures on him to compromise with the Pathet Lao. Then, in May 1962, the Pathet Lao launched a successful offensive against the Phoumi garrison of 5,000 troops at the provincial capital of Nam Tha. The Royal Lao troops fled. This brought Pathet Lao forces close to the Mekong River, which formed the Laotian border with Thailand.

Proposals for military action were again raised in Washington. At a National Security Council meeting on May 10 Harriman and Roger Hilsman, director of the State Department's bureau of intelligence and research, recommended three actions: moving elements of the Seventh Fleet into the Gulf of Siam; moving a thousand Marines to Thailand; and moving a United States Army battle group, in Thailand on SEATO maneuvers, to the Laotian border. Pentagon representatives counterproposed diplomatic protests, moving the Seventh Fleet units, and increased arms, equipment, and training for Phoumi's army. That day President Kennedy approved moving the Seventh Fleet elements but did not approve the other recommendations. On May 12 he went further, approving the deployment of Marines to Thailand and the movement of the army battle group to the Laotian border.[79] This was not itself overt military intervention, since the forces were not autho-

[77] Dommen, *op. cit.*, p. 194.
[78] *The New York Times,* December 12, 1961, 21:1.
[79] Hilsman, *op. cit.*, pp. 145–46.

rized to move against defended objectives in either Thailand or Laos without prior authorization from Washington. It was a show of force.

Almost as quickly as these actions were taken, events suggested to decision-makers that it was not necessary to go further. On May 12 Premier Khrushchev spoke to the British ambassador, reaffirming his support for a negotiated neutral and independent coalition government in Laos. The premier repeated this the next day to United States Ambassador Llewellyn Thompson. Also, intelligence reports indicated that the Pathet Lao offensive had halted.[80] The chances for settlement were much improved. The successful attack on his forces had made Phoumi Nosovan more willing to accept a coalition government. The Pathet Lao, who could have pushed all the way to the Thai border, had stopped, despite pressure from some of their leaders to continue.[81] Then, in late May, the monsoon rains began, preventing further Pathet Lao advances. On June 11 an agreement was announced in Laos under which Souvanna Phouma would be premier of a new government and Phoumi Nosovan and Prince Souphanouvong of the Pathet Lao would be vice-premiers. At Geneva the Declaration on the Neutrality of Laos was signed on July 23, 1962.

President Kennedy and his advisers accepted the coalition government, doing so in the apparent belief that Laotian non-Communists would be strong enough to prevent a takeover by a Communist government. Ambassador Harriman explained the reasoning in a *New York Times* article in May:

> The United States believes that the framework gives satisfactory assurances that a non-Communist political control can be evolved in Laos. This belief is based upon several factors: the natural disposition of the overwhelming majority of the Lao people, the degree of political sophistication among the non-Communist Lao leaders, and most of all, the unpopularity of the Pathet Lao because of the stigma which attaches to them for having introduced the ancient Vietnamese enemy of the Laotian people into Laos during the past two years.[82]

Harriman's estimate of non-Communist strength within the coalition was apparently correct, at least for a few years.

The coalition did little more than legitimize a partition of the country between Pathet Lao-controlled and Royal Lao Army-controlled re-

---

[80] *The New York Times,* May 14, 1962, 1:8.   [81] Dommen, *op. cit.,* p. 219.
[82] W. Averell Harriman, "What We Are Doing in Southeast Asia," *The New York Times Magazine,* May 27, 1962, p. 55.

NO MILITARY INTERVENTION

gions. The coalition soon collapsed with the withdrawal of Prince Souphanouvong, and the factions fought again. North Vietnam continued to provide the Pathet Lao with war materiél and troops. The United States continued to assist the Royal Lao Army with money and equipment, as well as covert combat assistance provided by Air America; beginning in 1961 the United States also trained, supplied, and paid a paramilitary force formed of Meo tribesmen to fight the Pathet Lao. Nevertheless, the factions maintained an equilibrium. Each dry season, usually beginning in January, the North Vietnamese and Pathet Lao undertook an offensive that enlarged the area of their control. Then, when the monsoon season began in June, they would withdraw, and the Royal Lao Army and Meo tribesmen would recapture the land. In this process Souvanna Phouma's government controlled about two-fifths of the country's land, but 80 percent of the population.[83]

Despite the equilibrium, United States military involvement grew after 1963. In 1964 Air America began flying covert air strikes against Pathet Lao and North Vietnamese troops in Laos. In 1965 the United States Air Force started bombing missions, expanding the overt military intervention in South Vietnam. Most of these missions were directed against infiltration routes from North to South Vietnam that passed through Laos, but some were against Pathet Lao-North Vietnamese troop concentrations and supply areas. Not until the winter of 1969–70 did these overt actions gain much public attention in the United States. That year the Communist offensive was particularly successful, and the United States Air Force flew a larger number of missions than usual.

United States overt military intervention did begin in 1965, simultaneously with the start of the continuous bombing of North Vietnam. It could have begun in 1961 or 1962, but did not because the Kennedy Administration still believed that non-Communist Laotians were strong enough, for the moment, to prevent a total Pathet Lao victory. It was obviously an uncertain view, and military planning continued despite it. Yet it was enough to prevent consummation of military intervention despite the very nearness of it. One cannot but wonder what other decision-makers would have done in the same circumstances. Had Kennedy been Eisenhower and his chief adviser Dulles, rather than McGeorge Bundy, would the small step have been taken of providing close combat support or deploying the Marines from Thailand to Laos? The question is not answerable, since there was no situation

[83] Robert Shaplen, *Time Out of Hand* (New York: Harper & Row, 1968), p. 345.

like the Laotian one during the Eisenhower presidency. But the possibility does exist that in some situations individual differences among major decision-makers may make them view differently whether lesser actions have made overt military intervention unnecessary.

THREATS OF COMMUNIST GOVERNMENT IN "JUST ANOTHER COUNTRY"

"Just another country" is one that United States decision-makers perceive as neither part of a Communist-threatened region nor of special interest to the United States. Appendix A-3 lists thirteen deadly armed conflicts posing an evident threat to government in these other countries where major foreign affairs policy-makers may have perceived the possibility of a Communist government, but where United States overt military intervention did not occur. As a condition for overt military intervention in this class of situations, American leaders appear to require overt military intervention by another country that the United States can condemn.

In each of the thirteen situations at least one restraint appeared to operate. Four, however, are sufficiently interesting to merit further discussion: the Algerian war of 1954–62; the Indonesian civil war of 1948–62; the Indonesian conflict of 1965–66; and the Cyprus conflict of 1963–64.

Algeria, 1954–62

It has never been clear whether major United States decision-makers saw a significant possibility of a Communist government in Algeria at any time during that country's struggle for independence from France, of which it was technically a part. Arthur Schlesinger suggests those of the Kennedy Administration did not.[84] The possibility may have been entertained, however, by the decision-makers of the Eisenhower Administration. Armed conflict began late in 1954, when, on November 1, Algerian guerrillas, demanding independence, launched simultaneous attacks at thirty points where French troops were stationed around the country. France claimed the Communist party supported the guerrillas and in September 1955 outlawed the Communist party in Algeria. The Eisenhower Administration, torn between supporting a major ally and supporting nationalist aspirations, continued military

[84] Schlesinger, *op. cit.*, pp. 564–65.

NO MILITARY INTERVENTION

assistance to France but would not give verbal support to its attempt to put down the insurgents. As early as 1955 there were reports of United States-French friction over the Algerian problem.[85] In 1956 France offered evidence before the United Nations Security Council that Egypt was supplying military assistance to the guerrillas. By 1958 there was some possibility of United States military intervention. During the political crisis in France engendered by the Algerian struggle, French military units seized control of Algeria. The United States was reported to be preparing military contingency plans.[86]

There were, however, restraints on United States overt military intervention, even if the major decision-makers did perceive a significant possibility of a Communist government in Algeria. Although either the French government or a military government in Algeria could have requested military intervention by the United States, the situation lacked overt military intervention by a country the United States could condemn. The United Arab Republic was providing only military assistance. The only country engaging in overt military intervention in Algeria was France, and it would have been difficult to accept a request and condemn French intervention at the same time. The major decision-makers of the Eisenhower Administration may also have believed it unnecessary to approve overt military intervention, for they seem to have believed that the non-Communists among the guerrillas were much stronger than the Communists among them. Perhaps for that reason, if not because he perceived no threat at all, President Eisenhower reports disagreeing with West German Chancellor Konrad Adenauer during their Bonn meeting of April 1959 over the severity of the Communist threat in Algeria.[87] After General de Gaulle assumed power in France, France moved in the direction of granting independence to Algeria, recognizing Algeria as an independent nation in July 1962. The armed conflict between the guerrillas, the French forces, and the right-wing Secret Army Organization, which had begun fighting after 1958, abated.

The point in time when there probably existed the greatest danger of a Communist government in Algeria, if there was such a threat, was late in 1961, during the period before independence, but after the Kennedy Administration took office. In August 1961 Benyoussef Ben Khedda, often described as a "left-wing extremist," became premier of the nationalist rebels' government. Ben Khedda's ascent could have been viewed as a signal that the Communists were gaining dominance

---

[85] *The New York Times,* June 15, 1955, 30:5.   [86] *Ibid.,* May 29, 1958, 1:8.
[87] Eisenhower, *Waging Peace,* p. 417.

over the nationalists among the rebels. But as already noted, Schlesinger suggests that the Kennedy Administration's decision-makers did not perceive a significant possibility of a Communist government in Algeria. Even if they did, United States overt military intervention would have been restrained by the same lack of moral legitimation that could have restrained United States overt military intervention in the 1950's. There was no other country the United States could condemn that was engaging in overt military intervention in Algeria. When Algeria did gain independence in 1962, Ahmed Ben Bella, a neutralist and thereafter an independent actor in international affairs, returned from Europe to head the government.

Indonesia, 1958–62

The Indonesian civil war of 1948–62 is more clearly a conflict in which United States overt military intervention may have been restrained merely by lack of sufficient moral legitimation for the act. That conflict began before Indonesia gained independence from the Netherlands in 1949 and reached its greatest intensity in 1958.

President Eisenhower's memoirs give but one brief mention to what was probably very intense concern that a Communist government might be established in Indonesia.[88] In this conflict it was not the antigovernment forces who advocated a Communist government. On the contrary, the Indonesian Communist party sided with President Achmed Sukarno against the rebels. The antigovernment forces were composed of the Darul Islam organization, a right-wing nationalist group, and other military and civilian opponents of President Sukarno and the Indonesian Communist party. By 1958 the antigovernment forces had gained control over areas of the outer islands of Indonesia and proclaimed their own government in February of that year. By that time the Eisenhower Administration's fear of a Communist government in Indonesia was seemingly great. The United States Information Agency reported in late 1957 that the Indonesian Communist party had prepared detailed plans for taking over the government.[89] There were apparent leaks to the press by high American officials in March 1958 that the Soviet Union was providing military assistance to the Indonesian government.[90] However, Secretary Dulles had to say at a press conference a few days after the apparent leak that Soviet assis-

[88] *Ibid.*, p. 266.   [89] *The New York Times*, January 4, 1958, 3:3.
[90] *Ibid.*, March 31, 1958, 1:1.

NO MILITARY INTERVENTION

tance to Indonesia probably did not include arms.[91] There were also rumors that the Indonesian "rebel" government had requested assistance from the United States—rumors Secretary Dulles denied.[92] Further, Peking publicly offered to intervene on behalf of the antirebel forces.[93] In this situation the United States provided covert military assistance to the antigovernment forces, parachuting supplies to the rebel forces from planes, reportedly flown by CIA-hired pilots, based in Malaya and the Philippines.[94] At least one American, Allen Pope, flew a bomber for the antigovernment forces. Shot down on a mission, Pope was captured and exhibited by the Indonesian government along with evidence that he had been hired by the CIA.

It can be asked why United States decision-makers did not approve overt military intervention to prevent the perceived possibility of a Communist government. There was conflict, and the Indonesian Communist party was not being weakened by the covert aid being given the rebels. Yet the situation seemed to lack sufficient moral legitimation for United States overt military intervention; that is, it lacked the degree of outside force that seems to be required for overt military intervention in countries not of special interest and not part of Communist-threatened regions. Peking may have been providing military equipment to the antirebel forces that Washington could have documented and condemned. No outside country, however, was engaging in overt military intervention. There would also have been difficulty in claiming that the rebel government had any degree of *de facto* control in Indonesia, outside the North Celebes, were United States policymakers to entertain its request.

In the latter half of 1958 the antigovernment forces weakened, and government troops quickly captured many of the major objectives previously held by the rebels. United States decision-makers then proceeded in a different direction. Economic assistance was again extended to the Indonesian government, and Indonesia was permitted to buy military equipment in the United States. As both Roger Hilsman and Hanson Baldwin have suggested, the major United States decision-makers were strengthening the Indonesian army to balance the strength of the Indonesian Communist party.[95] In 1962 the civil war ended with the capture of the last major Darul Islam leader.

[91] *Ibid.*, April 2, 1958, 12:2.   [92] *Ibid.*, April 9, 1958, 1:5.
[93] *Ibid.*, May 16, 1958, 1:8.   [94] Hilsman, *op. cit.*, p. 369.
[95] Hilsman, *op. cit.*, pp. 372–73; and *The New York Times,* May 28, 1958, 7:3.

APPEAL TO FORCE

Indonesia, 1965–66

The Indonesian government under Sukarno moved further left during 1964 and 1965. In 1965 Indonesia withdrew from the United Nations. A cabinet change of late March 1965 was reportedly viewed by United States decision-makers as marking an even larger role in government for the Indonesian Communist party.[96] Then, at the beginning of October 1965, large-scale armed conflict broke out again, the details of which are still unclear. Apparently elements of the Indonesian Communist party attempted to seize control of the government. Some army elements contested the attempt, and the conflict continued for several days. On October 4 six anti-Communist generals were discovered murdered. Only days later army forces, apparently led by General Suharto, had largely defeated the insurgents. President Sukarno appointed General Suharto, known to be anti-Communist, chief of staff of the army. A wave of anti-Chinese and anti-Communist violence swept Indonesia. It has been estimated that 100,000 Communists and Chinese were killed in reprisals by year's end.[97] The reprisals continued into 1966. In the aftermath of the apparent attempted coup, General Suharto gradually eroded the power of President Sukarno, eventually coming to lead the government himself. That there was no United States overt military intervention in the conflict is perhaps not surprising. There was no overt military intervention by any other country; and it is doubtful that any Indonesian government would have requested United States intervention.

Cyprus, 1963–64

Cyprus was yet another of the "other countries" where American leaders may have perceived the possibility of a Communist government. Cyprus was torn by conflict from 1954 to 1959 between its Greek and Turkish communities and British troops stationed there. In 1960 it was made an independent nation and gained a government with Archbishop Makarios as president. Britain reduced its garrison on the island, and many hoped that the strife had ended. Deadly armed conflict

---

[96] *The New York Times,* April 1, 1965, 8:5.
[97] *Ibid.,* January 13, 1966, 1:3. John Hughes, in *Indonesian Upheaval* (New York: David McKay, 1967), pp. 184–89, suggests that 200,000 may be an even more accurate estimate.

NO MILITARY INTERVENTION

again erupted, however, in December 1963. Under a treaty by which Turkey, Greece, and Great Britain guaranteed the Cypriote government, Turkey threatened overt military intervention.

By 1963 the Kennedy Administration was reportedly concerned about the possibility of a Communist government on Cyprus; the party was growing and President Makarios was doing little to answer that growing strength.[98] The fighting continued into 1964. United States decision-makers considered sending American troops, under United Nations or NATO auspices.[99] The United States and Great Britain formally proposed a NATO peace-keeping force, a proposal the Soviet Union quickly attacked. Instead, the United Nations Security Council approved a United Nations peace-keeping force at the beginning of March. The United States and Great Britain contributed half the cost of the operation, but the United States contributed no combat troops. Amid Turkish threats of intervention, United Nations forces arrived and by the end of March replaced British troops policing the country. Turkey continued to threaten intervention, and in August 1964 Turkish planes attacked targets on Cyprus. President Johnson in June had sent a strong warning to the Turkish government against taking military action. Nevertheless, when the Turkish planes attacked, the president did not approve sending United States combat forces. By the end of 1964 conflict subsided and some accommodations were reached among the Cypriote communities.

The Cypriote conflict lacked the kind of condemnable overt military intervention by other powers that United States decision-makers seem to require for overt military intervention by the United States in "just other" countries. British troops engaged in some fighting in January 1964 and after, but President Johnson would not likely condemn Great Britain's actions in the situation. Turkish overt military intervention never materialized until August 1964; then it was brief and insignificant. There was also the problem of obtaining a request for intervention. President Makarios headed the only government of Cyprus; there was no rival government. A press report of January 1964 said United States decision-makers were considering sending American troops if the Cyprus government would approve.[100] Makarios, however, was reportedly opposed to such action and even opposed United States participation in a United Nations peace-keeping force.[101] Even

[98] *The New York Times,* August 26, 1963, 26:4.
[99] *Ibid.,* January 30, 1964, 1:7.   [100] *Ibid.*
[101] *Ibid.,* February 16, 1954, 31:1.

had major United States leaders considered Cyprus a country of special interest, overt military intervention might have been restrained for lack of a request and by the action of the United Nations.

THREATS OF COMMUNIST GOVERNMENT IN "DISPUTED TERRITORY AT THE MARGINS OF COMMUNIST STATES"

"Disputed territory at the margins of Communist states," as used here, refers to territory not under a Communist government but for which the neighboring Communist party-governed state makes a public claim supported by legalistic arguments. This classification includes West Berlin, Nepal, Sikkim and Bhutan, the northern borders of India and Burma, the Chinese offshore islands, as well as Tibet in 1949–51 and Trieste in 1946–53. There have been eight situations of deadly armed conflict posing an evident threat to government in such territory since 1946 (see Appendix A-4). United States overt military intervention occurred in none of them, although Peking used overt military intervention in five of the eight. When Peking bombarded some of the Chinese offshore islands in 1954 and 1958, when it invaded India's frontier in 1959–62, and when it invaded Tibet in 1950, none of the restraints on United States overt military intervention would seem to have operated. Yet such intervention did not occur. It might be thought that United States overt military intervention will not occur in disputed territory at the margins of Communist states, yet there is an aspect of unpredictability in such situations.

A central consideration for major United States decision-makers appears to be how much disputed territory the Communist state gains. In 1954 Peking gained control of certain of the offshore islands, including Ichiang and the Tachens, and in 1959–62 it captured some of India's northern boundary. But both times Peking failed to gain as much as it demanded. It did not push as far as some feared it might, perhaps because it perceived the possibility of overt military intervention by the United States. However, Communist Chinese troops completely subdued Tibet in 1950, in effect gaining all the disputed territory.

Would major United States decision-makers approve overt military intervention under any circumstances to protect disputed territory? There are some indications they might. President Eisenhower received congressional approval on January 28, 1955, to use military force to defend the offshore islands of Quemoy and Matsu if an attack on those

NO MILITARY INTERVENTION

islands were deemed a prelude to an attack on Taiwan and the Pescadores.[102] (Taiwan is itself claimed by Peking, but the United States formed a bilateral defense agreement with the government of Taiwan in December 1954 and that island is probably now best regarded as of special interest to the United States.) President Eisenhower also claims that he might have used overt military intervention to protect Quemoy and Matsu in 1958 if he perceived a threat to Taiwan.[103] Arthur Schlesinger also indicates that in 1962, during the Chinese-Indian conflict, the Kennedy Administration informed Indian Prime Minister Nehru that "in case the war intensified, India could expect American assistance." [104] By November 1962 the United States had already made air defense arrangements with India and was using twelve United States planes and crews to move Indian troops and supplies to the northern border. Under these circumstances, "American assistance" could have meant overt military intervention. On the other hand, no country, including the United States, seemed prepared to contest Peking's claim of suzerainty over Tibet in 1950.[105]

There appears to be no consistent point at which United States overt military intervention will occur in conflicts in disputed territory at the margins of Communist states—if it will occur at all. There appears to be no particular point at which the major decision-makers will consider the conflict serious enough to merit that action. President Eisenhower has noted that in authorizing Admiral Felix B. Stump, in January 1955, to evacuate Chinese Nationalist forces from the Tachens, which were being abandoned to Peking, he also authorized the admiral to bomb airfields on mainland China "if self-defense so required." [106] Had such bombing occurred, it would have been overt military intervention. (It must be noted that it is still not publicly known whether this directive required Admiral Stump to clear an attack on the airfields with the president before undertaking the action. Some "authorizations" have fewer strings attached than others.) It may be that United States overt military intervention can occur in deadly armed conflicts in disputed territory at the margins of Communist states only if there is condemnable overt military intervention by another and no other restraint operates. The absence of American military intervention in the disputes involving Tibet, the Indian frontier, and

---

[102] Eisenhower, *Mandate for Change*, pp. 467–69.
[103] Eisenhower, *Waging Peace*, p. 295.   [104] Schlesinger, *op. cit.*, p. 531.
[105] George Ginsburgs and Michael Mathos, *Communist China and Tibet: The First Dozen Years* (The Hague: Martinus Nijhoff, 1964), p. 6.
[106] Eisenhower, *Mandate for Change*, p. 469.

the Chinese off-shore islands—when these conditions were met—suggests that more is needed for intervention to occur. Symbolic importance comparable to that of West Berlin may be a necessary condition. On the other hand, the complete absence of American military intervention in disputed territories could mean that American leaders do not think these situations serious enough to warrant drastic action.

THREATS OF SOMETHING OTHER THAN NEW COMMUNIST GOVERNMENTS

All conflicts threatening non-Communist governments of foreign countries can pose some degree of threat to the United States, even when American decision-makers do not perceive in them a significant possibility of a Communist government. The hypothesis of this study, however, is that the major decision-makers will not perceive such situations sufficiently threatening to approve overt military intervention—even if there is condemnable overt military intervention by another country and no other restraint operates. Appendix A-5 lists fifty-three of these conflicts since World War II. United States overt military intervention occurred in none of them.

Among these fifty-three situations are a number where United States overt military intervention might have been expected, either as partisan or as peace-keeping, had the major American leaders perceived a significant possibility of a Communist government. These include situations in which no restraints seemed to operate: the Palestinian conflict in 1946–49; the Israeli-Arab war of 1967; the India-Pakistan war of 1965; the seizure of Goa in 1961; the Kashmir conflict in 1947–49; the Yemen civil war of 1962–67; the Nigerian civil war of 1966–69; the Anglo-French-Israeli invasion of Suez in 1956; and the conflict that broke out in the West Irian dispute between Indonesia and the Netherlands in 1962.

The latter two conflicts serve to indicate the boundary between a perception of a significant possibility of a Communist government and its absence. President Eisenhower reports he saw "serious Communist penetration in the Middle East" in 1955 when President Nasser of Egypt negotiated to buy arms from Czechoslovakia.[107] Seeing "penetration" or influence, however, does not necessarily mean the major decision-makers perceive a significant possibility of a Communist government. As Eisenhower has noted, President "Nasser was able to deal

[107] Eisenhower, *Waging Peace*, p. 24.

NO MILITARY INTERVENTION

with Communists and accept their aid with some degree of safety simply because he demanded that all Soviet operations be conducted through himself." [108] In Syria, on the other hand, Eisenhower believed the Soviet Union dealt directly with government agencies and other organizations. The only concern of major United States decision-makers for the possibility of a Communist government in the Middle East during the Suez conflict appears to have been the fear that the Soviet Union would take retaliatory action elsewhere in the region.[109]

Apparently the Kennedy Administration did not perceive an imminent possibility of a Communist government in the West Irian fighting in 1962, either. Indonesia made a public claim for West New Guinea (West Irian) as soon as it gained independence in 1949. Nevertheless, the Netherlands continued to control West Irian until 1962. That year President Sukarno, having won his own civil war, threatened invasion. In response, the Netherlands sent troops to West Irian. Sukarno sent token numbers of paratroops in overt military intervention. To the consternation of the Netherlands, Washington advocated that the territory be transferred to Indonesia. President Kennedy and his advisers may have seen the possibility of a Communist government in Indonesia (which would mean West Irian, too, if Indonesia gained it), but they apparently did not believe the possibility imminent. A Communist government was seemingly thought most likely *after* Sukarno retired; United States support for the transfer of West Irian was apparently thought a means to strengthen the non-Communist forces in Indonesia.[110] Indonesia and the Netherlands, with the mediation of United States Ambassador Ellsworth Bunker, reached an agreement in August 1962 to transfer the territory to Indonesia. The armed conflict ended before it ever reached serious proportions.

DEVELOPMENTS IN COMMUNIST STATES

There have been a few situations of deadly armed conflict posing an evident threat to government in Communist-governed states since 1946 (see Appendix A-6 for a list of nine). United States overt mili-

---

[108] *Ibid.*, p. 197n.   [109] *Ibid.*, p. 91.

[110] Schlesinger, *op. cit.*, pp. 533–35; Hilsman, *op. cit.*, pp. 366–67, 371–72. Arthur Krock strongly criticized United States actions in the conflict, but appeared to impute similar perceptions to the major decision-makers. *The New York Times*, May 25, 1962, 32:4; May 29, 1962, 30:4; August 1, 1962, 1:8; and August 17, 1962, 22:4.

tary intervention, however, has not occurred in such situations. This has been true despite Soviet overt military intervention in Hungary in 1956 and Czechoslovakia in 1968, and Communist Chinese overt military intervention in Tibet in 1959. It was even true when the United States-supported invasion of Cuba's Bay of Pigs failed in 1961.

In late October 1956 revolt broke out in Hungary against the government of Janos Kádár. Within a few days the Hungarian army had moved to the side of the revolutionaries and the revolutionaries announced an independent government under Imre Nagy. It was announced that Soviet troops would leave Hungary. Then, on November 1, Soviet forces returned to Budapest. In the midst of bloody fighting in the city's streets, Nagy appealed to the United Nations for action. Neither the United States nor any other Western nation (Britain and France were at that moment engaged at Suez) offered overt military intervention. Soviet forces reinstated the Kádár government on November 3, 1956. Before October 26 Hungary had a Communist government, but between October 27 and November 2 there was a period during which major United States decision-makers might have thought Hungary no longer had such a government. United States overt military intervention was ostensibly then restrained only by the presence of Soviet troops; to intervene would have been to fight the Soviet Union.

The same restraint applied to Czechoslovakia in 1968. The Czech government under President Ludwig Svoboda and the Communist party under Alexander Dubcek had been progressively loosening controls on individual citizens since January 1968, actions that apparently dismayed the Soviet leadership. When Warsaw Pact maneuvers in Czechoslovakia ended in July, the Soviet Union refused to remove its troops and did not remove all of them until the beginning of August. Czech and Russian leaders met in high-level conferences at Bratislava and Cierna, where the Soviet Union attempted to persuade the Czechs to slow the liberalization program. When no change followed, Warsaw Pact troops from the Soviet Union, East Germany, Poland, Hungary, and Bulgaria invaded Czechoslovakia on August 20 and occupied the country. There was limited resistance, but the invasion was very quickly successful, with the result that the troops controlled the country. The invaders did not overthrow the government, although they did briefly capture Dubcek and other leaders, all of whom were soon released. The troops remained, however. Over the following months the Soviet Union was able to gain concessions on programs and personnel

NO MILITARY INTERVENTION

without bloodshed. Unlike Hungary, there was no time when Czechoslovakia lacked a government that called itself Communist. Nor was there any request for outside assistance publicly expressed by the Czech government. Had there been a request, United States overt military intervention would still have been restrained by the presence of Soviet troops.

There were no Soviet troops in Tibet in 1959. That restraint did not apply. Between May 1951, when Tibet and Communist China signed the agreement on "Measures for the Peaceful Liberation of Tibet," and 1959, Peking succeeded in establishing a *de facto* Communist government in Tibet.[111] President Eisenhower seems to have recognized that fact in 1959.[112] In 1959 Khamba tribesmen, who had sporadically fought Chinese Communist troops in the country for years, arose again in a major revolt. This time the tribesmen were joined by others in Lhasa. The Dalai Lama fled to India. Eventually, the Dalai Lama made a public appeal to the United Nations for assistance. Yet United States overt military intervention did not occur, although no other restraints operated and although there was condemnable overt military intervention by another country, Communist China. China assumed full control of the country.

Most puzzling of these instances is why the United States did not use overt force at Cuba's Bay of Pigs in 1961. It did go so far as to sponsor, train, and transport Cuban exiles for an invasion, which took place April 17, but United States combat troops did not accompany the invaders, and United States military planes were not among those bombing the island. Even when the invasion began to fail, Washington did not attempt to assure success by committing United States forces.

The invasion was planned by the Central Intelligence Agency. President Eisenhower on March 17, 1960, had approved the training of Cuban exiles for future action against Castro.[113] The original plan was to train guerrillas who would enter Cuba surreptitiously in small groups, but the plan changed while the exiles were being trained. By November 1960 the CIA envisaged a conventional assault.[114] Eventually, it was decided that the invaders should land at the Bay of Pigs on the south coast of Cuba.

It was understood from the very beginning that United States mili-

---

[111] Ginsburgs and Mathos, *loc. cit.*   [112] Eisenhower, *Waging Peace*, p. 326.
[113] *Ibid.*, p. 533; and Karl E. Meyer and Tad Szulc, *The Cuban Invasion: The Chronicle of a Disaster* (New York: Praeger, 1962), p. 77.
[114] Haynes Johnson, *The Bay of Pigs* (New York: W. W. Norton, 1964), pp. 53–54.

tary forces were not to be a direct part of any covert action in Cuba. This was understood by all who engaged in the planning under the Eisenhower Administration; indeed, Arthur Schlesinger has called it a "CIA ground rule."[115] The Kennedy Administration continued this restriction. President Kennedy himself emphasized the need to avoid United States overt military involvement. He did so at a meeting with advisers on March 11, and again at a meeting on April 4.[116] Nevertheless, lending the operation moral legitimation was a major preoccupation. In January 1961 the plan was again amended. It was decided to form a provisional government for Cuba in the United States and fly it in; and if the invaders sustained themselves for ten days or two weeks, the provisional government could be recognized. It could then formally request United States assistance, but aid would be logistic and would not include United States troops.[117] A provisional government had first to be formed, and the exile leaders in the United States were divided into two factions: the Democratic Revolutionary Front and the Revolutionary Movement. On March 18 representatives of the CIA met with the leaders of the two factions and pressured them to unite as a condition for United States support. They agreed to form a Cuban Revolutionary Council and chose Dr. Miro Cardona provisional president.[118] The provisional government was announced March 22 and issued a statement of its intentions when it achieved power in Cuba. It was a conservative program, which disturbed the Kennedy Administration. So Adolph Berle, head of President Kennedy's Latin American task force, Philip Bonsal, former United States ambassador to Cuba, and Arthur Schlesinger, the president's special assistant, met Miro and urged him to include some social welfare planks in the council's platform. It was an unsuccessful effort. Nonetheless, on April 3 the White House issued a "white paper" stating that the Castro government posed a danger to the hemisphere. It mentioned no conflict and no foreign meddling in a Cuban conflict, for there was no significant fighting in Cuba before the exile invasion.

    A decisive meeting of the major decision-makers occurred on April 4, 1961. This was not the last meeting before the invasion, and President Kennedy retained until the last minute the means to abort the plan. On this day, however, all the principals involved met and approved the plan. It can be said that the decision to land the exiles was

[115] Schlesinger, *op. cit.,* p. 234.
[116] *Ibid.,* pp. 241–43; and Johnson, *op. cit.,* p. 69.
[117] Schlesinger, *op. cit.,* p. 237.
[118] *Ibid.,* pp. 243–44.

NO MILITARY INTERVENTION

thereafter firm. The group met at the State Department. Present were the president, Secretary Rusk, Secretary McNamara, Treasury Secretary Douglas Dillon, then Assistant Secretary of State for Inter-American Affairs Thomas Mann, Assistant Secretary of Defense for International Security Affairs Paul Nitze, Chairman of the Joint Chiefs of Staff General Lyman Lemnitzer, Director of the Central Intelligence Agency Allen Dulles, Deputy Director for Plans of the CIA Richard Bissell, the three presidential advisers Adolph Berle, Richard Goodwin, and Arthur Schlesinger, and Senator J. William Fulbright.[119] It was agreed, as the president insisted, that no United States forces should participate directly. The 1,400 exiles would be transported in United States vessels assigned to the CIA. Old United States B-26 attack bombers would destroy the Cuban air force before the landing, but the pilots would be Cubans or CIA-hired United States civilians.

Pointedly excluded from this and later discussions were some American officials who might have opposed the plan. The United States ambassador to the United Nations, Adlai Stevenson, was one. On April 15 Ambassador Stevenson found himself denying in good faith before an emergency session of the United Nations Political Committee that the B-26 attack on Cuba of that morning was United States-supported. Also excluded was Edward R. Murrow, head of the United States Information Agency. And most important, Cleveland Amory, deputy director for intelligence of the CIA, was not among those informed or consulted. The omission of these persons may have precluded opposition to the plan. All those who did attend the April 4 meeting, except Senator Fulbright, supported it.

The invasion, planned for April 10, was postponed for a week and was executed very early in the morning of April 17. Although some American civilians were present, military personnel were not. It was a covert operation rather than overt military intervention. This limitation is understandable. Cuba was a Communist-governed state, and overt action could not be morally justified: there was no conflict to deplore, no government yet in Cuba that would issue a request, and no nation to condemn for meddling in a conflict.

It is more interesting to ask why the United States did not commit its military forces when it became apparent the exiles were losing. The invasion was a fiasco. The B-26 bombing attack of April 15 failed to destroy Cuba's air force. Some of the vessels in the invading fleet were sunk by fire or by hitting reefs. Elements of the Cuban army were on hand to contain the assault. By the afternoon of April 18 Washington

[119] *Ibid.*, pp. 251–52; and Johnson, *op. cit.*, pp. 67–70.

knew the plan was perilously close to abject failure. That evening President Kennedy met at the White House with Vice-President Johnson, Secretary Rusk, Secretary McNamara, McGeorge Bundy, Walt Rostow, Richard Bissell, Arthur Schlesinger, and Chief of Naval Operations Arleigh Burke.[120] Bissell and Burke proposed overt military intervention in the form of a concealed air strike from the United States aircraft carrier *Essex* stationed near Cuba, but the president rejected it. He did agree to permit unmarked United States planes to fly air cover for a second strike by the B-26 bombers the next morning, but they were not to be permitted to engage in the overt action of bombing or strafing. Events prevented the execution of even this near-military intervention. A mix-up resulted in the B-26's arriving over their targets an hour before the unmarked cover planes from the *Essex*. The invasion no longer had hope of success. Within days virtually all the exiles were captured.

President Kennedy explained his decisions in a speech to the American Society of Newspaper Editors in Washington on April 20. The invasion had begun only three days before, but it was already dead. The first thing he did was to explain why overt force was not used—the open use of military force would not have been morally justified. His words were:

> I have emphasized before that this was a struggle of Cuban patriots against a Cuban dictator. While we could not be expected to hide our sympathies, we made it repeatedly clear that the armed forces of this country would not intervene in any way.
>
> Any unilateral American intervention in the absence of an external attack upon ourselves or an ally would have been contrary to our traditions and to our international obligations . . . .[121]

There followed a vague threat that "our restraint is not inexhaustible," and the United States might use open force in the future despite tradition.

Even after the invasion began, United States overt military intervention was still restrained. The president articulated one of the restraints. Although conflict existed, the only nation that could be condemned for intervention was the United States itself. And there was no government to request United States involvement—certainly Castro would not do so, and Miro Cardona's government did not have

---

[120] Schlesinger, *op. cit.*, pp. 277–78.
[121] *The New York Times*, April 21, 1961, 2:2.

NO MILITARY INTERVENTION

the chance to land in Cuba, much less establish control over any part of the country, before the invasion collapsed. In addition, of course, intervention was restrained by the fact that Cuba already had a Communist government. Although its presence in the hemisphere was unpleasant, the threat it posed to the United States was not seen as grave enough to justify an open military expedition with its attendant cost in lost international prestige and the risk that a large number of United States combat troops might for some time have to be employed for fighting in, and occupation of, a Caribbean nation of uncertain strategic value.

SUMMARY

United States overt military intervention is a rare event, having occurred since World War II only when armed conflict threatened a foreign government. But American forces have been committed to only a few of the postwar conflicts. Its frequent absence, which is otherwise puzzling, is explicable by the theory of restraints. When overt military action did not occur, one or more requirements for it were not met. In some instances American leaders did not see a threat of a new Communist government. In other instances one or more restraints of the international system, decision-making process, or operational code were present. No conflict between 1948 and 1971 fully met all the requirements for intervention, except those in Korea, Lebanon, Vietnam, and the Dominican Republic. The only event between 1945 and 1947 when intervention appeared unrestrained but failed to happen was the Paraguayan civil war of 1947, but it is not certain that the Truman Administration saw in it a threat of Communist government despite the alarms raised by Paraguay's right-wing president. It is equally evident that neither extraordinary significance of a threatened nation (as China), nor failure of a covert intervention (as in Cuba in 1961), nor humanitarian appeals for intervention to restore peace (as in the Nigerian civil war of 1966-69) have been sufficient to induce American leaders to use military force when a restraint acted on it.

Although the requirement of a Communist threat and the several restraints can prevent the beginning of overt military intervention, they do not prohibit lesser actions, including covert intervention, as was undertaken in Cuba in 1961. Nor do they prevent the expansion of intervention in a region to countries where it would not otherwise occur. For example, intervention in Southeast Asia did not begin in

Laos in 1961 because the Kennedy Administration perceived local actors strong enough to prevent a Communist takeover, but intervention in South Vietnam, which was begun in 1961, expanded to Laos in 1965 although the Laotian situation had not markedly worsened. United States policy-makers treat the beginning of overt military intervention as a threshold. It can be crossed only under precisely limited conditions. There are fewer restraints on action short of direct military involvement: noncombat military assistance is freely given, and covert operations are more frequent than military interventions. Once the threshold is crossed and military action begun, the restraints are relaxed, and intervention may be enlarged within the country as well as expanded to neighboring countries.

6

THE PRESENT AND THE FUTURE IN THE UNITED STATES'S USE OF FORCE

United States overt military intervention since World War II has been tightly constrained. Constraint has lent pattern to the action. America has been predictable, whether or not its leaders have wanted it to be. Presidents and policy-makers have come and gone. Yet the pattern of American military intervention has persisted for more than twenty-five years. It is a truism that in international politics every situation is different, but in the resort to force, American policy-makers have treated each new situation in the same manner as earlier ones. Whatever differences there may have been in the purposes that different policy-makers have seen in the use of force, all have used it in the same way. The continuing restraints upon intervention have shaped its use to the same mold.

The pattern of American military intervention is a simple one. American leaders have appealed to force when, and only when, they believed that a Communist government might be established in a country that did not have one. And military intervention has occurred when, and only when, restraints of the international system, the top-level decision-making process, and the shared moral values of foreign policy leaders have not operated. On those occasions when a Communist threat was thought to exist and when none of the other restraints was operative, intervention has followed. In the absence of a perceived Communist threat or when one or more of the other restraints have operated, overt military intervention has not occurred.

The four times the United States commenced overt military intervention after World War II, no restraint operated to inhibit the action.

We have assumed that the American decision-makers' operational code defines a scale of seven categories, delineated on page 25 and discussed at length in Chapter 5, to rank the significance of different kinds of threats. Our theory hypothesizes that only a threat high on the scale (a perceived threat of a Communist government in a previously non-Communist country) would be sufficient to produce direct American military action. In North Korea's invasion of South Korea, Washington saw the possibility of a Communist government in just another country. In South Vietnam's long civil war, American leaders foresaw the chance of Communist government within the Communist-threatened region of Southeast Asia. A similar threat was seen in Lebanon for the Communist-threatened region of the Fertile Crescent. In the Dominican Republic, American decision-makers believed that a Communist government might arise within this special interest country. The importance of perception over reality is underlined by the possibility that American leaders may have been wrong in believing that Communist government threatened Lebanon and the Dominican Republic. Nevertheless, the United States has not practiced overt military intervention against threats of something other than a Communist government. It has abstained from the use of force within states that already had Communist governments, no matter what happened within them—at least it has so abstained at the outset of intervention within a region. The United States has also failed to use military force in disputed territory at the margins of Communist states. This suggests, in general, that only the threatened "loss" of entire countries will spur American overt military intervention. An exception may be these territories of great symbolic importance such as West Berlin. There is the possibility, if not the certainty, that the United States would act in Berlin despite its demonstrated unwillingness to intervene in less conspicuous places such as Tibet. In addition, the United States has not used force under a perception of true peril since World War II. The reason is simple: There have been no occasions of true peril since World War II, nor any instances when policy-makers thought the United States was in direct danger. If true peril were perceived, we assume that American military intervention would follow even if some of the other restraints were operating.

The other restraints were also inoperative for Korea, Lebanon, Vietnam, and the Dominican Republic. The theory suggests that several additional restraints could each prevent overt military action. The international system can prevent the use of force that would necessarily involve nuclear weapons or would require fighting the Soviet

THE PRESENT AND THE FUTURE

Union. The manner in which decisions are made can also act to restrain intervention. The president may permit another member of the policy-making group a veto. Or during the incremental process of decision making, less extreme actions may solve the problem, another acceptable nation or international organization may assume the burden, or local actors may be perceived by United States leaders as strong enough to resist the threat with only limited American assistance. The shared moral values of the operational code further demand a request from a government in the host country, the existence of armed conflict threatening the government, and demonstrable, condemnable intervention by another country. (How much "other-party" intervention is required depends upon the significance of the country.) The theory assumes that compliance with the restraints is not voluntary. The restraints have automatic effect. Thus, for the theory to be valid, no restraint may operate when intervention occurs.

The four times the United States resorted to overt military intervention after World War II none of the restraints operated. Nuclear weapons were not needed. No Russian troops were in the countries. The president permitted no veto; indeed, there was virtually no dissent among his advisers. Nor did extreme action become unnecessary. Verbal support and military assistance were tried early in each conflict, and each time these early efforts failed. It is true, of course, that the judgment that early efforts had failed came much more quickly in the Korean and Dominican crises than in the Lebanese and South Vietnamese conflicts. Nor did United States leaders believe that non-Communists were strong enough to resist a Communist government if given only limited assistance: not in South Korea on June 27, 1950, when the fall of Seoul was imminent; not in Lebanon on July 14, 1958, after the coup in Iraq; not in South Vietnam on November 15, 1961, after the Taylor-Rostow report; and not in the Dominican Republic on April 28, 1965, after the Molina Urena government fell and the anti-Bosch military effort stalled. In each instance there was a governmental request, although the Korean and South Vietnamese requests were vague, the Lebanese request was merely verbal, and the Dominican request came from a government that controlled only a small area near Santo Domingo. Each of the four countries suffered conflict threatening government. Last, there were other countries to condemn for intervention. Cuba gave "support" to revolutionaries in the Dominican Republic (a special interest country), mostly in the form of prior training. Syria gave insurgents in Lebanon military assistance, and North Vietnam provided military assistance to the Viet Cong in South Vietnam. Such assistance legitimized United States action in these Communist-threatened regions. And North Korea invaded South Korea, committing the overt military intervention necessary to legitimize the use of force by the United States in just another country.

The theory of restraints also appears to explain why overt military intervention has not been used at other times and places. When it didn't happen, one or more restraints operated and so prevented it. The fit of the model is ambiguous in one event—the Paraguayan civil war of 1947. We do not know for certain whether the Truman Administration saw in that country, at that time, the chance of a Communist government. It probably did not. If it did, however, intervention should have followed unless the "containment" pattern of intervention was not yet fully established in 1947. For all other situations, the theory makes accurate predictions. Everywhere else, at least one restraint operated.

The theory further suggests that one restraint alone should be enough to prevent the resort to force. Each of the restraints has proven its independent effect in at least one situation. During the Indian invasion of Goa in 1961 and the Nigerian civil war of 1966–69, no other restraint operated, but United States policy-makers did not believe either country was threatened by communism. All that prevented overt action in the Chinese civil war after 1947 was the necessity for nuclear weapons. It is possible that United States action in Hungary in November 1956, after the Imre Nagy government took power, was restrained only by the presence of Russian troops. Intervention in Indochina in 1954 was prevented only by the veto President Eisenhower granted leaders of Congress. Direct military action could have occurred in the guerrilla wars in Peru and Bolivia during the 1960's, but it became unnecessary when the governments of the countries suppressed the rebellions with the aid of United States equipment and advice. United States troops might have been sent to Malaya in 1948, had not Britain assumed the burden, and to the Congo in 1960, after the Soviet Union began aiding Lumumba, had not the United Nations Security Council already organized a peace-keeping force. All that seemed to restrain United States overt military intervention in Laos in 1961 was the Kennedy Administration's belief that non-Communist Laotians could prevent takeover by a Communist government although they could not eradicate the threat posed by the Pathet Lao. Burma, at least at points during its eleven-year civil war, 1948–58, met all requirements except that the government of U Nu would not request United States presence. American troops might well have fought in West Berlin in 1962, but conflict threatening the West Berlin government failed to arise—East Germany did not invade. And intervention has sometimes been restrained because other nations' involvement was insufficient to lend justification to United States action. Indonesia in 1958 (just another country) met all other tests, except there was no condemnable overt military intervention by another country. Iran in 1953 (part of a Communist-threatened region) might have received United States troops, but there was no documentable military assistance from outsiders that Washington could condemn. In the 1960's most of the insurrectionary wars in the special interest area of Latin America received "support" from Fidel Castro's government in Cuba, and condemnation of Cuba could be used to legitimize United States action in the region. But in some of the conflicts that preceded Castro's rise to power—as those in Peru in 1948, in Bolivia in 1952, and in Haiti in 1957—intervention was prevented by the absence of any external support Washington could condemn, although all other requirements were satisfied.

THE CRITICAL THRESHOLD OF OVERT MILITARY INTERVENTION

It may come as a surprise that American use of force exhibits so simple a pattern and that so simple and deterministic a theory can explain it. One cannot completely reject the possibility that the pattern is simply the product of chance. Any event as rare as overt military intervention might by chance fall into a pattern. The fit of the theory to both the presence and the absence of overt military intervention, however, reduces the probability that the pattern is accidental.

The seeming inflexibility of American military action is nonetheless startling. The notion that restraints may shape United States action is not a new one. Stanley Hoffmann wrote a brilliant essay on the subject some years ago.[1] That restraints may *determine* American behavior, however, is alien to most approaches to the subject of foreign policy.[2] Most areas of United States foreign policy do not reflect such precise patterning. The preferences and the values of individual deci-

---

[1] Stanley Hoffmann, "Restraints and Choices in American Foreign Policy," *Daedalus*, Vol. 91 (Fall 1962), pp. 668–704.

[2] Graham Allison limns three modal approaches to the study of foreign policy. None are deterministic models. See his *Essence of Decision: Explaining the Cuban Missile Crisis* (Boston: Little, Brown, 1971).

sion-makers appear to make a difference in other areas, while they do not on overt military intervention. It takes unusual conditions to negate the influence of individuals in the decision-making process.

One condition peculiar to overt military intervention is that the choice for it since World War II has always been made by the top decision-makers. This in itself can act to reduce the variability of the behavior. If many people with force at their command can elect to use it, the use of force is less likely to be consistent than if a smaller number of persons exercise the authority. It was not always the case that the top policy-makers controlled the appeal to force; they did not do so in the early nineteenth century. It is not that American military officers now lack the physical ability to act independently. Rather, professional military officers now share an ethic asserting that top-level approval *ought* to be a condition for direct military action.

The centralization of decision-making does not by itself assure that choice will be determined. That choices on overt military intervention have been group choices rather than individual decisions may be a second peculiarity of this aspect of American behavior. Groups that interact often and over long periods of time have a remarkable ability to routinize their decisions. It is advantageous for them that they do so, for no group can survive recurrent acrimonious dispute on major issues. The process of routinization need not be a conscious effort. Indeed, most participants in routine processes of group choice do not realize how predictable their decisions are. The patterning of group decisions is more often the result of the sharing of values and the general acceptance of the legitimacy of particular outside constraints. Group processes do not necessarily become routine, of course; it is just that it is sometimes easier for this routinization to happen in group processes than in individual choices.

The beginning of overt military intervention in a region is both routinized and centralized. Other kinds of decisions in foreign affairs are not strictly controlled. Routinization and centralization of decisions for the starting of direct military action may exist in part because American policy-makers regard the first use of overt force as a critical threshold in the scale of violence. They act as if it were a threshold. American leaders threaten force under diverse circumstances—over the Chinese offshore islands, over Berlin, and over missiles in Cuba. Yet the threats are not always fulfilled; they are fulfilled only when the restraints on intervention are inoperable. Washington will often skirt the border of the threshold, seemingly being careful not to cross it, as in the military assistance program to Greece in the late 1940's, the military adviser program in Laos between 1959 and 1965, and the conspicuous covert invasion of Cuba in 1961.

Below the threshold of overt military intervention American action does not appear to be so tightly constrained as it is at the crossing point. For instance, the United States has established programs of military assistance with eighty different countries since 1945. It has also participated in more covert or "black" political and paramilitary operations than military interventions. In some cases covert action has been a substitute for overt force when Washington feared the formation of a new Communist government but when the standards of moral legitimation for direct military action could not be met. The black operations in the Philippines in 1950, Iran in 1953, Guatemala in 1954, Indonesia in 1958, and Cuba in 1961 occurred when either request, conflict, or condemnable intervention by others was lacking. Sometimes, however, when overt intervention cannot be justified, nothing is done, as in the several Iraqi conflicts after 1958 and the Haitian uprising of 1957. The choice among alternative actions below the threshold —military assistance, show of force, threat, covert action, or something else—being relatively unrestrained, is also unprogrammed. What lesser alternative will be chosen is not highly predictable. It cannot be predictable, because below the threshold of overt military intervention the choice among alternative actions is not necessarily made by the group of major foreign policy decision-makers. For lesser issues decision making is often dispersed among the middle levels of the foreign policy establishment. Action may be different depending upon where the decision is made. Bureaucrats in the Agency for International Development are likely to move in different directions from bureaucrats in the State Department, the CIA, the Department of the Air Force, or the Office of the Secretary of Defense. Given the number of events that occur abroad requiring decision, and given the lack of communication and coordination among agencies that is so much a problem in Washington, it is sometimes a matter of chance who gets to make the decision on a lesser foreign policy issue.

The choice of what form of overt force to use first is also unprogrammed. The rules controlling the beginning of intervention do not distinguish between combat troops, naval shelling, aerial bombing, and close combat support. The choice between them is left to the decision-makers. Action began in South Korea with bombing, in Lebanon with an amphibious Marine landing, in the Dominican Republic with an aerial Marine landing, and in South Vietnam with close combat support. The differences depended heavily upon professional military calculations of what the United States could effectively do, the location of United States units, the nature of existing contingency plans, and bargaining among top leaders.

Once intervention is begun, action is also relatively unrestrained. One kind of military action can lead to the use of other kinds. Bombing and naval shelling in South Korea were followed by the landing of United States troops. Close combat support in South Vietnam was followed by air strikes, naval shelling, and American troops. But one form does not necessarily lead to another. Only combat troops were used in Lebanon and the Dominican Republic; there was no bombing and no shelling, although planes were available for air strikes. American leaders exercise discretion in determining the ultimate size of an intervention, too. The buildup of forces in the Dominican Republic was arrested at 22,000 men; that in Lebanon stopped at 14,000 men. In both instances no more troops were sent because it was concluded that no more were needed. On the other hand, after 550,000 servicemen had been sent to South Vietnam without achieving success and the United States military command in Southeast Asia in the spring of 1968 asked for 200,000 more, the request was not granted. President Johnson and his advisers were persuaded that a further enlargement would not produce a commensurable increase in the chances of success and would not justify its economic and political costs.[3] There is a tendency to escalate interventions once they are started, but escalation is not automatic.

Intervention can also expand to other countries, unrestrained by the rules that restrict the beginning of an intervention. From South Korea military action expanded to North Korea. From South Vietnam intervention expanded to North Vietnam, Laos, and Cambodia. Laos and Cambodia fit the requirements for beginning interventions, but loosely. In each instance some restraints were violated. For Laos there was no public request for United States intervention. For Cambodia there was no request, and the action came too soon in the incremental decision-making process—lesser actions had not had a chance to fail. There were threats of Communist government in the two countries, although in the case of Cambodia that threat was at the time of United States intervention still a potential one posed by the possible future action of North Vietnamese troops. American actions in Laos and Cambodia, however, were not primarily directed against the threats to the two countries themselves. Most of the bombing in Laos, but not all, was

[3] Townsend Hoopes, *The Limits of Intervention* (New York: David McKay, 1969), pp. 159–224.

directed against the Ho Chi Minh Trail, the infiltration route from North to South Vietnam that passed through Laos. The ground offensives in Cambodia and Laos were designed to clear Viet Cong and North Vietnamese sanctuaries that were used by those forces as bases for attacks into South Vietnam. In both cases the expansion of intervention seemed related primarily to Viet Cong activities in South Vietnam, not to any threats to Laos and Cambodia themselves.

The interventions in North Korea and North Vietnam do not fit the pattern of beginning interventions at all. These states were not threatened by communism since they already had Communist governments. In addition, the conditions for moral justification—request, conflict, and the condemnable intervention of others—were wholly lacking.

It is evident that the rigid rules governing intervention become flexible once intervention is begun in a region. They can be interpreted loosely to permit intervention in neighboring non-Communist states and ignored completely to permit action against "aggressor" Communist nations. Intervention will not necessarily expand to other countries, however. From Lebanon it was not extended into Jordan, Syria, or Iraq. The action in the Dominican Republic remained limited to that country. Nor will expansion into a neighboring state necessarily escalate. The bombing of Laos was not immediately followed by the dispatch of United States troops, although the bombing of Cambodia was. After North Korea had been shelled and bombed for some months, the United States sent troops into it. But there was no invasion of North Vietnam despite the heavy bombing of it. Once intervention is begun in a region, decisions give greater consideration to matters that are largely ignored when intervention is begun. Urging expansion are the sense of commitment, the feeling that the nation's "prestige" is at stake, the desire to "win," the need to protect United States servicemen, the wish to demonstrate to opponents one's "will" to fight, and that most American of assumptions, the belief that the United States cannot be defeated in a war. Restraining expansion are the tacit bargains that are struck between adversaries in efforts to keep limited wars limited. The United States avoided attacks on China during the Korean War. The lesson of Chinese intervention after the United States entered North Korea suggested during the Southeast Asia war that no United States ground troops should enter North Vietnam.

No rigid rules evidently control what the United States shall do once intervention in a region is begun. American leaders are free to cope with the many competing demands upon them. It is not that United States policy-makers are free to do as they wish once United

APPEAL TO FORCE

States force is committed, but that they are thereafter free to exercise judgment in deciding what demands and restraints to consider, and how to weigh them. It is precisely this exercise of judgment on what factors to consider that is proscribed for decisions to initiate overt military intervention.

Military force is not forever free once it is unleashed in a region. There is a higher threshold at the point of using nuclear weapons, where choice is circumscribed by rules that top policy-makers impose upon themselves. One might have thought that the use of chemical and biological weapons constituted another higher threshold, but the casual use of chemical devices in Vietnam suggests that American leaders no longer regard it so. The rule against nuclear weapons appears to be an absolute prohibition. This may, however, be a wrong inference. It may be that nuclear weapons have not been used since 1945 merely because no threat has been thought severe enough to justify them. Were the United States to be directly attacked or were it thought an attack was imminent, nuclear-armed missiles and bombers could be employed. This possibility is the threat on which American strategists rely to deter an attack upon the United States. It is also possible that an overt military intervention abroad could expand under some conditions to include the use of nuclear weapons even if the United States were not directly threatened. What those conditions are is unknowable, since nuclear weapons have not yet been used; perhaps even American leaders will not know until it happens.

The critical threshold at the point of beginning overt military intervention is arbitrary. The behavioral difference between covert invasion and military equipment and training, on the one hand, and bombing missions and close combat support, on the other, is small. Nevertheless, United States policy-makers draw a sharp distinction between overt military intervention and lesser actions. One reason for this, observed by Henry Kissinger, is that Americans think of war and peace as distinct, "separate and successive phases of policy." [4] Peace is thought to be the normal state of relations among nations. Thus the breaking of the peace is not to be done lightly. Once war has begun, however, different, less restrictive rules are believed to apply. Yet where peace leaves off and war begins is ambiguous. Does war begin with the granting of military equipment? Covert invasion? "Police action," as the operation in Korea was once officially called? Or only

---

[4] Henry A. Kissinger, *The Necessity for Choice* (New York: Harper, 1960), p. 176.

with a declaration of war? What kind of action shall be considered critical, and thus rigidly controlled, is arbitrary.

Critical thresholds are not necessarily immutable either. The threshold for the kind of action considered critical was seemingly once higher. Before 1928 minor landings of Marines and seamen were extraordinarily common. Large actions by the United States Army were not frequent, however. Until after World War II the army was generally used only after elaborate justifications had been given and the act had been legitimized by a congressional resolution. The infrequency of army campaigns before 1928 reflects in part the small size of the army between wars and the difficulties involved in transporting it abroad. The rarity of its use, however, suggests also that the dispatch of the army was considered a grave action. The frequency of Marine landings before 1928 and the variety of conditions under which they occurred suggest that a minor naval landing was thought less than critical. Until the twentieth century, Marine landings were minor compared to army campaigns. The Marines rarely remained long, their directives usually called for no more than the restoration of order or the defense of specific objectives (such as an American legation), and their role was often described as one of "peace keeping." After 1928 even minor Marine landings were subject to rigorous restraint, and no new ones occurred in the following decade. The change originally occurred when American leaders wished to be less involved in world affairs. The critical threshold remained in the same place after World War II, although it may have been continued for reasons other than those that instituted it. Among the reasons for its continuance after World War II were greater international criticism of any form of military intervention, greater American sensitivity to the political consequences to a host country of even a minor landing, and a reduced need for minor precautionary deployments as the navy increased its ability to deploy Marines quickly and thus wait longer before acting.

INFLEXIBLE RESPONSE

Although the present pattern of United States overt military intervention is rigid, it does not emerge from a grand plan designed by American policy-makers. It is a pattern of unconscious response. It is not that American leaders act purposelessly. Individually, presidents, secretaries of state, and others at the top probably make their proposals and weigh the proposals of others in the light of goals they value. But individual purposes become confounded in the processes of making choices within the constraints of limited time and limited information and under the psychological pressures imposed by the grave risks and threats inherent in crises.[5] American decisions to begin overt military intervention are by definition crisis choices. The result has been that decision-makers, without necessarily meaning to do so, have let their actions be patterned by rules acceptable to the group. Whether or not they are good in principle, the rules are arbitrary, and their rigid application may not produce results that are always satisfying.

The way of measuring national security is an instance of arbitrariness. It may be laudable that American leaders demand a threat to United States security as one condition for approving direct military action. The risks and costs of war are great. The "containment" measure of national security, however, is an arbitrary standard. It is doubtful that every new Communist government, no matter what part of the world it is in, poses a significant long-term threat to the United States. But when this is the standard, political figures in other countries may be able to precipitate American intervention by stressing the threat of Communist government. The anti-Bosch military officers did just that in the Dominican Republic in 1965. On the other hand, the containment measure, because it emphasizes the formation of new Communist governments, may peremptorily dismiss some other significant threats. If communism does truly pose a long-range threat, one wonders what is so peculiarly significant about new governments, as opposed to governments "influenced" by the Soviet Union or China, or governments that include Communist party members in a coalition. It is interesting that the members of the Eisenhower Administration considered the possibility of a Communist government in Lebanon in 1958 more threatening than they did Egyptian control of the Suez Canal in 1956 when they saw President Nasser "influenced" by the Soviet Union. It is equally interesting that the Kennedy Administration believed the threat of a Communist government in Vietnam in 1961 was more significant than that posed by a coalition government containing Communists in Laos, which they accepted in 1962. The ostensible assumption is that Communist governments once established are irremovable, while almost all other kinds of situations are to some degree subject to change.

---

[5] Charles Hermann has examined the "irrational" effects crises have on foreign policy decisions in *Crises in Foreign Policy: A Simulation Analysis* (Indianapolis, Ind.: Bobbs-Merrill, 1969).

The requirement of moral justification for intervention also can produce undesirable effects, although the principle of moral standards for the use of force is commendable. The arbitrary and inflexible rules for moral legitimation accepted by American policy-makers create the problem. The rigid demand for conflict, request, and intervention by others as preconditions for American military action means United States leaders can be manipulated by the moral context of situations. That covert operations are sometimes undertaken without all three legitimizing conditions suggests that American decision-makers do not wholly lack the Machiavellian virtues. Nevertheless, United States overt military intervention may have been prevented in some situations, as in Cuba in 1961, by the absence of conflict, request, or intervention by others, when the action might otherwise have been desirable. The ultimate effects of the Castro government in Cuba are uncertain, and an overt invasion to overthrow it would not necessarily have been beneficial. Nevertheless, the absence of open military action was determined, not by strategic considerations, but by arbitrary moral rules. More serious is the possibility that American standards of moral legitimation sometimes work the other way, impelling toward overt military intervention by their presence, even when that action is not desirable. It is possible that President Chamoun was able to force United States military intervention in Lebanon in 1958 by so loudly denouncing the United Arab Republic's assistance to the opposition and demanding United States action.

The consequence of these arbitrary rules is that American policy-makers may be unable to manipulate the values of other nations' leaders but may be susceptible to having their own values used by others and by circumstances. The rules that govern when military force shall be applied are set; its use awaits the proper circumstances to trigger it. American policy-makers are imprisoned by the very values to which they are committed. They differ from Metternich, who has been credited with manipulating the moral assumptions of other European leaders in order to protect the interests of Austria after the 1815 Congress of Vienna.[6]

It is easy to condemn United States policy-makers for their inflexibility. To do so assumes that they are less than they can be expected to be, less imaginative, perhaps, than the leaders of other countries. Such criticism may reflect wishful thinking. Routinization of critical choices may be a price paid for collective decision making. Groups are

[6] Henry A. Kissinger, *A World Restored: Metternich, Castlereagh and the Problems of Peace, 1822–32* (Boston: Houghton Mifflin, 1957), p. 315.

seldom noted for their flexibility and imagination. Those times in world history when a state has seemed the master of its own destiny in the use of force, one man of unusual mind and will has usually so controlled the foreign policy machinery of his government that he could shape the nation's actions to his own vision. Metternich, Bismarck, and Napoleon were men of such heroic cast.[7] But the era of heroes seems over. Joseph Stalin and, to a lesser extent, Charles de Gaulle may represent the last of the breed in the major industrialized nations, although Mao Tse-tung, Sukarno, Nasser, and Castro have continued the tradition in developing states. Affluence has not robbed the privileged nations of men of vision. Rather, since World War II most major nations have turned to group processes for major decisions in foreign policy. They do so as a means of handling the information explosion created by large intelligence networks and the general growth in international communications, as well as to reduce the chance of inadvertent action at a time when nations are more interdependent and nuclear weapons magnify the cost of unwanted war. Groups have advantages over individuals in bringing to bear large quantities of information. In so doing, they may also reduce the risk of inadvertent action. The foreign policy of other major nations has not been markedly more flexible or imaginative than America's. Britain, France before and after De Gaulle, Russia since Stalin, Germany, and Japan have relied upon collective decisions in at least some major areas of foreign policy. It is possible that the appeal to force by these states, too, is programmed, although the patterns would be different, reflecting different standards of threat and moral justification. One does not suggest that the United States revert to the practices of earlier times and give the president complete control of foreign policy. The costs of error are too great. There is no assurance that a remarkable man would manipulate world politics to the United States's long-term advantage. Metternich was successful in protecting Austria, and Bismarck was successful in building Germany. But other heroes, from Napoleon to Hitler, reaped disaster, and the long-term effect of Stalin and De Gaulle is unclear. Nor is there assurance that the president will always be a remarkable man. For the United States, greater flexibility requires both that innovative solutions emerge in high councils and that they survive the arduous process of fact-finding, discussion, and decision. Neither requirement is easily met. Thus, flexibil-

---

[7] Sidney Hook has defined the hero as the event-making man who shapes events by the exercise of his will and his ideas, as opposed to the eventful man who merely reacts to events. *The Hero in History* (New York: The Humanities Press, 1950), p. 154.

ity in the resort to force, and abstention from it may be difficult to achieve.

THE FUTURE

The question arises whether the pattern of military intervention that has existed since World War II will continue long into the future. That the pattern did not exist before 1945 demonstrates that it is not a permanent part of American foreign policy. That the basis of it is a set of arbitrary rules implies that change is possible if only some of the rules are altered. What counts is the chance for change in the rules.

One possibility is immediately apparent. If it is true that American policy-makers have acted in a pattern of which they are not aware, they might decide to change when they realize what they have been doing. Told that American intervention is predictable, major leaders might choose to violate the pattern in order to make their actions less foreseeable. To be predictable is not always a blessing after all. If the actions of the United States are predictable, other nations that know the pattern will less often miscalculate what America will do. This is desirable from the American point of view when United States leaders mean the threats they utter and fear that other nations will not take the threats seriously. But predictability does destroy the effectiveness of bluffs. Worse, United States intervention is not wholly subject to American control in that other nations are the ones that create the conditions that determine whether intervention will or will not occur. If other nations knew the conditions under which American military force would be used, they could act with impunity abroad merely by avoiding those conditions. If America's friends and allies knew the bounds within which force would be used, they might sometimes be tempted to create the conditions necessary to force United States intervention in conflicts that were purely their own.

The implications of rigidity for the United States's strategic posture, in particular, give incentives for changing the pattern. In the 1950's the United States threatened "massive retaliation" by nuclear weapons against "Communist aggression" anywhere in the world. The strategy was changed in the 1960's when it was concluded that this was not a credible threat. Now the posture is one of "graduated response," under which the United States still threatens the use of tactical nuclear weapons in the event of attack on Western Europe and nuclear retaliation against the cities and military installations of the

Soviet Union if conventional forces and tactical nuclear weapons cannot contain the assault. This, too, may not be a credible threat. The pattern in America's use of force since World War II raises doubts that United States leaders would authorize the use of any kind of nuclear weapons, or that they would attack the Soviet Union with even conventional force, if they did not believe the United States itself to be in imminent peril. It is just this kind of questioning that may have prompted France to build its own nuclear deterrent. If the Soviet Union's leaders reached the same conclusion on the basis of America's past performance, they might conclude that they could act in Europe with relative impunity; and the value of the nuclear deterrent for Europe would be lost.

The probabilities of willful change are uncertain, however. One possibility is that the critical threshold could be raised, permitting a wider range of free action below it. A consideration underlying its present position at the point of the beginning of overt military intervention is that death and destruction usually follow any open use of force. As the accuracy of United States aerial weapons is further improved, however, a capability for a true "surgical" strike may be created. It may become possible to destroy a large military target by missile or plane with confidence that persons and property in areas surrounding it would be slightly damaged. This could lead American decision-makers to consider surgical air strikes as below the critical threshold. Another Cuban missile crisis might then see the offending targets destroyed, even if there were no request and no conflict in the country.

Other chances for change depend upon how resistant to change the rules are. Some of the restraints seem more permanent than others. Those of the decision-making process—the possibility of a veto and the practice of incremental choice with the attendant opportunities for overt action becoming unnecessary before it is approved—are fixtures of the group decision-making process. No change in them would seem likely. The restraints of the international system also appear highly resistant to change. The world has been greatly transformed since the immediate postwar years; in consequence, so has the international system. Europe and the People's Republic of China have larger roles in the system than they did a few years ago. This does not mean, however, that the United States and the Soviet Union are likely to abandon their tacit agreements not to use nuclear weapons and not to use their forces against one another. Agreements, explicit as well as tacit, may be abridged in a moment; but both United States and Russian strategists seem still to assume these accords. Indeed, as other nations—

particularly China—become stronger, American and Soviet decision-makers may come to count more heavily on agreements with each other. The 1972 agreements to limit the numbers of offensive missiles and bombers and of anti-ballistic missile sites point in this direction. Also, as nuclear weapons proliferate and other nations develop them, agreements prohibiting their use will assume more, not less, importance in the international system.

The way of measuring threats to national security may be more malleable. The containment vision that new Communist governments are always a threat to the United States is under attack. Some persons at the margins of the group of major decision-makers are among the attackers, such as Senators James W. Fulbright, Mike Mansfield, and George McGovern, Representative Paul McCloskey, and former Senator Eugene McCarthy. The criticism offers some possibilities that the rule will be changed. Some who are critics could become top leaders. If they did, it would presumably be by election rather than appointment. If these men's minds were not changed by holdover members of the group, they could shape group decisions to a different pattern. The critics face obstacles, however. The containment view is shared by large numbers of the party activists who nominate presidential candidates and by a major portion of the American public that elects presidents. And once elected, a man of different vision would have to resist the counsel of many respected men around him who would urge the continuation of past practices.

Another possibility is the chance that criticism may encourage those who have traditionally accepted the containment way of thinking to modify it. They could come to interpret it more loosely. At least one of the other restraints on intervention has already been subject to loose interpretation, that is, the requirement of a request. The requesting government in the Dominican Republic in April 1965 was reportedly created with the assistance of United States representatives. It could claim a degree of *de facto* control because it was the only functioning government, but the area it actually ruled extended little beyond the boundaries of San Isidro air base. The request itself was rewritten, if not originally drafted, by American direction. At some point, always poorly defined, free interpretation becomes functionally equivalent to the denial of a standard.

Superficially, it appears that the containment measure of threat to national security has also been subject to loose interpretation. It was not, for example, self-evident on July 14, 1958, that a Communist government would be established in Lebanon. Nevertheless, Washington concluded that a significant risk existed. This is not the same as a loose interpretation of the standard, however. The notion that new Communist governments are always threatening has been strictly applied. What has been subject to interpretation is whether there was a risk of a Communist government's being established. When it has been uncertain whether a Communist government was in the offing, United States decision-makers have sometimes concluded that one was, as in Lebanon and the Dominican Republic. It is possible that the fear of communism has encouraged such judgments, but American leaders have not consistently erred on the side of seeing Communist threats where there were none. Sometimes ambiguity has been interpreted in the opposite direction, as the Eisenhower Administration did in looking at the war against Batista in Cuba during the late 1950's, which led to the rise of Fidel Castro. When United States policy-makers have decided that a Communist government was a possibility, however, there has been no looseness in their judgment of the threat this entailed. It has always been assumed that this possibility posed a threat to the United States and that America ought to do something about it, including overt military intervention if the other conditions were right.

This way of seeing United States national security—and the pattern of intervention it creates—is not merely the product of lack of information, the distortion of information, or misperceptions of reality. If it were, it might be easily modified. The introduction of more information into the deliberations of the group of major foreign affairs leaders and the airing of competing views of the situations at hand might then be enough to produce change. Instead, the containment vision has a much more fundamental base—the root assumption that all new Communist governments do, in the long run, threaten the United States. This is a value judgment. Value assumptions are harder to change than deficiencies in information networks or even misperceptions. Lack of information can be erased by technical means. Misperceptions can be altered by forcing the testing of them against reality. But value assumptions cannot be directly affected in either way. This condition raises grave obstacles to the modification of values, particularly values that are shared by a group and reinforced for each member of the group by the fact that other members share them.

Values can be altered, of course. If they could not be, very little of men's behavior could change, since values underlie much of what men do. It has been suggested by both academic observers and pundits that, as a reaction to the long, costly, and indecisive war in Southeast Asia, the public mood is changing from support for military endeavors to opposition to them. It is commonly assumed that this will lead American leaders to weigh national security more restrictively and use military force less often.[8] This belief overemphasizes the impact of public moods. It overlooks the fact that there was much public antipathy to the war in Korea after it had dragged on for two years, but that public war-weariness did not break the pattern. It overlooks the fact that public dislike of the Vietnam War did not prevent the Nixon Administration's expansion of it by sending forces into Cambodia, by approving more blatant action in Laos, and by resuming large-scale air strikes across the border of North Vietnam. Policy-makers can choose to accept the direction of public opinion, but they do not have to do so. They may choose to resist the public mood in the belief that the public is wrong and that continued action is in the national interest.

The belief that the United States may intervene less often in the future when Washington sees the chance of a new Communist government is also commonly based on a reading of United States history that describes American foreign policy in terms of alternating periods of isolationism and internationalism.[9] The period of the 1890's until after World War I, for example, was internationalist. That between World Wars I and II was isolationist, and that from 1940 until the present has been another internationalist period. The notion is that the current internationalist phase is drawing to an end. It is undeniable that Americans in the 1970's are increasingly preoccupied with the problems of American society and less with those of other countries. What is wrong with this reading is that American foreign policy is not now, if it ever was, unidimensional. It is true that the United States after World War II gave its overt support to international organizations that it did not give after World War I. It is true that in the first ten years after 1945 the United States formally committed itself to treaties of alliance with an unprecedented number of nations. It is also true that massive military and economic assistance programs to other countries were begun in the postwar period. Nevertheless, the actual use of military force since World War II has reflected a curious blending of isolationist and internationalist beliefs. It has been simultaneously global and strictly circumscribed. United States military intervention has occurred all over the world since 1945 when leaders

---

[8] This possibility is raised at several points in Richard M. Pfeffer, ed., *No More Vietnams?* (New York: Harper, 1968).

[9] Frank L. Klingberg wrote the classic statement of this interpretation of the history of United States foreign policy: "The Historical Alternation of Moods in American Foreign Policy," *World Politics,* Vol. 4 (January 1952), pp. 239–73.

APPEAL TO FORCE

perceived the possibility of a new Communist government—in the Caribbean, in the Near East, and twice in Asia. Yet, when the possibility of a new Communist government has not been perceived, overt military action has not occurred. One of the tenets of the isolationist faith in the United States before World War II was the dictum, "Stay out of others' quarrels." In the presence of a believed threat of a new Communist government United States military power exhibits extraordinary reach. But without it American military force still seems to keep the isolationist faith—it does "stay out of others' quarrels." Earlier periods of presumed isolationism were also partially internationalist on the issue of military intervention. Except for the decade of the 1930's there has been no lengthy period since 1800 in which the United States wholly abstained from the overt use of force abroad.

Since American foreign policy is not unidimensional, increasing public preoccupation with domestic problems does not assure that United States military intervention will occur less often in the future. The public mood could have such an effect only if it were to erect an absolute prohibition against international intercourse, as happened before only in the 1930's. The public mood offers no promise of being so extreme, however. The chance that America will cut itself off from the rest of the world is small. It is so deeply involved in alliances, aid programs, private investments abroad, and international trade that it can hardly extricate itself. Thus a change in the pattern of United States intervention will probably have to come from some other source.

The practice of intervention could also change through alterations in the rules of moral justification. The chances for change depend in part upon how widely accepted the rules are. The need to see one's acts as moral ones, especially destructive acts such as the use of military force, may be universal. But the particular conception that moral legitimation consists of a request, prior conflict, and someone else to blame is not shared by many other nations. If these rules are peculiar to the group of major United States foreign policy decision-makers, the opportunities for change in them is greater than if they are cultural values shared by most Americans. If they are part of the American culture, it would be unlikely that anyone would join the group who did not already believe in them.

The requirement of a request in situations that do not pose true peril to the United States is probably not a cultural value. It has been widely believed by Americans since World War II that the United States intervenes abroad to assist other countries to resist aggression.

That the other countries asked for help is taken for granted. The attitude that force ought only to be sent upon request, however, may be shared only by a segment of the population that is highly educated and usually "liberal" in its politics. For the rest of Americans this attitude competes with the contradicting paternalistic one that the governments of other countries of the world do not always know what is good for themselves or their people. Requests were never required for American intervention until after 1945, not even for major wars involving the army. It appears to be a value that emerged only in this century and became significant only after World War II, and whose source is not the American culture but an attention to international law. Thus it could be modified relatively easily, but it could change either to be more strict or less binding.

The requirements of conflict and condemnable intervention by others are more fundamental. These are arbitrary rules, to be sure, but they reflect the basic American belief that it should not fire the first shot. These standards were accepted even before World War II, although they were not rigidly applied. The public justification for the Spanish-American War was the sinking of the battleship *Maine*. General Pershing's 1916 expedition into Mexico was preceded by attacks by Mexicans against Texans. The joining of World War I was publicly justified in terms of the existence of destructive war in Europe that had been started by the Central Powers. Americans have traditionally placed emphasis on the role of others in starting conflicts that the United States later enters. The concept of preventive war is not well accepted. American use of force has reflected a need to see itself moral in the sense of not starting conflicts.[10]

The root of this attitude may lie deep in the culture. Margaret Mead has noted that all cultures convey norms to children about the conditions that make fighting legitimate.[11] Different cultures convey different norms. American mothers teach their children the contradictory values that they must stand up for themselves ("don't be a sissy"), but that they should not start a fight ("don't be a bully"). The American parent, confronted with an eight-year-old son returned home battered, bloody, bruised, and crying from a fight, starts looking into the justice of the matter by asking first, "Who started it?" The result is a society of persons who feel they must be prepared to fight, and willing to

---

[10] Dexter Perkins, *The American Approach to Foreign Policy* (Cambridge: Harvard University Press, 1952), p. 79.

[11] Margaret Mead, *And Keep Your Powder Dry* (New York: William Morrow, 1942), pp. 138–57.

fight, but only if they are not the ones to land the first blow. The popular preoccupation with "the first blow" and with the beginning of war condemns the physical act of starting military conflict where there was none. It also condemns the symbolic act of being the first outsider to intervene, especially by the blatant application of military might, and so make international war of mere domestic civil strife. American policy-makers have enacted literally the popular demand for pre-existing conflict; their only contribution is the definition of how much intervention by others gives moral justification for American military intervention. Because of the United States's unusually secure position in the world, Americans have been able to carry this attitude into the conduct of their foreign policy without adverse consequences. That this attitude has not brought failure in international affairs has meant that there has been no challenge to it, and the value has remained a strong one and, as a consequence, highly resistant to change.

None of the factors that underlie the pattern of United States overt military intervention since World War II is likely to change quickly or easily. The containment definition of threats to national security is still widely accepted by persons in and around the foreign policy establishment. There is little reason to expect change in the tacit agreements between the United States and the Soviet Union restricting the use of force against one another's troops and prohibiting the use of nuclear weapons. The possibility of veto and the incremental nature of top-level decision-making practices seem durable parts of the governmental structure. The peculiar standards for the moral legitimation of intervention are, in the main, deeply held values. Nor is it likely that the many demands for the resort to force made upon American leaders will suddenly abate. Yet the pattern of military intervention that has characterized the era of containment is not likely to be permanent. There are simply too many factors on which the pattern depends that are subject to change. That intervention is practiced in accordance with some set of precise decision rules is likely to be durable, however, and the specific rules that underlie the containment pattern seem likely to be with us for at least a few years more.

APPENDICES

APPENDIX A

CONFLICTS, 1946–71, IN WHICH OVERT MILITARY INTERVENTION BY THE UNITED STATES DID NOT OCCUR

A NOTE ON THE METHOD OF LISTING ARMED CONFLICTS

A complete catalog of the world's armed conflicts since World War II is not yet available. Several groups are presently preparing such compilations, but they are not yet completed. The 149 conflicts in the period 1946–71 considered here are drawn from lists published by Bloomfield, K. J. Holsti, Huntington, Luard, Modelski, Richardson, Tanter, and Wright, with the addition of other conflicts found in the press, memoirs, and the works of other writers.[1] This list may not include all incidents that have occurred since World War II. However, since it was drawn from several sources, each of which had different reasons for mentioning particular situations, there is no reason to suspect that the list embodies any systematic bias toward situations that

[1] Lincoln P. Bloomfield, et al., *The Control of Local Conflict*, Vol. I, prepared for the U.S. Arms Control and Disarmament Agency (Washington: Government Printing Office, 1967), p. 8; K. J. Holsti, "Resolving International Conflict," *Journal of Conflict Resolution*, Vol. 10 (September 1966), pp. 272–96; Samuel P. Huntington, "Patterns of Violence in World Politics," in Samuel P. Huntington, ed., *Changing Patterns of Military Politics* (New York: Free Press of Glencoe, 1962), pp. 17–50; Evan Luard, *Peace and Opinion* (London: Oxford University Press, 1962), pp. 35–37; George Modelski, "International Settlement of Internal War," in James N. Rosenau, ed., *The International Aspects of Civil Strife* (Princeton: Princeton University Press, 1964), pp. 150–53; Lewis F. Richardson, *Statistics of Deadly Quarrels* (Pittsburgh: Boxwood Press, 1960); Raymond Tanter and Manus Midlarsky, "A Theory of Revolution," *Journal of Conflict Resolution*, Vol. 11 (September 1967), pp. 264–80; and Quincy Wright, *A Study of War*, 2d ed. (Chicago: University of Chicago Press, 1965), pp. 1544–47.

APPENDIX A

will fit the theory being tested. Also, since the list includes nearly all known armed conflicts threatening foreign governments, it may be that most of those situations not listed embodied no great threat, or if they did, were not perceived as such by major United States decision-makers.

The New York Times Index (which tends to emphasize violence and threats to governments), the memoirs of Presidents Truman, Eisenhower, and Johnson and the "insider" accounts of Schlesinger and Hilsman on the Kennedy Administration were used to analyze all suspected situations of armed conflict threatening a foreign government.[2] Those conflicts that did not involve armed conflict or did not threaten government were excluded from the list. When a situation was in doubt, as the conflict in East Berlin in 1953, which was reported as "riots" and "demonstrations," not as armed conflict, it was included. When an ongoing conflict changed during its course in a manner particularly significant to United States policy-makers, as did Greece in 1947 when Great Britain announced it would withdraw its troops, that conflict was divided, with each part listed separately.

Those armed conflicts that did threaten a foreign government were analyzed further. They were classified by (1) their significance for United States national security as perceived by United States leaders according to the seven-point scale from "true peril" to "developments in Communist states," and (2) whether or not each of the several restraints on overt military intervention operated (see Appendices A-1 through A-6). Where perceived significance for national security was in doubt, the situation was placed in the higher class. Thus China in 1946–49 is listed as a situation of "special interest" because it is unclear what significance United States decision-makers attached to China at that time. When it was unclear whether a particular restraint operated, the restraint is treated as though it did operate or as uncertain. For example, it is not often known whether United States representatives were approached with a request for intervention or tried to obtain a request. Hence, a request is registered as absent only if a request from someone who could claim to represent a government is implausible.

---

[2] Harry S. Truman, *Memoirs* (2 vols.; Garden City, N.Y.: Doubleday, 1955–56); Dwight D. Eisenhower, *The White House Years* (2 vols.; Garden City, N.Y.: Doubleday, 1963–65); Roger Hilsman, *To Move a Nation* (Garden City, N.Y.: Doubleday, 1967); Arthur M. Schlesinger, *A Thousand Days* (Boston: Houghton Mifflin, 1965); and Lyndon B. Johnson, *The Vantage Point: Perspectives of the Presidency, 1963–1969* (New York: Holt, Rinehart and Winston, 1971).

A-1
THREATS OF COMMUNIST GOVERNMENT IN "SPECIAL INTEREST COUNTRIES"

SITUATIONS

Bolivia, 1952	Revolt ousts government
Bolivia, 1965	Government troops battle miners
Bolivia, 1965–68	Communist guerrilla war
Brazil, 1965–68	Communist guerrilla war in northeast
British Guiana, 1962	Race riots
China, 1946–47	Civil war
China, 1947–49	Civil war
Colombia, 1960–	Communist guerrilla war
Costa Rica, 1948	Army revolt against government
Cuba, 1956–59	Anti-Batista war
Dominican Republic, 1961	Disorders
Formosa, 1947	Independence riots
Greece, 1946–47	Civil war
Greece, 1947–49	Civil war
Guatemala, 1954	Castillo Armas invasion
Guatemala, 1960	Unsuccessful revolt
Guatemala, 1964–	Communist guerrilla war
Haiti, 1957	Disorders, changes in government
Haiti-Dominican Republic, 1963	Unsuccessful exile invasion
Nicaragua, 1960	Fighting, Costa Rica border
Panama, 1966–68	Guerrilla conflict
Paraguay, 1947	Civil war
Peru, 1948	Unsuccessful Aprista revolt
Peru, 1962–65	Communist guerrilla war
Philippines, 1946–50	Huk war
Philippines, 1950–54	Huk war
Philippines, 1970–	Renewed Huk violence
Uruguay, 1968–	Tupamaro urban guerrilla war
Venezuela, 1958	Series of revolts
Venezuela, 1960	Unsuccessful revolt
Venezuela, 1963–	Communist guerrilla war

RESTRAINTS

Not able without nuclear weapons	Would fight USSR	President permits veto	Lesser acts successful	Another takes burden	Locals strong enough	No request	No armed conflict	No overt military intervention to condemn	No military assistance	No outside support
o	o	o	x	o	?	o	o	x	x	x
o	o	o	x	o	x	o	o	x	x	o
o	o	o	x	o	x	o	o	x	?	o
o	o	o	x	o	x	o	o	x	?	o
o	o	o	?	x	?	o	?	x	x	?
x	o	o	?	o	o	o	o	x	o	o
x	o	o	o	o	o	o	o	x	o	o
o	o	o	x	o	x	o	o	x	?	o
o	o	o	?	o	?	x	o	o	o	o
o	o	o	?	o	x	o	o	x	x	x
o	o	o	x	o	?	o	?	x	x	o
o	o	o	x	x	x	?	o	x	x	x
o	o	o	x	x	o	o	o	x	o	o
o	o	o	x	o	o	o	o	x	o	o
o	o	o	o	o	o	?	o	x	x	x
o	o	o	x	o	o	o	o	x	x	o
o	o	o	x	o	?	o	o	x	?	o
o	o	o	x	o	?	?	o	x	x	x
o	o	o	x	o	o	o	o	x	o	o
o	o	o	x	o	x	o	o	x	x	o
o	o	o	x	o	x	o	o	x	?	o
o	o	o	?	o	?	?	o	x	x	o
o	o	o	x	o	?	o	o	x	x	x
o	o	o	x	o	x	o	o	x	?	o
o	o	o	x	o	x	?	o	x	x	o
o	o	o	x	o	o	?	o	x	x	o
o	o	o	x	o	x	o	o	x	o	o
o	o	o	x	o	x	o	o	x	x	o
o	o	o	x	o	x	o	o	x	x	x
o	o	o	x	o	x	o	o	x	x	x
o	o	o	x	o	x	o	o	x	x	o

o = Restraint did not appear to operate. ? = Unclear whether or not restraint operated.
x = Restraint may have operated.

A-2
THREATS OF COMMUNIST GOVERNMENT IN "COMMUNIST-THREATENED REGIONS"
S I T U A T I O N S

Burma, 1948–49	Civil war
Burma, 1950–53	Civil war
Burma, 1953–58	Civil war
Burma, 1962	Renewed civil violence
Burma, 1970–	Renewed civil violence
Cambodia, 1969	Viet Cong–government troops battle
Congo, 1960–64	Multifaction civil war
Ethiopia, 1960	Coup against Haile Selassie
Ethiopia-Somalia, 1963–68	Conflict on Ethiopian border
Ghana, 1966	Army coup ousts Nkrumah
Indochina, 1945–50	Viet Minh war
Indochina, 1950–53	Viet Minh war
Indochina, 1954	Viet Minh war
Iran, 1946	Presence of USSR forces
Iran, 1951–52	Isolated disorders
Iran, 1953	Anti-Mossadegh coup
Iraq, 1958	Kassim coup
Iraq, 1959	Communist–nationalist conflict
Iraq, 1962–63	Kurdish revolt
Iraq, February 1963	Army removes Kassim
Iraq, November 1963	Army overthrows Ba'athists
Jordan, 1957	Demonstrations against Hussein
Laos, 1959–62	Multifaction civil war
Lebanon, May–June 1958	Civil war
Malagasy Republic, 1971	Disorders in Tuléar region
Malaya, 1947–60	Communist guerrilla war
Malaysia, 1970	Communist guerrilla flare-up
Rwanda-Burundi, 1961–62	Watusi tribe violence
Sudan, 1964	Riots, Abboud removed
Syria, August 1949	Army coup
Syria, January 1954	Druze Mountains uprisings
Syria, February 1954	Army revolt
Syria, 1961	Military revolt against UAR
Syria, 1966	Ba'ath party revolt
Thailand, 1965–	Communist guerrilla war

RESTRAINTS

Not able without nuclear weapons	Would fight USSR	President permits veto	Lesser acts successful	Another takes burden	Locals strong enough	No request	No armed conflict	No overt military intervention to condemn	No military assistance	No outside support
o	o	o	x	o	o	x	o	x	x	o
o	o	o	x	?	o	?	o	x	o	o
o	o	o	x	o	?	x	o	o	o	o
o	o	o	x	o	?	?	o	x	o	o
o	o	o	x	o	x	?	o	x	o	o
o	o	o	x	o	x	?	o	?	o	o
o	o	o	x	x	?	o	o	x	o	o
o	o	o	x	o	?	o	o	x	x	?
o	o	o	x	o	x	o	o	?	o	o
o	o	o	x	o	?	x	o	x	x	?
o	o	o	x	x	o	o	o	x	x	o
o	o	o	?	x	o	o	o	x	o	o
o	o	x	o	o	o	o	o	x	o	o
o	x	o	?	o	o	o	o	o	o	o
o	o	o	x	o	?	?	?	x	?	o
o	o	o	o	o	o	o	x	x	x	o
o	o	o	o	o	o	x	o	x	x	o
o	o	o	x	o	?	x	o	x	?	o
o	o	o	x	o	?	x	o	?	o	o
o	o	o	x	o	?	x	o	x	?	o
o	o	o	x	o	?	x	o	x	?	o
o	o	o	x	o	o	o	x	x	x	o
o	o	o	x	o	x	o	o	x	o	o
o	o	o	x	o	x	o	o	x	o	o
o	o	o	x	o	x	o	o	x	x	o
o	o	o	o	x	o	o	o	x	o	o
o	o	o	x	o	x	o	o	x	o	o
o	o	o	x	o	x	?	o	x	o	o
o	o	o	x	o	x	x	?	x	x	x
o	o	o	x	o	x	x	o	x	x	x
o	o	o	x	o	x	x	o	x	x	o
o	o	o	x	o	x	x	o	x	x	?
o	o	o	x	o	o	x	o	o	o	o
o	o	o	x	o	o	x	o	x	?	o
o	o	o	x	o	x	o	o	x	o	o

o = Restraint did not appear to operate.
x = Restraint may have operated.
? = Unclear whether or not restraint operated.

A-3
THREATS OF COMMUNIST GOVERNMENT IN "JUST ANOTHER COUNTRY"

SITUATIONS

Algeria, 1954–62	War against France
Ceylon, 1971	PLF revolt
Cyprus, 1954–59	"Enosis" conflict
Cyprus, 1963–64	Civil conflict
India, 1947	Violence
India, Hyderabad, 1947–48	Hyderabad accession
Indonesia, 1945–49	War of independence
Indonesia, 1948–62	Civil war
Indonesia-Malaysia, 1963–66	"Confrontation"
Indonesia, 1965–66	Attempted coup
Kenya, 1952–56	Mau Mau terrorism
South Korea, 1948	Unsuccessful revolts
South Yemen, 1968	Liberation Front attacks

RESTRAINTS

Not able without nuclear weapons	Would fight USSR	President permits veto	Lesser acts successful	Another takes burden	Locals strong enough	No request	No armed conflict	No overt military intervention to condemn	No military assistance	No outside support
o	o	o	x	x	?	o	o	x	o	o
o	o	o	x	o	x	o	o	x	o	o
o	o	o	x	x	?	o	o	x	o	o
o	o	o	?	x	?	x	o	x	o	o
o	o	o	x	o	x	x	o	x	x	?
o	o	o	x	o	x	o	o	?	?	?
o	o	o	x	x	x	o	o	?	?	o
o	o	o	?	o	o	?	o	x	o	o
o	o	o	x	x	x	o	o	o	o	o
o	o	o	o	o	o	?	o	x	o	o
o	o	o	o	x	x	o	o	x	?	o
o	o	o	?	o	?	o	o	x	o	o
o	o	o	x	o	x	?	o	x	?	o

o = Restraint did not appear to operate. ? = Unclear whether or not restraint operated.
x = Restraint may have operated.

A-4
THREATS OF COMMUNIST GOVERNMENT IN "DISPUTED TERRITORY AT THE MARGINS OF COMMUNIST STATES"

SITUATIONS

Burma, 1956	Chinese invasion of north
China offshore islands, 1954	Bombardment by Peking
China offshore islands, 1958	Bombardment by Peking
India frontier, 1959–62	Chinese invasion
Nepal, 1950	Congress party revolt
Nepal, 1960	Revolt
Nepal, 1962	Guerrilla conflict
Tibet, 1950	Chinese invasion

RESTRAINTS

Not able without nuclear weapons	Would fight USSR	President permits veto	Lesser acts successful	Another takes burden	Locals strong enough	No request	No armed conflict	No overt military intervention to condemn	No military assistance	No outside support
o	o	o	?	o	?	x	o	o	o	o
o	o	o	o	o	o	o	o	o	o	o
o	o	o	o	o	o	o	o	o	o	o
o	o	o	o	o	o	o	o	o	o	o
o	o	o	o	o	o	o	o	x	o	o
o	o	o	o	o	o	o	o	x	o	o
o	o	o	o	o	o	o	o	x	o	o
?	o	o	o	o	o	o	o	o	o	o

o = Restraint did not appear to operate. ? = Unclear whether or not restraint operated.
x = Restraint may have operated.

A-5

THREATS OF SOMETHING OTHER THAN NEW COMMUNIST GOVERNMENTS

SITUATIONS

Aden, 1954–59	Tribal violence
Angola, 1961–	Uprising against Portuguese
Argentina, 1955	Civil war against Perón
Argentina, 1962	Revolts after Frondizi ousted
Bolivia, 1946	President Villaroel killed by mob
Bolivia, 1947	Isolated revolts
Brunei, 1962	Azahiri revolt
Chad, 1965–	Rebel violence in northeast
Colombia, 1948–53	Civil war
Colombia, 1957	Riots against President Rojas
Costa Rica-Nicaragua, 1955	Nicaragua seizes border
El Salvador-Honduras, 1969	The "football war"
Ethiopia, Eritrea, 1965–	Eritrean Liberation Movement
French Cameroons, 1955–60	Opposition violence
Gabon, 1964	French forces restore President Mba
Goa, 1961	India seizes Goa, Diu, and Damao
Haiti, 1946	Disorders, military seize power
Honduras-Nicaragua, 1957	Nicaragua seizes border
India, 1949–63	Naga tribe violence
India, 1966–	Naxalite guerrilla movement
India–Pakistan, 1965	Brief war
Iraq, 1965–66	Kurdish violence in north
Israel–Arab States, 1967	June war
Jordan–Syria, 1970	Civil war in Jordan; Syria intervenes
Kashmir, 1947–49	India-Pakistan conflict
Kuwait, 1961	Iraqi invasion
Lebanon, 1969	Army–Arab guerrilla conflicts
Madagascar, 1947	Revolt, French repression
Malaysia, 1969	Racial violence
Morocco, 1953–56	Independence movement

RESTRAINTS

Not able without nuclear weapons	Would fight USSR	President permits veto	Lesser acts successful	Another takes burden	Locals strong enough	No request	No armed conflict	No overt military intervention to condemn	No military assistance	No outside support
o	o	o	These			o	o	?	o	o
o	o	o	restraints			o	o	x	o	o
o	o	o	are not			x	o	x	?	?
o	o	o	relevant			x	o	x	x	x
o	o	o	to these			x	o	x	x	x
			situations.							
o	o	o				x	o	x	x	x
o	o	o				?	o	x	?	?
o	o	o				?	o	x	?	o
o	o	o				o	o	x	o	o
o	o	o				x	o	x	x	x
o	o	o				o	o	x	o	o
o	o	o				o	o	o	o	o
o	o	o				o	o	x	o	o
o	o	o				x	o	x	x	x
o	o	o				x	o	x	x	x
o	o	o				o	o	o	o	o
o	o	o				x	o	x	x	x
o	o	o				o	o	o	o	o
o	o	o				x	o	x	?	o
o	o	o				o	o	x	o	o
o	o	o				o	o	o	o	o
o	o	o				x	o	x	x	o
o	o	o				o	o	o	o	o
o	o	o				o	o	o	o	o
o	o	o				o	o	o	o	o
o	o	o				o	?	?	?	?
o	o	o				o	o	x	o	o
o	o	o				x	o	o	o	o
o	o	o				o	o	x	x	?
o	o	o				o	o	x	o	o

0 — Restraint did not appear to operate.
x = Restraint may have operated.
? = Unclear whether or not restraint operated.

A-5 (continued)

S I T U A T I O N S

Morocco-Algeria, 1962–63	Border dispute
Mozambique, 1964–	Guerrilla war against Portuguese
Muscat & Oman, 1956–58	Uprising against sultan
Muscat & Oman, 1968–	Guerrilla conflict
Nigeria, 1953	Moslem People's Congress riots
Nigeria, 1966–69	Biafran secession
Northern Ireland, 1969–	Catholic street uprisings
Pakistan-India, 1971	Civil war in Pakistan; India intervenes
Palestine, 1946–49	Arab–Israeli–British conflict
Portugese Guinea, 1961–	Guerrilla war against Portuguese
South Korea, 1960	Demonstrations against Rhee
South Korea, 1961	Street fighting
Spanish Morocco, 1957–58	Anti-Spanish guerrilla war
Sudan, 1955–	Secessionist movement in south
Sudan-Egypt, 1958	Egypt invades north
Suez, 1950–55	Anti-British violence
Suez, 1956	Anglo–French–Israeli invasion
Syria-Lebanon, 1946	Anti-French violence
Trinidad and Tobago, 1970	Black power riots and army mutiny
Tunisia, 1951–56	Independence movement
West Irian, 1962	Indonesian "invasion"
Yemen, 1959	Garrison mutiny
Yemen, 1962–70	Civil war

RESTRAINTS

Not able without nuclear weapons	Would fight USSR	President permits veto	Lesser acts successful	Another takes burden	Locals strong enough	No request	No armed conflict	No overt military intervention to condemn	No military assistance	No outside support
o	o	o	These			x	o	o	o	o
o	o	o	restraints			?	o	x	?	o
o	o	o	are not			o	o	x	o	o
o	o	o	relevant			?	o	x	x	o
o	o	o	to these			x	o	x	x	x
o	o	o	situations.			o	o	x	o	o
o	o	o				o	?	x	x	x
o	o	o				o	o	o	o	o
o	o	o				o	o	o	o	o
o	o	o				o	o	x	o	o
o	o	o				o	o	x	x	x
o	o	o				x	o	x	x	x
o	o	o				o	o	o	o	o
o	o	o				o	o	x	o	o
o	o	o				o	o	o	o	o
o	o	o				o	o	x	x	x
o	o	o				o	o	o	o	o
o	o	o				o	o	o	o	o
o	o	o				o	o	x	x	?
o	o	o				o	o	x	o	o
o	o	o				o	o	o	o	o
o	o	o				x	o	x	x	o
o	o	o				?	o	o	o	o

0 = Restraint did not appear to operate.   ? = Unclear whether or not restraint operated.
x = Restraint may have operated.

A-6

DEVELOPMENTS IN COMMUNIST STATES

SITUATIONS

Communist China, 1966–68	Red Guard violence
Cuba, 1961	Bay of Pigs invasion
Czechoslovakia, 1968	Warsaw Pact invasion
East Berlin, 1953	Riots and demonstrations
Hungary, 1956	Revolution
Poland, 1956	Poznań riots
Poland, 1970	Rioting in port cities
Tibet, 1959	Khamba uprising
USSR–China, 1969	Border conflict

R E S T R A I N T S

Not able without nuclear weapons	Would fight USSR	President permits veto	Lesser acts successful	Another takes burden	Locals strong enough	No request	No armed conflict	No overt military intervention to condemn	No military assistance	No outside support
x	o	o	These			x	o	x	x	?
o	o	o	restraints			o	o	x	x	x
o	x	o	are not			?	o	o	o	o
o	x	o	relevant			?	?	x	o	o
o	x	o	to these			o	o	o	o	o
o	x	o	situations.			?	o	x	o	o
o	x	o				?	?	x	o	o
?	o	o				o	o	o	o	o
x	?	o				x	o	o	o	o

o = Restraint did not appear to operate.   ? = Unclear whether or not restraint operated.
x = Restraint may have operated.

APPENDIX
B

UNITED STATES OVERT MILITARY INTERVENTIONS, 1789–1940

Most of the events in this chronology, and all of the landings by Marines and seamen, were drawn from two sources: David M. Cooney, *A Chronology of the U.S. Navy, 1775–1965* (New York: Franklin Watts, 1965); and Colonel Robert D. Heinl, Jr., *Soldiers at Sea: The United States Marine Corps 1775–1962* (Annapolis, Md.: U.S. Naval Institute, 1962).

Date	Place	Description
May 1800	Puerto Rico	80 Marines seize fort, Puerto Plata
Sept. 1800	Curaçao	20 Marines assist Dutch to resist French
1801–16	Tripoli, Algiers	Minor landings in war with Barbary pirates
1811–12	Spanish Florida	Capt. John Williams's adventures against Spanish and Indians
1812–14	Pacific	One navy ship attacks British whaling ports in the Pacific
July 1817	Haiti	48 Marines land at Port-au-Prince after U.S. consul expelled
1817–21	Haiti	Ship's companies land at Cap Haitien on three occasions during unrest
April 1818	Spanish Florida	Andrew Jackson's punitive expedition against Indians

Date	Place	Description
1821–23	Cuba	At least seven landings of ship's companies to suppress piracy
Nov. 1824	Puerto Rico	Ship's company lands at Fajardo to seek reparations for insults and damages
Nov. 1827	Greece	Ship's company burns pirate town of Miconi in the Cyclades Islands
Nov. 1827	Greece	Ship's company burns pirate town of Andros
Jan. 1832	Falkland Islands	Small unit of Marines lands to secure release of three American whalers
Feb. 1832	Sumatra	Ship's company lands and destroys pirate stronghold of Qualla Battoo
Oct. 1833	Argentina	Ship's company lands at Buenos Aires during disorder
Dec. 1835–Jan. 1836	Peru	Small unit of Marines lands near Lima to protect U.S. consulate during disorder
Jan. 1839	Sumatra	360 men attack Qualla Battoo in reprisal for murder of U.S. seamen
July 1840	Fiji Islands	70 men destroy two towns in reprisal for murder of seamen
Feb. 1841	Samoa	70 men destroy three villages at Upolu in reprisal for murders
April 1841	Gilbert Islands	80 men destroy villages on Drummond Island in reprisal for murders
Oct. 1843	Mexican California	Capture of Monterey
Dec. 1843	Liberia	Several small landings to restore order and suppress slave trading
July 1844	China	Small unit of Marines lands at Canton during disorder
1846–48	Mexico	Mexican-American War
Feb. 1852	Argentina	Small unit of Marines lands at Buenos Aires during disorder

Appendix B (continued)

Date	Place	Description
Sept. 1852	Argentina	Small unit of Marines lands at Buenos Aires during disorder
March 1853	Nicaragua	Ship's Marine guard lands at San Juan del Norte during disorder
April 1854	China	90 Americans join British brigade fighting imperial troops at Shanghai during Taiping Rebellion
July 1854	Okinawa	20 Marines land to demand punishment for murder of an American
July 1854	Nicaragua	Ship's company lands at San Juan del Norte after attack on U.S. consular officer
Nov. 1854	Okinawa	Small landing of Marines to enforce treaty signed in July
May 1855	China	Ship's Marine guard lands at Shanghai during disorder
1855	China	U.S. Marines join British Marines in attack on pirate base near Hong Kong
August 1855	Uruguay	Minor Marine landing at Montevideo during disorder
Sept.–Oct. 1855	Fiji Islands	Three landings of Marines after piracy and disorder at Viti Levu and Nukulau
Nov. 1855	Uruguay	100 sailors and Marines land at Montevideo during disorder
Sept. 1856	Panama	160 men land during disorder
Oct.–Nov. 1856	China	287 sailors and Marines land near Canton and destroy channel forts
Jan. 1858	Uruguay	Minor landing at Montevideo during disorder
Oct. 1858	Fiji Islands	54 men land at Waya, destroy two villages in reprisal for murders

Date	Place	Description
June 1859	China	U.S.S. *Powhatan* assists British and French in attack on Pa Ho River forts (This may be the first instance of U.S. "close combat support" abroad.)
August 1859	China	Minor landing at Shanghai during unrest
Feb. 1860	Kissembo (Angola)	Minor landing of Marines to aid U.S. Navy in suppressing slave trading
Sept. 1860	Panama	U.S. Marines join British Marines at Panama City in effort to restore order
June 1866	China	50 Marines and seamen land at New Chwang to assure punishment for attack on U.S. consul
June 1867	Formosa	181 sailors land, destroy village, after murder of U.S. crewmen
Feb. 1868	Japan	Two minor landings, Hioga and Nagasaki, during unrest
Feb. 1868	Uruguay	Two landings at Montevideo in disorders, both involving only small parties
April 1868	Japan	25 Marines land at Yokohama during unrest
Nov. 1868	Japan	Ship's company lands at Hioga during unrest
June 1870	Mexico	Ship's company attacks pirates in Teacapan River
June 1871	Korea	650 Marines and sailors attack forts north of Inchon
May 1873	Panama	200 sailors and Marines land near Panama City during disorder
Sept.–Oct. 1873	Panama	190 sailors and Marines land again in renewed disorders
Feb. 1874	Hawaii	150 sailors and Marines land during disorder
May 1876	Mexico	Small number of Marines and sailors land at Matamoros during disorder

Appendix B *(continued)*

Date	Place	
July 1882	Egypt	73 Marines and 60 sailors join 4,000 British troops at Alexandria
March–June 1885	Panama	1,000 Marines and seamen land at Colón during revolution
1888	Haiti	Minor Marine landing during unrest
June 1888	Korea	25 men land near Seoul during unrest
Nov. 1888	Samoa	Minor Marine landing at Apia during unrest
July 1889	Hawaii	Minor Marine landing at Honolulu during election disturbances
July 1890	Argentina	Minor Marine landing at Buenos Aires during disorders
June 1891	Haiti	Marines land at Navassa Island, maintain order
August 1891	Chile	Ship's company lands at Valparaiso during unrest
Jan. 1893	Hawaii	Minor Marine landing at Honolulu during disorder
July 1894	Korea	Ship's company lands near Seoul during Sino-Japanese War
July 1894	Nicaragua	Minor Marine landing at Bluefields during disorder
Dec. 1894– March 1895	China	Small Marine landings in North China, during unrest in Chefoo and Tientsin
March 1895	Panama	Minor landing at Bocas del Toro during unrest
May 1896	Nicaragua	Minor landing at Corinto during unrest
Feb. 1898	Nicaragua	Minor landing at San Juan del Sur during unrest
May–Dec. 1898	Cuba, Philippines, Guam, and Puerto Rico	Spanish-American War

Date	Place	Description
1899–1916	Philippines	Philippines insurrection. Large army and Marine units until 1905; smaller units remain until 1916.
Feb. 1899	Samoa	Ship's company lands at Apia during unrest
Feb. 1899	Nicaragua	Minor Marine landing at Bluefields during disorder
April 1899	Samoa	60 Americans join 62 British and 100 friendly natives in effort to restore order
May–Dec. 1900	China	U.S. joins international relief expedition to North China during Boxer Rebellion
Nov. 1900– Dec. 1901	Panama	U.S. Colombian Expeditionary Force makes series of minor landings
April 1902	Panama	Landing at Bocas del Toro during insurrection; minor
May 1902	Panama	Minor landing at Panama City during disorder
Sept.–Nov. 1902	Panama	Battalion-size Marine landing at Colón during disorder
Jan. 1903	Panama	Ship's company of Marines lands at Colón during disorder
March 1903	Honduras	Battalion-size Marine landings at Puerto Cortés and La Ceiba during unrest
April 1903	Dominican Republic	Minor Marine landing at Santo Domingo during revolt
Sept. 1903	Syria	Minor landing at Beirut during unrest
Nov. 1903– Feb. 1904	Panama	Marines land at various points before and during successful revolt for independence from Colombia
Jan. 1904	Dominican Republic	Minor Marine landing at Puerto Plata during revolt
Jan.–April 1904	Korea	100 Marines land near Seoul during Russo-Japanese War

Appendix B (continued)

Date	Place	Description
Feb. 1904	Dominican Republic	300 Marines land during revolt
May 1904	Morocco	Ship's guard of Marines lands at Tangiers during unrest
Jan. 1905	Dominican Republic	Marines sent from Panama during unrest
Sept. 1906	Cuba	120 Marines and sailors land during unrest at request of Cuban governor
April–June 1907	Honduras	Minor landing at Laguna during Honduran-Nicaraguan War
May 1909–Sept. 1910	Nicaragua	Marines land at Bluefields and remain during disorders
Feb. 1911	Honduras	Marine landing at San Pedro during disorders
Oct. 1911–Jan. 1914	China	Marines make series of minor landings at Shanghai, Taku, and in other parts of China during revolution
May–Aug. 1912	Cuba	More than 2,500 Marines land to maintain order during uprisings
Aug. 1912–Jan. 1913	Nicaragua	Marines land near Managua, Corinto, and San Juan del Sur during disorders; more than 1,000 Marines eventually
Feb. 1914	Haiti	Small landing parties of Marines at Cap Haitien and Port-de-Paix during unrest
1914–17	Mexico	Mexican Revolution. Marines seize Veracruz. Army under Pershing later pursues Pancho Villa.
July 1914	Haiti	Marines land at Port-au-Prince to transfer gold to U.S. during unrest
Oct. 1914	Dominican Republic	Marines land at Santo Domingo to restore order

Date	Place	Description
July 1915–June 1934	Haiti	Marines land in period of disorder, then form Gendarmerie d'Haiti with U.S. Marine officers to stay until 1934
May 1916–Sept. 1924	Dominican Republic	Marines land in period of disorder. Occupation declared in Nov. 1916. Guardia Nacional Dominica formed with U.S. Marine officers.
Jan. 1917–Feb. 1922	Cuba	Marine landing during unrest, then occupation. Two companies remain until 1922.
1917–18	Western Europe	World War I
1918–20	Russia	U.S. forces join those of Britain, France, and Japan at two points—Archangel and Vladivostok.
May 1922	China	Marine landing at Shanghai in revolution
Feb. 1923	China	Ship's company of Marines lands at Matsu Island during disorders
Nov. 1923	China	Small detachment of Marines lands at Tungshan during continuing revolution
Feb.–March 1924	Honduras	150–200 Marines and sailors make series of landings at La Ceiba, Puerto Cortés, Tela, and Tegucigalpa during civil war
Aug. 1924–Dec. 1927	China	Yangtze River Patrol (U.S. Marines) makes series of landings during revolution
Sept. 1924	Honduras	110 Marines and seamen land at La Ceiba during disorder
April 1925	Honduras	Minor landing at La Ceiba during unrest
May 1926–Jan. 1933	Nicaragua	Landing of Marines during revolution. Guardia Nacional organized under U.S. Marine officers. Marine units also remained.

SELECTED BIBLIOGRAPHY

INTERVENTION

Books

Barnet, Richard J. *Intervention and Revolution: The United States in the Third World*. New York: World Publishing Company, 1968.
Bosch, Juan. *Pentagonism: A Substitute for Imperialism*. New York: Grove Press, 1968.
Kolko, Gabriel. *The Roots of American Foreign Policy*. Boston: Beacon Press, 1969.
Oglesby, Carl, and Richard Shaull. *Containment and Change*. New York: Macmillan, 1967.
Pfeffer, Richard M., ed. *No More Vietnams? The War and the Future of American Foreign Policy*. New York: Harper & Row, 1968.
Pusey, Merlo J. *The Way We Go to War*. Boston: Houghton Mifflin, 1969.
Schwarz, Urs. *Confrontation and Intervention in the Modern World*. Dobbs Ferry, N.Y.: Oceana Publications, 1970.
Steel, Ronald. *Pax Americana*. New York: Viking Press, 1967.

Articles

Deutsch, Karl W. "External Involvement in Internal War," *Internal War*, ed. Harry W. Eckstein. New York: Free Press of Glencoe, 1964. Pp. 100–10.
———, and Morton A. Kaplan. "The Limits of International Coalitions," *International Aspects of Civil Strife*, ed. James N. Rosenau. Princeton, N.J.: Princeton University Press, 1964. Pp. 170–84.

SELECTED BIBLIOGRAPHY

Gallois, Pierre. "U.S. Foreign Policy: A Study in Military Strength and Diplomatic Weakness," *Orbis*, Vol. 9 (Summer 1965), pp. 338–57.

Kaplan, Morton A. "Intervention in Internal War: Some Systemic Sources," *International Aspects of Civil Strife*, ed. James N. Rosenau. Princeton, N.J.: Princeton University Press, Pp. 92–121.

Modelski, George. "The International Relations of Internal War," *International Aspects of Civil Strife*, ed. James N. Rosenau. Princeton, N.J.: Princeton University Press, 1964. Pp. 14–44.

Rosenau, James N. "Internal War as an International Event," *International Aspects of Civil Strife*, ed. James N. Rosenau. Princeton, N.J.: Princeton University Press, 1964. Pp. 45–91.

———. "The Concept of Intervention," *Journal of International Affairs*, Vol. 22 (Summer 1968), pp. 165–76.

Yarmolinsky, Adam. "American Foreign Policy and the Decision to Intervene," *Journal of International Affairs*, Vol. 22 (Summer 1968), pp. 231–35.

Young, Oran R. "Intervention and International Systems," *Journal of International Affairs*, Vol. 22 (Summer 1968), pp. 177–87.

AMERICAN STYLE

Books

Kissinger, Henry A. *The Necessity for Choice*. New York: Harper, 1960. Pp. 175–98.

Mead, Margaret. *And Keep Your Powder Dry*. New York: William Morrow, 1942.

Perkins, Dexter. *The American Approach to Foreign Policy*. Cambridge, Mass.: Harvard University Press, 1952.

Tucker, Robert. *The Just War*. Baltimore, Md.: Johns Hopkins Press, 1960.

Articles

Hoffmann, Stanley. "Restraints and Choices in American Foreign Policy," *Daedalus*, Vol. 91 (Fall 1962), pp. 668–704.

Klingberg, Frank L. "The Historical Alternation of Moods in American Foreign Policy," *World Politics*, Vol. 4 (January 1952), pp. 239–73.

May, Ernest R. "The Nature of Foreign Policy: The Calculated Versus the Axiomatic," *Daedalus*, Vol. 91 (Fall 1962), pp. 653–67.

SELECTED BIBLIOGRAPHY

DECISIONS

Books

Allison, Graham. *Essence of Decision: Explaining the Cuban Missile Crisis.* Boston: Little, Brown, 1971.
De Rivera, Joseph. *The Psychological Dimension of Foreign Policy.* Columbus, Ohio: Charles E. Merrill, 1968.
Hermann, Charles. *Crises in Foreign Policy: A Simulation Analysis.* Indianapolis: Bobbs-Merrill, 1969.
Hook, Sidney. *The Hero in History.* New York: The Humanities Press, 1950.
Leites, Nathan. *A Study of Bolshevism.* New York: Free Press, 1953.
Schelling, Thomas C. *The Strategy of Conflict.* Cambridge, Mass.: Harvard University Press, 1960.

Articles

George, Alexander. "The 'Operational Code': A Neglected Approach to the Study of Political Leaders and Decision-Making," *International Studies Quarterly,* Vol. 13 (June 1969), pp. 190–222.
Lindblom, Charles E. "The Science of 'Muddling Through,' " *Public Administration Review,* Vol. 19 (Spring 1959), pp. 79–88.
Merton, Robert K. "Bureaucratic Structure and Personality," *Reader in Bureaucracy,* ed. Robert K. Merton, *et al.* New York: Free Press, 1960. Pp. 361–71.

KOREA

Books

Acheson, Dean G. *Present at the Creation: My Years at the State Department.* New York: W. W. Norton, 1969. Pp. 354–58, 402–25.
Futrell, Robert F., *et al. The United States Air Force in Korea, 1950–1953.* New York: Duell, Sloan and Pearce, 1961.
Goodrich, Leland M. *Korea: A Study of U.S. Policy in the United Nations.* New York: Council on Foreign Relations, 1956.
Halperin, Morton H. *Limited War in the Nuclear Age.* New York: Wiley, 1963.
Lyons, Gene M. *Military Policy and Economic Aid: The Korean Case, 1950–1953.* Columbus: Ohio State University Press, 1961.
MacArthur, Douglas. *Reminiscences.* New York: McGraw-Hill, 1964.

SELECTED BIBLIOGRAPHY

Neustadt, Richard E. *Presidential Power: The Politics of Leadership.* New York: Wiley, 1960. Pp. 123–51.

Paige, Glenn D. *The Korean Decision, June 24–30, 1950.* New York: Free Press, 1968.

Rovere, Richard H., and Arthur M. Schlesinger, Jr. *The General and the President, and the Future of American Foreign Policy.* New York: Farrar, Straus and Young, 1951.

Spanier, John W. *The Truman-MacArthur Controversy and the Korean War.* Cambridge, Mass.: Belknap Press, 1959. Pp. 15–103.

Truman, Harry S. *Memoirs,* Vol. II. Garden City, N.Y.: Doubleday, 1956. Pp. 316–93.

Articles

George, Alexander L. "American Policy-Making and the North Korean Aggression," *World Politics,* Vol. 7 (January 1955), pp. 209–32.

Hammond, Paul Y. "NSC 68: Prologue to Rearmament," *Strategy, Politics and Defense Budgets,* by Warner R. Schilling, Paul Y. Hammond, and Glenn H. Snyder. New York: Columbia University Press, 1962. Pp. 267–378.

Kaufmann, William W. "Limited Warfare," *Military Policy and National Security,* ed. William W. Kaufmann. Princeton, N.J.: Princeton University Press, 1956. Pp. 102–36.

Lichterman, Martin. "To the Yalu and Back," *American Civil-Military Decisions,* ed. Harold Stein. University, Ala.: University of Alabama Press, 1963. Pp. 569–642.

Smith, Beverly. "Why We Went to War in Korea," *Saturday Evening Post,* Vol. 224 (November 10, 1951), pp. 22–23+.

Warner, Albert L. "How the Korean Decision Was Made," *Harper's,* Vol. 202 (June 1951), pp. 99–106.

Government Publications

Appleman, Roy E. *South to the Naktong, North to the Yalu.* Washington: Office of the Chief of Military History, Department of the Army, 1961.

U.S. Department of State. *The Conflict in Korea: Events Prior to the Attack on June 25, 1950.* Publication No. 4266. Far Eastern Series No. 45. Washington: Government Printing Office, 1951.

———. *United States Policy in the Korean Crisis.* Publication No. 3922. Far Eastern Series No. 34. Washington: Government Printing Office, 1950.

Speeches

Acheson, Dean G. "Crisis in Asia: An Examination of U.S. Policy." Address before the National Press Club, Washington, D.C., January 12,

SELECTED BIBLIOGRAPHY

1950. *Department of State Bulletin,* Vol. 22 (January 23, 1950), pp. 111–18.

LEBANON

Books

Adams, Sherman. *Firsthand Report: The Story of the Eisenhower Administration.* New York: Harper, 1961. Pp. 287–93.
Campbell, John C. *The Defense of the Middle East.* New York: Harper, 1958.
Chamoun, Camille. *Crise au Moyen-Orient.* Paris: Gallimard, 1963.
Copeland, Miles. *The Game of Nations.* London: Weidenfeld and Nicolson, 1969. Pp. 191–207.
Cremeans, Charles D. *The Arabs and the World: Nasser's Arab Nationalist Policy.* New York: Praeger, 1963.
Cutler, Robert. *No Time for Rest.* Boston: Little, Brown, 1966. Pp. 362–65.
Deen, Said Taky. *Bridge Under the Water: This Is How We Chased Eisenhower Out of La République Libanaise.* Arab World Series No. 2. N.p.: by the author, 1958.
Dulles, Eleanor Lansing. *John Foster Dulles: The Last Year.* New York: Harcourt, Brace and World, 1963.
———. *American Foreign Policy in the Making.* New York: Harper & Row, 1968. Pp. 268–83.
Eisenhower, Dwight D. *Waging Peace.* Garden City, N.Y.: Doubleday, 1965. Pp. 262–91.
Hughes, Emmet John. *The Ordeal of Power: A Political Memoir of the Eisenhower Years.* New York: Atheneum, 1963. Pp. 262–64.
Karami, Nawwaf, and Nadia Karami. *The Truth About the Lebanese Revolt.* Beirut: n.p., 1959.
McClintock, Robert. *The Meaning of Limited War.* Boston: Houghton Mifflin, 1967. Pp. 98–123.
Meo, Leila M. T. *Lebanon: Improbable Nation.* Bloomington: Indiana University Press, 1955.
Murphy, Robert D. *Diplomat Among Warriors.* Garden City, N.Y.: Doubleday, 1964. Pp. 394–418.
Qubain, Fahim I. *Crisis in Lebanon.* Washington: The Middle East Institute, 1961.
Salibi, Kemal S. *The Modern History of Lebanon.* New York: Praeger, 1965. Pp. 199–204.
Seale, Patrick. *The Struggle for Syria: A Study of Post-War Arab Politics.* London: Oxford University Press, 1965.
Stewart, Desmond. *Turmoil in Beirut.* London: Allan Wingate, 1958.
Taylor, Maxwell D. *The Uncertain Trumpet.* New York: Harper, 1960.
Thayer, Charles W. *Diplomat.* New York: Harper, 1959.

SELECTED BIBLIOGRAPHY

Twining, Nathan F. *Neither Liberty nor Safety.* New York: Holt, Rinehart and Winston, 1966.

Articles

"America's Search for a Policy," *Foreign Report* (Economist News Service, Ltd.), No. 582 (July 31, 1958).

"Austrian Role for Lebanon," *Foreign Report* (Economist News Service, Ltd.), No. 581 (July 24, 1958).

Baldwin, Hanson W. "Strategy of the Middle East," *Foreign Affairs,* Vol. 35 (July 1957), pp. 655–65.

Braestrup, Peter. "Limited War and the Lessons of Lebanon," *The Reporter,* Vol. 20 (April 30, 1959), pp. 25–27.

Faris, Nabih Amin. "Reflections on the Lebanon Crisis," *SAIS Review,* Vol. 3 (Autumn 1958), pp. 9–14.

Frye, William R. "Lebanon: Story Behind the Headlines," *Foreign Policy Bulletin,* Vol. 38 (November 1, 1958), pp. 25–26.

Hadd, Harry A. "Who's a Rebel? The Lesson Lebanon Taught," *Marine Corps Gazette,* Vol. 46 (March 1962), pp. 50–54.

———. "Orders Firm but Flexible," *U.S. Naval Institute Proceedings,* Vol. 88 (October 1962), pp. 81–89.

Hottinger, Arnold. "Zu'ama' and Parties in the Lebanese Crisis of 1958," *Middle East Journal,* Vol. 15 (Spring 1961), pp. 127–40.

Kerr, Malcolm H. "Lebanese Views on the 1958 Crisis," *Middle East Journal,* Vol. 15 (Spring 1961), pp. 211–17.

Knebel, Fletcher. "Day of Decision," *Look,* Vol. 22 (September 16, 1958), pp. 17–19.

Laquer, Walter Z. "The Appeals of Communism in the Middle East," *Middle East Journal,* Vol. 9 (Winter 1955), pp. 17–27.

McClintock, Robert. "The American Landing in Lebanon: Summer of 1958," *U.S. Naval Institute Proceedings,* Vol. 88 (October 1962), pp. 64–79.

Nour, Francis. "Particularisme Libanais et Nationalisme Arabe," *Orient,* No. 7 (1958), pp. 29–42.

O'Donnell, James P. "Operation Double Trouble," *Saturday Evening Post,* Vol. 231 (September 20, 1958), pp. 42+.

Sights, Albert P., Jr. "Lessons of Lebanon: A Study in Air Strategy," *Air University Review,* Vol. 16 (July–August 1965), pp. 28–43.

Steward, Hal D. "The U.S. Army and Public Relations in Lebanon," *Irish Defense Journal,* Vol. 18 (October 1958), pp. 490–93.

"Story of a Decision," *U.S. News and World Report,* Vol. 45 (July 25, 1958), pp. 68–70.

Viccellio, Henry. "The Composite Air Strike Force 1958," *Air University Review,* Vol. 11 (Summer 1959), pp. 3–17.

Wade, Sydney S. "Operation Bluebat," *Marine Corps Gazette,* Vol. 43 (July 1959), pp. 10–23.

SELECTED BIBLIOGRAPHY

———. "Lebanon," *Marine Corps Gazette*, Vol. 49 (November 1965), p. 86.

"Washington's Heap of Trouble," *Foreign Report* (Economist News Service, Ltd.), No. 579 (July 10, 1958), pp. 1–2.

Government Publications

Shulimson, Jack. *Marines in Lebanon 1958*. Marine Corps Historical Reference Pamphlet. Washington: U.S. Marine Corps Headquarters, G-3 Division, Historical Branch, 1966.

U.S. Department of State. Bureau of Intelligence and Research. *World Strength of the Communist Party Organizations*. Annual Report No. 10. Washington: Department of State, 1958.

Statements and Speeches

Eisenhower, President Dwight D. Radio-television message, July 15, 1958. *Department of State Bulletin*, Vol. 39 (August 4, 1958), pp. 183–86.

Hart, Parker T. "Tensions and U.S. Policy in the Near and Middle East." Address made before the Foreign Policy Association of Pittsburgh, May 1, 1959. *Department of State Bulletin*, Vol. 40 (May 18, 1959), pp. 715–20.

Treaties

U.S. Treaty. *Status of United States Forces in Lebanon, Agreement Between the United States of America and Lebanon, Effected by Exchange of Notes Dated at Beirut July 31 and August 6, 1958*. Treaties and Other International Acts Series No. 4387. Washington: Government Printing Office, 1958.

United Nations Security Council Documents

United Nations. Security Council. *Complaint of Lebanon: Resolution of the Security Council*, June 11, 1958, S/4023.

United Nations. Security Council. *First Report of the United Nations Observation Group in Lebanon*, July 3, 1958, S/4040.

United Nations. Security Council. *Official Comments of the Government of Lebanon on the First Report of the United Nations Observation Group in Lebanon*, July 8, 1958, S/4043.

SELECTED BIBLIOGRAPHY

Unpublished Documents

Princeton University. John Foster Dulles Oral History Project. Interview with Robert Murphy. Section II. June 8, 1965.
Princeton University. John Foster Dulles Papers. Conference Dossiers, 1958. Correspondence, 1958. Engagements, 1958–59.

VIETNAM

Books

Fall, Bernard. *The Two Vietnams*. New York: Praeger, 1963.
———. *Vietnam Witness, 1953–66*. New York: Praeger, 1966.
Fulbright, James W. (ed.). *The Vietnam Hearings*. New York: Random House, 1966.
Goulden, Joseph C. *Truth Is the First Casualty: The Gulf of Tonkin Affair—Illusion and Reality*. Chicago: James B. Alder, Inc., in association with Rand McNally, 1969.
Hilsman, Roger. *To Move a Nation*. Garden City, N.Y.: Doubleday, 1967. Pp. 411–537.
Hoopes, Townsend W. *The Limits of Intervention*. New York: David McKay, 1969.
Jordan, Amos. *Foreign Aid and the Defense of Southeast Asia*. New York: Praeger, 1962.
Kraslow, David, and Stuart H. Loory. *The Secret Search for Peace in Vietnam*. New York: Vintage Books, 1968.
Lacouture, Jean. *Vietnam: Between Two Truces*. New York: Random House, 1966.
Montgomery, John D. *The Politics of Foreign Aid*. New York: Praeger, for the Council on Foreign Relations, 1962.
Pike, Douglas. *Viet Cong: The Organization and Techniques of the National Liberation Front of South Vietnam*. Cambridge: Massachusetts Institute of Technology Press, 1966.
Schlesinger, Arthur M., Jr. *A Thousand Days*. Boston: Houghton Mifflin, 1965. Pp. 536–50, 981–98.
Scigliano, Robert. *South Vietnam: Nation Under Stress*. Boston: Houghton Mifflin, 1963.
Sorensen, Theodore C. *Kennedy*. New York: Harper & Row, 1965. Pp. 648–61.

SELECTED BIBLIOGRAPHY

Articles

Eidenburg, Eugene. "The Presidency: Americanizing the War in Vietnam," *American Political Institutions and Public Policy*, ed. Allan P. Sindler. Boston: Little, Brown, 1969. Pp. 69–126.

Thomson, James C., Jr. "How Could Vietnam Happen: An Autopsy," *The Atlantic*, Vol. 221 (April 1968), pp. 47–53.

Government Publications

U.S. Congress. House. Committee on Armed Services. *United States-Vietnam Relations, 1945–1967*. A Study Prepared by the Department of Defense. 12 vols. Washington: Government Printing Office, 1971.

U.S. Department of State. *Aggression from the North*. Publication No. 7839. Far Eastern Series No. 130. Washington: Government Printing Office, 1965. Reprinted as House Document 136 (U.S. 89th Congress, 1st Sess.), 1965.

———. *A Threat to the Peace: North Viet-Nam's Effort to Conquer South Viet-Nam*, 2 parts. Publication No. 7308. Far Eastern Series No. 110. Washington: Government Printing Office, 1961.

Interviews and Speeches

Ball, George W. "Viet-Nam: Free-World Challenge in Southeast Asia." Based on an address to the Economic Club of Detroit, April 30, 1962. Department of State Far Eastern Series No. 113. Washington: Government Printing Office, 1962.

Bundy, William P. "The Path to Viet-Nam: A Lesson in Involvement." An address prepared for delivery before the National Student Association 20th Annual Congress, August 15, 1967. Department of State East Asian and Pacific Series No. 166. Washington: Government Printing Office, 1967.

Kennedy, President John F. "NBC Interview with Huntley-Brinkley," September 9, 1963. *Department of State Bulletin*, Vol. 49 (September 30, 1963), pp. 499–500.

DOMINICAN REPUBLIC

Books

Center for Strategic Studies, Georgetown University. *Dominican Action —1965: Intervention or Cooperation*. Special Report Series No. 2. Washington: Center for Strategic Studies, 1966.

SELECTED BIBLIOGRAPHY

Draper, Theodore. *The Dominican Revolt.* New York: Commentary, 1968.
Evans, Rowland, and Robert Novak. *Lyndon B. Johnson: The Exercise of Power.* New York: The New American Library, 1966. Pp. 510–29.
Geyelin, Philip. *Lyndon B. Johnson and the World.* New York: Praeger, 1966.
Johnson, Lyndon B. *The Vantage Point: Perspectives of the Presidency, 1963–1969.* New York: Holt, Rinehart and Winston, 1971. Pp. 187–205.
Kurzman, Dan. *Santo Domingo: Revolt of the Damned.* New York: Putnam, 1965.
Lowenthal, Abraham. *The Dominican Intervention.* Cambridge, Mass.: Harvard University Press, 1972.
Martin, John Bartlow. *Overtaken by Events.* Garden City, N.Y.: Doubleday, 1966.
Slater, Jerome. *Intervention and Negotiation: The United States and the Dominican Republic.* New York: Harper & Row, 1970.
Szulc, Tad. *Dominican Diary.* New York: Delacorte Press, 1965.

Articles

Bonsal, Philip W. "Open Letter to an Author, The Dominican Republic: Days of Turmoil," letter from Philip Bonsal to John Bartlow Martin, *Foreign Service Journal,* Vol. 44 (February 1967), pp. 40–42.
Dare, James A. "Dominican Diary," *U.S. Naval Institute Proceedings,* Vol. 91 (December 1965), pp. 36–45.
Draper, Theodore. "Dominican Crisis: A Case Study in American Policy," *Commentary,* Vol. 40 (December 1965), pp. 33–68.
———. "The Dominican Intervention Reconsidered," *Political Science Quarterly,* Vol. 86 (March 1971), pp. 1–36.
Plank, John. "The Caribbean: Intervention, When and How?" *Foreign Affairs,* Vol. 44 (October 1965), pp. 37–48.
Quello, J. I., and Narcissa Isa Conde. "Revolutionary Struggle in the Dominican Republic and Its Lessons," part I, *World Marxist Review,* Vol. 8 (December 1965), pp. 92–103.
Tompkins, R. McC. "Ubique," *Marine Corps Gazette,* Vol. 49 (September 1965), pp. 32–39.

Government Publications

U.S. Department of State, Bureau of Intelligence and Research. *World Strength of the Communist Party Organizations.* Annual Report No. 17. Washington: Department of State, 1965.

SELECTED BIBLIOGRAPHY

Statements and Speeches

Ball, George. "Principles of Our Policy Toward Cuba." Address before the Omicron Delta Kappa Society, Roanoke, Va., April 23, 1964. *Department of State Bulletin*, Vol. 50 (May 11, 1964), pp. 738–44.

Bunker, Ellsworth. "The United States and Latin America: 'Special Ties of Interest and Affection.'" Address before the Pan American Liaison Committee of Women's Organizations, Washington, D.C., January 30, 1965. *Department of State Bulletin*, Vol. 52 (March 1, 1965), pp. 301–4.

Fulbright, James W. "The Situation in the Dominican Republic," *Congressional Record* (daily, Senate), September 15, 1965, pp. 22998–23008.

Johnson, President Lyndon B. "The State of the Union." Address to Congress, January 4, 1965. *Department of State Bulletin*, Vol. 52 (January 25, 1965), pp. 94–100.

———. Statement of April 28. *Department of State Bulletin*, Vol. 52 (May 17, 1965), pp. 738–39.

———. Statement of April 30 broadcast over radio and television. *Department of State Bulletin*, Vol. 52 (May 17, 1965), pp. 742–43.

———. Statements of May 1. *Department of State Bulletin*, Vol. 52 (May 17, 1965), pp. 743–44.

———. Statement of May 2 broadcast over radio and television. *Department of State Bulletin*, Vol. 52 (May 17, 1965), pp. 744–48.

———. Statement to members of Congress at the White House, May 4. *Department of State Bulletin*, Vol. 52 (May 24, 1965), pp. 816–22.

Mann, Thomas. "The Dominican Crisis: Correcting Some Misconceptions." Address before the Inter-American Press Association, San Diego, Calif., October 12, 1965. *Department of State Bulletin*, Vol. 53 (November 8, 1965), pp. 730–38.

OTHER CONFLICTS

China, 1946–49

Acheson, Dean G. *Present at the Creation: My Years at the State Department*. New York: W. W. Norton, 1969. Pp. 202–11, 302–07.

Shaw, Henry I., Jr. *The United States Marines in North China, 1945–1949*. Reprinted. Washington: U.S. Marine Corps Headquarters, G-3 Division, Historical Branch, 1968.

Truman, Harry S. *Memoirs*, Vol. II. Garden City, N.Y.: Doubleday, 1956. Pp. 61–92.

Tsou, Tang. *America's Failure in China, 1941–50*. Chicago: University of Chicago Press, 1963.

SELECTED BIBLIOGRAPHY

The Congo, 1960–64

Hilsman, Roger. *To Move a Nation*. Garden City, N.Y.: Doubleday, 1967. Pp. 233–71.

Lefever, Ernest W. *Crisis in the Congo*. Washington: The Brookings Institution, 1965.

Merriam, Alan P. *Congo: Background to Conflict*. Evanston, Ill.: Northwestern University Press, 1961.

Schlesinger, Arthur M., Jr. *A Thousand Days*. Boston: Houghton Mifflin, 1965. Pp. 574–99.

Sorensen, Theodore C. *Kennedy*. New York: Harper & Row, 1965. Pp. 635–39.

Cuba, 1961

Johnson, Haynes. *The Bay of Pigs*. New York: W. W. Norton, 1964.

Meyer, Karl E., and Tad Szulc. *The Cuban Invasion: The Chronicle of a Disaster*. New York: Praeger, 1962.

Schlesinger, Arthur M., Jr. *A Thousand Days*. Boston: Houghton Mifflin, 1965. Pp. 215–85.

Sorensen, Theodore C. *Kennedy*. New York: Harper & Row, 1965. Pp. 294–309.

Cuba, 1962

Abel, Elie. *The Missile Crisis*. Philadelphia: J. B. Lippincott, 1966.

Allison, Graham. *Essence of Decision: Explaining the Cuban Missile Crisis*. Boston: Little, Brown, 1971.

Hilsman, Roger. *To Move a Nation*. Garden City, N.Y.: Doubleday, 1967. Pp. 159–229.

Kennedy, Robert F. *Thirteen Days*. New York: W. W. Norton, 1969.

Schlesinger, Arthur M., Jr. *A Thousand Days*. Boston: Houghton Mifflin, 1965. Pp. 795–830.

Sorensen, Theodore C. *Kennedy*. New York: Harper & Row, 1965. Pp. 667–718.

Guatemala, 1954

Slater, Jerome. *The OAS and United States Foreign Policy*. Columbus: Ohio State University Press, 1967. Pp. 115–33.

Westerfield, H. Bradford. *The Instruments of America's Foreign Policy*. New York: Crowell, 1963. Pp. 422–39.

SELECTED BIBLIOGRAPHY

Indochina, 1954

Devillers, Philippe, and Jean Lacouture. *End of a War.* New York: Praeger, 1969.
Donovan, Robert J. *Eisenhower: The Inside Story.* New York: Harper, 1956. Pp. 259–68.
Eisenhower, Dwight D. *Mandate for Change.* Garden City, N.Y.: Doubleday, 1963. Pp. 332–75.
Ely, Paul. *Memoires,* Vol. I, *L'Indochine dans la Tourmente.* Paris: Plon, 1964.
Gurtov, Melvin. *The First Vietnam Crisis: Chinese Communist Strategy and United States Involvement, 1953–4.* New York: Columbia University Press, 1967.
Randle, Robert F. *Geneva 1954: The Settlement of the Indochinese War.* Princeton, N.J.: Princeton University Press, 1969.
Roberts, Chalmers M. "The Day We Didn't Go to War," *The Reporter,* Vol. 11 (September 12, 1954), pp. 31–35.
Warner, Geoffrey. "Escalation in Vietnam: The Precedents of 1954," *International Affairs* (London), Vol. 41 (April 1965), pp. 267–77.

Indonesia, 1965

Hughes, John. *Indonesian Upheaval.* New York: David McKay, 1967.
Ra'anan, Uri. "Indonesia, 1965," *The Politics of the Coup D'Etat,* ed. William G. Andrews and Uri Ra'anan. New York: Van Nostrand, Reinhold, 1969. Pp. 43–64.

Laos, 1959–62

Dommen, Arthur J. *Conflict in Laos.* New York: Praeger, 1964.
Fall, Bernard B. *Street Without Joy.* Harrisburg, Pa.: Stackpole, 1963. Pp. 323–33.
———. *Anatomy of a Crisis: The Laotian Crisis of 1960–1961,* ed. Roger M. Smith. Garden City, N.Y.: Doubleday, 1969.
Harriman, W. Averell. "What We Are Doing in Southeast Asia," *The New York Times Magazine* (May 27, 1962), pp. 7+.
Hilsman, Roger. *To Move a Nation.* Garden City, N.Y.: Doubleday, 1967. Pp. 91–155.
Modelski, George. "SEATO: Its Function and Organization," *SEATO: Six Studies,* ed. George Modelski. Melbourne: F. W. Cheshire for the Australian National University, 1962. Pp. 12–17.
Schlesinger, Arthur M., Jr. *A Thousand Days.* Boston: Houghton Mifflin, 1965. Pp. 323–42, 512–18.

SELECTED BIBLIOGRAPHY

Shaplen, Robert. *Time Out of Hand*. New York: Harper & Row, 1968. Pp. 342–70.

Simpson, O. R. "Thailand," *Marine Corps Gazette*, Vol. 49 (November 1965), pp. 87–89.

Sorensen, Theodore C. *Kennedy*. New York: Harper & Row, 1965. Pp. 639–48.

Toye, Hugh. *Laos: Buffer State or Battleground?* London: Oxford University Press, 1968.

Warner, Dennis. *The Last Confucian*. New York: Macmillan, 1963. Pp. 194–223.

INDEX

Acheson, Dean: Iran and, 147; Korea and, 43, 44, 72–73, 91, 96, 102–103, 125
Adana, Turkey, 49, 77
Aden, 5, 212–13(tab)
Adenauer, Konrad, 163
Adoula, Cyrille, 149
advisers, see military assistance
Afif al-Bizri, 76
Africa, 88; sub-Sahara, 27, 142
Agency for International Development, 155, 185
aggression, 17, 20, 33–35, 198–99; "indirect," 75–76, 80; defined, 17. See also armed conflict (prior to U.S. military intervention); intervention by others
Air America, 159, 161
air warfare, 188; in Bay of Pigs, 175, 176; Cuban crisis (1962) and, 131–32, 194; in Dominican Republic, 62, 64–65, 66, 67, 185, 186; Indochina War, 53, 150, 151, 152, 153; in Indonesia, 165; in Korea, 4, 15, 43–44, 45, 74, 97, 99, 103, 112, 127, 185, 187; in Laos, 2, 58–59, 87, 127–28,

air warfare (cont.)
159, 161, 186–87; in Lebanon, 49, 100; in Syria (1957 threat of), 77; in Vietnam, 2, 3, 57, 58, 59–60, 101, 106, 115, 116, 128, 129, 186
Albania, 135
Alexandria, Egypt, 10
Algeria, 34, 133, 162–64, 208–209(tab); Moroccan dispute (1962–63), 5, 214–15(tab)
Alliance for Progress, 26
allies, 21, 26, 197, 198; intervention decisions and, 32, 34, 109–11, 193; non-intervention decisions and, 135–36, 147, 153–54; South Vietnam alliance request, 56; Taiwan, 169. See also areas of strategic interest such as "Communist-threatened" regions; "disputed territories;" "just another country" states; "special interest" countries
American Society of Newspaper Editors, 154, 176
Amory, Cleveland, 175
Anderson, Robert, 95
Angola, 5, 212–13(tab), 221

241

INDEX

Ankara, Turkey, 77
Antarctica, 9
Arab League Council, 119
Arab States, 28, 77, 112. June War (1967) and, 170, 212–13(*tab*)
Arbenz Guzman, Jacobo, 137–38
Argentina, 6, 10–11, 142, 212–13(*tab*), 219, 220, 222
Armas, Castillo, 134, 138
armed conflict (prior to American intervention), 34, 36, 37(*tab*), 93, 181, 198–200, 204–17(*tab*); absence of, 39, 76–77, 131–33, 142, 191; in Algeria, 162, 163; in Burma, 143, 144, 145; in Communist states, 171–73; in Congo (Kinshasa), 148–50; in Cyprus, 166–67; in disputed territories, 168, 169–70; Dominican, 60–61, 62, 89–90, 117; in Greece, 134; in Guatemala, 137–38; Indonesian, 165, 166; in Iran, 145, 146, 148; in Korea, 35, 42, 70, 73–74, 117, 124–25, 131; in Lebanon, 45–46, 117; listing (1946–71) of, 202–17; "peace-keeping" ethic and, 17, 20, 21, 189; in Vietnam, 35, 54, 55, 117, 131
Asia, *see* Far East; Near East
Associated States of Indochina (French Union), 53, 152
Asunción, Paraguay, 141
Australia, 85
Austria, 191

Baghdad, Iraq, 48
Baghdad Pact, 114
Balaguer, Joaquin, 61, 68
Baldwin, Hanson, cited, 53, 84, 135, 144, 165
Ball, George W., 107, 132; cited, 89, 121–22
Bangladesh, *see* East Pakistan

Barkley, Alben, 102–103
Barnet, Richard, 18
Batista, Fulgencio, 134, 138–39, 196
Battle Line (newsletter), 121
Bay of Pigs invasion (1961), 3, 7, 133, 172, 173–77, 185, 216–17(*tab*)
Beirut, Lebanon, 10, 45–46, 47, 109, 113; Marine assault (1958) on, 3, 49, 78–79, 80–82, 101–102, 105
Beirut Telegraph (newspaper), 46, 47, 78
Belgium, 12, 148–50
Ben Bella, Ahmed, 164
Ben Khedda, Benyoussef, 163–64
Bennett, William Tapley: Dominican intervention (1965) and, 61, 62–63, 64, 65, 66–67, 90, 107, 123–24
Benoit, Pedro Bartolene, 63, 65–66, 123–24
Berle, Adolph A., 174, 175
Bhutan, 25, 28, 168
Bismarck, Otto von, 192
Bissell, Richard, 175, 176
Blair House Conferences (1950), Washington, 43–44, 71, 96–97, 102–103, 109, 110, 111–12, 118
BLUEBAT, 79, 80, 100, 105
Bolivia, 6, 11, 12, 141, 142, 183, 204–205(*tab*), 212–13(*tab*); conflict (1965), 33, 182, 204–205(*tab*)
bombing, *see* air warfare; naval warfare; nuclear weapons
Bonn, West Germany, 163
Bonnelly, Rafael F., 68
Bonsal, Philip, 88, 174
Bosch, Juan, 60–61, 68; Dominican opposition forces, 62, 63, 64, 109, 116, 123, 181, 190
Boun Oum, Prince, 156
Bowles, Chester, 144
Bradley, Omar, 43, 44, 96, 102, 112

INDEX

Brasília, Brazil, 133
Bratislava Conference (1968), 172
Brazil, 6, 11, 12, 68, 133, 204–205(*tab*)
Bridges, Styles, 103, 104
Britain, 8, 76, 80, 145, 154, 192; Burma and, 143; Cyprus and, 166, 167; Greece and, 134, 135, 203; Jordan and, 49–50, 81; Laos civil war (1959–62) and, 158, 160; Lebanon and, 47, 48, 79, 83, 105, 110–11, 113, 114, 118; Malayan civil war and, 32, 111, 182; Suez invasion (1956) and, 5, 110, 170, 172
British Guiana, 6, 133, 204–205(*tab*)
Brown, Charles R., 51
Brunei, 5, 212–13(*tab*)
Budapest, Hungary, 7, 172
Bulgaria, 135, 172
Bundy, McGeorge, 68, 106, 107, 161; Cuba and, 131, 176
Bundy, William, 54
Bunker, Ellsworth, 67, 68, 88, 171
burden of intervention, assumption by others, 32–33, 109–111, 134, 138, 167
bureaucracy, *see* group decision-making
Burke, Arleigh, 176
Burma, 6, 84, 85, 150, 157; civil war (1948–58), 142, 143–45, 148, 182, 206–207(*tab*); as disputed territory, 28, 168, 210–11(*tab*)
Byrnes, James F., 145

Caamaño Deno, Francisco, 63, 65, 68
Caceres Troncoso, Ramon, 60, 62
California, 219
Cambodia, 6, 53, 54, 206–207(*tab*); Laos civil war (1959–62) and, 87, 156, 157; Viet-

Cambodia (*cont.*)
nam war expansion into, 2, 4, 11, 52, 59, 86, 127, 128, 129, 186–87, 197
Canada, 25
Caracas, Venezuela, 21, 132
Cardona, Miro, 174, 176–77
Caribbean, 41, 158, 177, 198; combat-ready troops in, 101, 123; Western Hemisphere defense doctrine and, 26, 27
Castro, Fidel, 173, 174, 176; Cuban civil war (1956–59) and, 7, 8, 138–39, 196; Latin American influence of, 89, 183, 191, 192
Castro, Raoul, 139
casualties, 3, 69, 99, 117
Center for Strategic Studies, 90
Central America, 11, 26, 27. *See also specific countries*
centrism, 13
Ceylon, 208–209(*tab*)
Chaco War (1930–35), 12
Chad, 6, 212–13(*tab*)
Chamoun, Camille, 45–46, 61, 77; Murphy and, 50–51, 82; pre-intervention support for, 47, 48, 109, 110, 112–13, 114, 118–20, 191
Chang, John M., 118
chemical weapons, 101, 188
Chiang Kai-shek, 6, 109, 139, 140; Burma and, 143–44
Chile, 11, 17, 133, 222
China, Empire of: pre-revolution U.S. interventions in, 219, 220, 221, 222, 223, 224, 225
China, People's Republic of (Peking), 6, 7, 12, 21, 80, 157, 190, 194, 216–17(*tab*); Burma and, 143, 144; Indochina War (1954) and, 52, 53, 85, 150, 151, 152; Indonesia and, 85, 165, 166; Korea and, 2, 45, 71, 97, 101, 110, 112, 187; nuclear weapons and, 28–29, 99, 100, 101, 140–41, 182,

243

INDEX

China (*cont.*)
 195; offshore islands dispute, 5, 28, 100, 168–69, 170, 184, 210–11(*tab*); Tibet and, 28, 168, 169, 172, 173, 210–11(*tab*)
China, Republic of (Taiwan), 5, 12, 204–205(*tab*); Formosa establishment of, 6, 28, 100, 139–40, 143–44, 169; Korea and, 71, 73, 109
Chinese Civil War (1927–49), 53, 71, 80; Burma and, 143–45; U.S. intervention restraints in, 6, 12, 17, 19, 134, 139–41, 177, 182, 203, 204–205(*tab*)
Chouf, Lebanon, 46
Churchill, Winston, 154
CIA, *see* United States Central Intelligence Agency (CIA)
Cierna Conference (1968), 172
citizen protection, *see* nationals, protection of
Clark, Joseph, cited, 65–66
Clark air base, Philippines, 136
Clements, Earle, 153
close combat support, 221(*tab*); defined, 4; in Korea, 44–45, 112; in Vietnam, 56, 58, 94, 101, 105–106, 115–16, 121–22, 185, 186
Collins, J. Lawton, 44, 96, 102
Colombia, 6, 11, 63, 204–205(*tab*); civil war (1948–53), 142, 212–13(*tab*)
Colorado party (Paraguay), 141
combat ready (forces), defined, 3
communism, 4, 8–9, 21, 69; Algeria and, 162–64; Burma and, 143–45; Cambodia and, 186; Chinese civil war and, 2, 6, 12, 80, 139–41; Congo (Kinshasa) and, 149; containment doctrine and, 11, 17, 24–29, 84–85, 111, 142, 145–46, 179, 182, 190, 195–97, 200; Cuba and, 138–39, 177, 196; Cyprus and, 166, 167; Dominican

communism (*cont.*)
 Republic and, 63, 64, 65, 67, 70, 87–91, 92, 107, 116, 117, 123, 126, 180, 196; Greece and, 134; Guatemala and, 137; Indochina War (1954) and, 150, 153, 154; Indonesia and, 164–65, 166, 171; intergovernment disputes of, 171–77, 180, 182, 187, 216–17(*tab*); Iran and, 145–48; Korea and, 42, 70–74, 91, 92, 111–12, 180; Laos civil war (1959–62) and, 155, 157, 158, 159, 160, 161, 178, 182, 190; Lebanon and, 46, 47, 70, 74–83, 91, 92, 104–105, 109, 112, 113, 114, 180, 190, 195–96; Paraguay and, 141–42, 177, 182; Philippines and, 136–37; "spheres of influence" theory and, 19–20; U.S. restraints on intervention in face of, 93, 133–34, 142, 150, 168–70, 176–77, 204–11(*tab*), 216–17(*tab*); U.S. scale of security threats from, 25–29, 35, 36, 38, 70, 126–27, 129, 133, 177, 180, 182, 193–94, 198; Vietnam and, 52, 54, 55, 70, 83–87, 91, 92, 180, 190
"Communist-threatened" region(s), 25, 74–83; defined, 27; Fertile Crescent as, 70, 74–78, 126–27, 180; restraints on intervention in, 35, 36, 37(*tab*), 142–62, 183, 206–207(*tab*); Southeast Asia as, 70, 84–87, 126–27, 180
Composite Air Strike Force (1958), 49, 100
Concepción, Paraguay, 141
Conde, Narcissa Isa, cited, 61
Congo (Brazzaville), 133
Congo, Republic of (Kinshasa), 5, 17, 111, 142, 148–50, 182, 206–207(*tab*)
Congo River, 149

244

INDEX

Congress of Vienna (1815), 191
Connally, Tom, 103
Connett, William, 61, 63, 64
conservatism, 18
contingency planning, 185–86; Algeria and, 163; Cuba and, 132, 173–77; Indochina War (1954) and, 151, 152–53; Korea and, 71–73; Laos civil war (1959–62) and, 157; the Near East and, 77, 78–79, 80, 82–83, 100, 105; Vietnam and, 115
Costa Rica, 5, 6, 204–205(*tab*), 212–13(*tab*)
costs of intervention, 3, 6, 53; Vietnam, 54–55, 69
covert military action, 3, 159, 161, 165, 173–77, 185
Cremeans, Charles D., cited, 77
Crockett, Kennedy M., 63
Cuba, 6, 183, 191; Bay of Pigs invasion, 3, 7, 133, 172, 173–77, 185, 216–17(*tab*); civil war (1956–59), 8, 134, 138–39, 196, 204–205(*tab*); Dominican Republic and, 35, 88, 89, 90, 107, 126, 127, 181; missile crisis (1962), 7, 26, 31, 131–32, 184, 194; pre-World War II interventions in, 11, 219, 222, 224, 225
Cuban Revolutionary Council, 174
Curaçao, 9, 11, 218
Cutler, Robert, 104
Cyprus, 5, 32, 162, 166–68, 208–209(*tab*); British troops in, 79, 81, 105, 110–11
Czechoslovakia, 133, 137, 170; invasion of (1968), 5, 7, 17, 28, 29, 172–73, 216–17(*tab*)

Dalai Lama, 173
Dare, James A., 63–64, 66
Darul Islam, 164, 165
decision-making: intervention rationales, 9, 10, 11, 12, 15–20, 73–74, 131, 176, 190–91, decision-making (*cont.*) 193–200; intervention restraints, 20–39, 93–129, 131–33, 150, 161–68, 168–70, 176–78, 187–88. *See also* group decision-making; individual decision-making
Democratic Party (U.S.), 2
Democratic Revolutionary Front (Cuba), 174
Detroit Economic Club, 122
Diaz, Carlos Enrique, 138
Diem, Ngo Dinh, 54; reforms and, 55, 56, 57, 58, 116, 120–21, 122; Viet Cong and, 55–56, 84, 114–15, 117
Dienbienphu, battle of, 7, 53, 84, 85, 150–51, 154; nuclear defense proposal and, 152
Dillon, Douglas, 152, 175
disputed territories, 25, 168–70, 180, 210–11(*tab*); defined, 27–28
Dominican Communist Party (PCD), 61, 89
Dominican Republic: pre-World War II interventions in, 26, 223, 224, 225; uprisings in (1961), 6, 142, 204–205 (*tab*)
Dominican Republic intervention (1965), 11, 14, 18, 20, 31, 60–68, 69, 126, 134, 177, 187; local military strength in, 62, 64, 109, 116, 117, 181; nuclear risk in, 100–101, 127; public reaction to, 1, 2, 19, 33, 35; request for, 21, 34, 65, 66, 107, 120, 123–24, 181, 195; Soviet confrontation risk in, 4, 94, 127; United Nations and, 111; U.S. Marines action in, 4, 17, 26, 60, 64, 66–67, 101, 108, 116, 123, 124, 185; U.S. perception of security threat in, 8, 19, 87–91, 92, 180, 190, 196
Dominican Revolutionary Party (PRD), 61, 62, 64, 65, 67, 68

245

INDEX

Dominican Socialist Party (PSP), 89
"domino theory," 27, 85, 86
Draper, Theodore, cited, 18
Drummond Island, Gilbert Islands, 10
Druze Mountains, 74
Dubcek, Alexander, 172
Dulles, Allen, 138, 175; Lebanon intervention and, 47, 78, 94–95, 96, 104, 110, 113
Dulles, John Foster, 11, 17, 161; Guatemala and, 137; Indochina and, 84–85, 152, 153, 154; Indonesia and, 164–65; Iran (1953) and, 148; Jordan and, 78, 81; Lebanon and, 47, 50, 94, 95, 96, 103, 104, 110, 112, 113–14, 118, 119; Syria and, 76–77

East Berlin, 203, 216–17(*tab*)
East Germany, 32, 133, 172, 183
East Pakistan (Bangladesh), 5, 6, 17, 28, 85
Ecuador, 12, 62
Egypt, 6, 47, 75, 77, 125, 163, 214–15(*tab*); Suez invasion (1956) and, 5, 110, 170–71, 172, 190, 214–15(*tab*); U.S. interventions in, 10, 222. *See also* United Arab Republic
Eisenhower, Dwight D., 13, 161–62, 203; Algeria and, 162–63; Burma and, 143, 144–45; Chinese offshore islands and, 168–69; Congo (Kinshasa) and, 148–49; Congress and, 31, 75, 153–54, 168, 182; Cuba and, 7, 138–39, 173, 174, 196; "domino theory" and, 27, 85, 86; Guatemala and, 137, 138; Indochina and, 53, 54, 84, 114, 151–52, 153–54; Indonesia and, 164; Iran and, 146, 147, 148; Jordan and, 78, 81; Laos civil war (1959–62) and, 156; Lebanon and, 2, 11, 47, 49,

Eisenhower, Dwight D. (*cont.*) 50, 74, 75, 79–80, 81, 82–83, 94, 95–96, 100, 104, 105, 108, 110–11, 112, 113, 114, 117, 118, 119, 190; on Nasser, 170–71; Syria and, 74, 76–77, 81, 83, 171; Tibet and, 173
Eisenhower Doctrine, 75
Ellis, Frank B., 106
El Salvador, 5, 17, 133, 212–13 (*tab*)
Ely, Paul, 150–51, 152, 153
Embajador Hotel, Santo Domingo, 64, 65, 66, 67
Eritrea, 212–13(*tab*)
Essex (vessel), 176
Ethiopia, 5, 12, 206–207(*tab*), 212–13(*tab*)
Europe, 9, 75, 199; Eastern, 19, 99, 111; Western, 20, 26, 28, 71, 87, 100, 193–94. *See also specific countries*

Faisal II, king of Iraq, 48, 77, 80, 119
Fajardo, Puerto Rico, 9
Falkland Islands, 219
Far East, 10, 19, 41, 198; Johnson on, 87; U.S. line of defense in, 71–73, 96–97. *See also specific countries*
Febrista Party (Paraguay), 141
Fertile Crescent: as "Communist-threatened" region, 27, 74–76, 79–80, 92, 94, 95, 114, 142, 180. *See also specific countries*
Fiji, 10, 219, 220
Finletter, Thomas K., 44, 96, 102
foreign aid, 3, 53. *See also* military assistance
foreign intervention (U.S.), *see* intervention
foreign intervention (other than American), *see* intervention by others
Formosa, Island of, 6, 139, 143–44, 204–205(*tab*). *See also* China, Republic of (Taiwan)

246

INDEX

Formosa Straits, 110
Fort Bragg, North Carolina, 64, 101
Fourteenth of June Movement, 89, 126
France, 5, 8, 12, 170, 172, 192, 194; Algeria and, 34, 133, 162, 163, 208–209(*tab*); Curaçao and, 9; Indochina and, 6–7, 52–54, 84, 85, 111, 142, 150–54; Laos civil war (1959–62) and, 155, 156; Lebanon and, 47, 48, 75, 110, 114, 118
French Cameroons, 5, 212–13 (*tab*)
French Secret Army Organization, 163
French Union (Associated States of Indochina), 53, 152
Fulbright, James William, 88, 104–105, 175, 195

Gabon, 212–13(*tab*)
Gallois, Pierre, cited, 18
Gambia, 27
Garcia-Godoy, Hector, 68
Gaulle, Charles de, 111, 163, 192
Gemayel, Pierre, 52
Geneva Conference (1954), 53–54, 85, 87, 154; (1962), 158, 159, 160
George II, king of Greece, 134
Georgia, 61
Germany, 12, 41, 81, 192. *See also* East Germany; West Germany
Geyelin, Philip, cited, 88, 90
Ghana, 133, 206–207(*tab*)
Gibraltar, 100
Gilbert Islands, 10, 219
Gilpatric, Roswell, 106
Gizenga, Antoine, 149
Goa, 5, 170, 182, 212–13(*tab*)
Goldwater, Barry, 13
Good Neighbor Policy, 26
Goodwin, Richard, 175
Grant, Ulysses, 11
Gray, David W., 79

Great Britain, *see* Britain
Greece, 6, 9, 219; civil war (1946–49), 76, 80, 129, 134–36, 184, 203, 204–205(*tab*); Cyprus and, 166, 167
Gromyko, Andrei, 158
ground warfare: in Cambodia, 87; in Dominican intervention, 60, 67; in Indochina War (1954), 151, 152, 153; in Korea, 45, 72, 73, 74, 99, 112, 127; in Lebanon, 47, 48, 49, 52, 81–82; in Vietnam, 2, 54, 55, 56, 57, 58, 59, 86, 91, 92, 106, 115, 117, 125–26, 185
group decision-making, 13–15; distortions in, 22, 91–92, 116–17, 180, 196; incremental process of, 31–33, 108–17, 127, 134, 149, 157, 181, 194, 200; levels of, 185; moral values and, 33–35, 36, 38, 69, 73, 117–27, 177, 184, 189–90, 191–92, 198; operational codes in, 22–24, 29, 34, 36, 37(*tab*), 38, 69–70, 74, 93, 117, 127, 133, 193–200; predictability of, 179–200; roles within, 30–31, 36, 38, 93, 102–108, 127, 150, 153–54, 169, 179, 181, 182, 183–84, 189–93, 194, 195, 200; secrecy and, 57, 106, 107, 175
Guam, 222
Guantanamo Bay, Cuba, 132
Guatemala, 6; invasion of (1954), 134, 137–38, 185, 204–205 (*tab*)
Guatemala City, Guatemala, 138
guerrillas: in Algeria, 162–63; in Bolivia, 182; in Greece, 134, 135–36; in Korea, 72, 73; in Laos, 58–59, 155, 156–57, 158, 160; in Peru, 182; in the Philippines, 136–37; in Vietnam, 54, 55, 56, 57, 58, 86, 91, 92, 117, 125–26
Guinea, 133

INDEX

Gulf of Siam, 159
Gurtov, Melvin, quoted, 154
Guzmán, Antonio, 68

Haina, Dominican Republic, 64
Haiti, 6, 8; disorders (1946), 212–13(*tab*); disorders (1957), 142, 183, 185, 204–205(*tab*); U.S. interventions in, 11, 12, 218, 222, 224, 225
Hanoi, North Vietnam, 151. *See also* North Vietnam
Hare, Raymond, 50
Harkins, Paul, 122
Harriman, W. Averell, 106, 159; quoted, 160
Hart, Parker T., cited, 75–76
Havana, Cuba, 139. *See also* Cuba
Hawaii, 221, 222
Hayes, Rutherford B., 11
Henderson, Loy, 77, 94
Hernando Ramirez, Miguel Angel, 63, 65
Herter, Christian A., 114, 125
Hickerson, John D., 96, 102
Hilsman, Roger, 159, 165, 203; quoted, 32
Hitler, Adolf, 192
Ho Chi Minh, 6–7, 52, 54, 84, 85, 87
Ho Chi Minh Trail, 58, 187
Hoffmann, Stanley, cited, 183
Holland, 9, 11, 12; West Irian and, 5, 170, 171
Holloway, James L., 50, 51, 79, 82
Honduras, 5, 17, 133, 212–13(*tab*); Guatemala and, 137, 138; U.S. interventions in, 223, 224, 225
"honor," as intervention justification, 21, 129, 132
Hoover, Herbert, 11, 13
Huk movement, 134, 136–37
Hungary, 6, 28, 29; uprising in (1956), 7, 172–73, 182, 216–17(*tab*)
Hussein I, king of Jordan, 48, 49, 77, 78, 81, 119

Ichiang Island, China, 168
Ileo, Joseph, 149
Imbert, Antonio, 68
"imperialism," 18
Incerlik air base, Turkey, 49, 77, 81
Inchon, South Korea, 43, 45, 99
incremental decision-making, 31–33, 108–17, 200; intervention restraint in, 32–33, 108, 134, 149, 157, 181, 194; war expansions and, 32, 127, 187–88
independence, wars of, 5–7, 9, 26, 52–54, 84, 145, 162–64. *See also specific wars*
Independence, Missouri, 43
India, 6, 173, 208–209(*tab*), 214–15(*tab*); frontiers of, 5, 28, 168, 169, 210–11(*tab*); Goa and, 5, 170, 182, 212–13(*tab*); Laos civil war (1959–62) and, 158
individual decision-making, 9–10, 169; executive, 1–2, 4, 10, 11, 13–15, 24, 161–62, 179, 181, 182 (*see also* United States presidency); group roles in, 30–31, 38, 102–108, 179, 189–93, 194, 195, 200; predictability of, 179, 183–84, 189–90, 192–93
Indochina, 5, 80; partition of, 85, 154, 155
Indochina War (1945–54), 5, 80, 84, 85, 111, 180; U.S. intervention restraints in, 6–7, 19, 31, 52–54, 142, 150–54, 206–207(*tab*)
Indonesia, 85, 162, 164–66, 183, 185, 208–209(*tab*); West Irian dispute (1962), 5, 170, 171, 214–15(*tab*)
Indonesian Communist Party, 164, 165, 166
Inter American Peace Committee, 65
Inter-American Peace Force, 68

248

INDEX

International Control Commission, 126, 158, 159
internationalism, 197–98, 199
intervention: criteria for, 4–8, 9, 15, 16–39, 69–70, 75, 76–77, 91–92, 93, 116–17, 127–29, 176, 180, 181–82, 187–89, 193–200; predictability, 179–200; rejection instances, 131–78, 180, 182–83. *See also* military assistance
intervention by others, 34–35, 36, 37(*tab*), 93, 117, 142, 143, 181, 182, 198; Algerian absence of, 34, 163, 164; within Communist states, 172–73, 182; in the Congo (Kinshasa), 148, 149–50, 182; Cuban absence of, 139, 176, 191; in Cyprus, 167; in the Dominican Republic, 126, 127, 181; Indonesian absence (1958–62) of, 164–65, 166, 183; in Iran, 145–47; in "just another country" situations, 162; in Korea, 124–25, 126, 182; in Laos civil war (1959–62), 155, 156–57; in Lebanon, 77, 109, 110–11, 119, 125, 126, 127, 181, 191; Syrian absence (1957) of, 76–77; in Vietnam, 84, 125–26, 127, 181
intervention requests, 35, 36, 37 (*tab*), 93, 117, 181, 203; Burmese absence of, 143, 144–45, 182; by Chiang Kai-shek, 140; by Congo (Kinshasa), 148, 149; Cuban absence of, 174, 176–77, 191; Cyprus absence of, 167–68; by Dominican Republic, 34, 65, 66, 120, 123–24, 181, 195; by Greece, 134, 135; Guatemalan absence of, 138; in Indochina War, 152; in Korea, 34, 118, 122, 124, 181; in Laos civil war (1959–62), 156, 157; by Lebanon, 48, 52, 110, 112–13, 114, 118–20,

intervention requests (*cont.*)
124, 181, 191; by Paraguay, 141; Philippine absence of, 137; Syrian absence of, 76–77; in Vietnam, 34, 56, 58, 120–23, 124, 181; war expansions and, 127–28, 186
investment interests, 18, 20, 21, 198; oil and, 83, 146, 147
Iran, 6, 7, 27, 29, 95, 111, 145–46; anti-Mossadegh coup (1953) in, 3, 76, 146–48, 183, 185, 206–207(*tab*)
Iraq, 6, 7, 74, 77, 81, 119, 185, 187, 212–13(*tab*); coup of 1958 in, 31, 48, 79, 80, 94, 100, 105, 109, 114, 181, 206–207(*tab*); oil and, 83
isolationism, *see* noninterventionism
Israel, 28, 77, 110, 111, 170; Hussein of Jordan and, 78; June war (1967) and, 5, 170, 212–13(*tab*)
Italy, 12

Jackson, Andrew, 9, 13, 218
Jamaica, 10
Japan, 8, 192, 221; China and, 12, 139, 140; U.S. occupation of, 27, 45, 71, 73, 99, 199; World War II surrender (1945), 41, 140
Jessup, Philip C., 96, 102
Johnson, Louis, 43, 96, 102
Johnson, Lyndon B., 13, 203; Cuba and, 126, 131, 176; Cyprus and, 167; Dominican intervention and, 2, 11, 14, 31, 61, 66, 67, 68, 87–88, 89, 90, 107, 108, 111, 116, 117, 123, 124, 126; Indochina War (1954) and, 153; Laos and, 86; Vietnam and, 1, 2, 15, 56, 92, 106, 115, 128, 186
Jones, Thomas, 9
Jordan, 5, 6, 7, 74, 105, 119, 187, 206–207(*tab*); Arab Union

249

INDEX

Jordan (cont.)
  and, 48; Britain and, 49–50, 81; civil war (1970), 212–13(tab); communism and, 75, 77–78, 79
Jordanian Communist Party, 75
Jordan Report, 121
Judeo-Christian tradition, force and, 33, 198–200
"just another country" states, 27; Korea as, 70, 73, 74; restraints on intervention in, 35, 36, 37 (tab), 187, 208–209

Kádár, Janos, 172
Kaisong, South Korea, 111–12
Karami, Rashid, 46, 51, 52
Karen Party (Burma), 143, 144
Kasavubu, Joseph, 148, 149
Kashmir, 5, 170, 212–13(tab)
Katanga Province, Congo (Kinshasa), 148, 149
Kellogg-Briand Pact, 33
Kennan, George, 24
Kennedy, John F., 13, 203; Algeria and, 162, 163–64; Cuba and, 7, 26, 88, 131–32, 174–75, 176; Cyprus and, 167; Dominican Republic and, 89; India and, 169; Laos civil war (1959–62) and, 157–58, 159, 160, 161, 178, 182, 190; Vietnam and, 2, 11, 55, 56–58, 83, 84, 86, 92, 106, 108, 111, 114, 115, 117, 120, 121, 122, 190; West Irian and, 171
Kennedy, Robert, 131, 132
Kenya, 5, 208–209(tab)
Keyes, Roger, 153
Key West, Florida, 158
Khamba tribesmen, 173, 216–17(tab)
Khoury, Bechara el-, 50
Khrushchev, Nikita, 158–59, 160
Kinshasa (Léopoldville), Congo, 149
Kissinger, Henry, quoted, 188
Knowland, William, 104, 153

Kong Le, 156, 157
Korea, 19, 27, 80; division of, 41–45; pre-World War II interventions in, 11, 221, 222, 223; U.S. occupation of (1945–49), 71–72. See also North Korea; South Korea
Korea, Democratic People's Republic of, see North Korea
Korea, Republic of, see South Korea
Korean War, 11, 19, 21, 31, 33, 35, 41–45, 107, 108, 126, 177, 182; casualties, 3, 69, 99; expansion and escalation of, 4, 15, 17, 43–44, 45, 52, 86, 99, 101, 105, 127, 131, 185–86, 187, 188; Formosan aid in, 109–10; intervention request, 34, 118, 122, 124, 128, 181; local military action in, 60, 111–12, 117, 181; nuclear war risk and, 99–100, 101, 127; public reaction to, 1–2, 102–103, 104, 197; Soviet confrontation risk in, 4, 94, 96–98, 127; United Nations and, 43, 44, 45, 108, 124–25; U.S. perception of security threat in, 8, 20, 27, 70–74, 91, 92
Kuomintang, see China, Republic of
Kurds, 145, 212–13(tab)
Kuwait, 212–13(tab)

Laniel, Joseph, 150, 152, 154
Lao Dong Party (North Vietnam), 84
Laos, 5, 53, 54; civil war (1959–62), 86–87, 115, 142, 154–62, 182, 185, 190, 206–207(tab); South Vietnam border and, 56, 58, 87, 161, 187; Vietnam War expansion into, 2, 4, 11, 52, 58 59, 127–28, 129, 161, 178, 186–87, 197
Laquer, Walter Z., cited, 75

INDEX

Latin America, 10–11, 12, 20, 32; Johnson on, 87–88; nonintervention situations listed, 204–205; U.S. "Western Hemisphere defense" doctrine and, 19, 26, 27, 71, 88, 111, 142, 177, 183. *See also specific countries*

League of Nations, 110

Lebanese Communist Party, 75

Lebanon, 5, 6, 206–207(*tab*), 212–13(*tab*). *See also* Lebanon intervention (1958)

Lebanon intervention (1958), 1, 2, 3, 4, 7, 11, 21, 33, 34, 41, 45–52, 60, 61, 69, 177, 185; expansion risks in, 94, 110–11, 187; local military strength in, 46, 108, 112–14, 117, 181; nuclear warfare risk in, 95, 100, 101–102, 127; United Nations and, 47–48, 103, 104, 105, 109, 110, 113, 119, 125; U.S. Congress and, 95, 104–105, 107, 125; U.S. perception of security threat in, 8, 17, 19, 20, 27, 74–83, 91, 92, 104–105, 126, 180, 190, 191, 195–96

Lefever, Ernest W., cited, 149

Leites, Nathan, cited, 23

LeMay, Curtis, 152

Lemnitzer, Lyman L., 106, 175

Léopoldville (Kinshasa), Congo, 149

Levi, Warner, cited, 22

Lhasa, Tibet, 173

Liberia, 219

Lie, Trygve, 43

Lindblom, Charles, cited, 31–32

Lloyd, Selwyn, 81

Lon Nol, 59, 128

Low Countries, *see* Belgium; Holland

Luang Prabang, Laos, 156

Lucas, Scott, 102

Lumumba, Patrice, 148–49, 182

Luzon, Philippines, 136

MacArthur, Douglas: Korean War and, 15, 44, 45, 99, 103, 109, 112

McCarthy, Eugene, 13, 195

McClintock, Robert: Lebanon intervention and, 47, 48, 50, 51–52, 113, 118, 120

McCloskey, Paul, 195

McCone, John A., 106

McCormack, John W., 102, 153

McGarr, Lionel, 120

McGovern, George, 195

McKinley, William, 11

Macmillan, Harold, 81, 158

McNamara, Robert S., 116; Cuba and, 131, 175, 176; Vietnam and, 106, 107, 121

Madagascar, 5, 212–13(*tab*). *See also* Malagasy Republic

Maddox (vessel), 128, 132

Magsaysay, Ramon, 137

Maine (vessel), 199

Makarios III, Archbishop, 166, 167

Malagasy Republic, 206–207(*tab*). *See also* Madagascar

Malaya, 5, 157, 165, 206–207(*tab*); Britain and, 32, 111, 182; communism and, 84, 85

Malaysia, 206–207(*tab*), 214–15(*tab*); Indonesia and, 5, 208–209(*tab*)

Malik, Charles, 47, 109, 112, 118

Manchuria, 12, 101

Mann, Thomas C., 175; Dominican intervention and, 61, 68, 90–91, 107, 116, 123–24

Mansfield, Mike, 103, 104, 105, 195

Mao Tse-tung, 6, 12, 28, 53, 71, 139, 140, 192

Marshall, George Catlett, 140

Martin, John Bartlow, 67–68; cited, 60, 90, 123

Martin, Joseph, 153

Matthews, Francis P., 96, 97

Matthews, H. Freeman, 97

Matsu Island, China, 28, 168–69

251

Mead, Margaret, cited, 199
Mediterranean Sea, 77, 78, 100, 135
Mekong River, 159
Menderes, Adnan, 77
Meo tribesmen, 161
Merton, Robert K., cited, 23
Metternich, Clemens, Fürst von, 191, 192
Meuchi, Patriarch, 46
Mexican War, 9, 219
Mexico, 9, 199, 219, 221, 224
Middle East, *see* Near East
military assistance, 3, 32, 33, 181, 182, 197, 198; in Algerian war, 163; to anti-Communist invasions and insurrections, 3, 7, 133, 137–38, 144, 149–50, 165, 172, 173–77, 178, 184–85, 188; to Cambodia, 59, 127; to China (Taiwan), 140; to the Congo (Kinshasa), 149; to Cuba, 139, 185; to Greece, 134, 135, 184; to India, 169; in Indochina War, 53, 150; to Indonesia, 165, 185; in Korea, 41, 43, 44–45, 72, 108, 112; to Laos, 155, 156, 157, 158, 159, 161, 185; to Lebanon, 109, 113; by other nations, 35, 36, 37(*tab*), 125, 126, 127, 137, 140, 142, 143, 144, 145, 149, 150, 152, 156, 164–65; to the Philippines, 136, 137, 185; to South Vietnam, 2, 4, 11, 54–55, 56, 57–58, 59, 94, 101, 105–106, 109, 111, 114, 115–16, 120–22, 185, 186
"military-industrial complex," 18–19
Milliken, Eugene, 153
Molina Urena, Rafael, 61, 62, 63, 65, 116, 181
Monroe Doctrine, 9, 26
Montas Guerrero, Salvador, 62
Monterey, Mexico, 9, 219
Montgomery, John, cited, 144
Mora, José, 68

moral values, 4, 117–27; change in, 196–200; covert intervention and, 174, 175, 176, 185, 188, 191; group decision-making and, 22–24, 33–35, 36, 38, 69–70, 102–108, 164, 181, 189–93; humanitarian, 177; individual predicability and, 179, 183–84, 189–90; presidential, 13, 24; surprise attack and, 132; war expansions and, 127–29, 178, 186, 188
Morínigo, Higinio, 141
Morocco, 5, 10, 11, 214–15(*tab*), 224
Moscow, Russia, 59. *See also* Soviet Union
Moslems, 46–47, 51
Mossadegh, Mohammed, coup against, 3, 146–48
Moyers, William, 107
Mozambique, 5, 214–15(*tab*)
Muccio, John J., 42, 43
Murphy, Robert D., 50–51, 82, 94
Murrow, Edward R., 175
Muscat and Oman, 6, 214–15(*tab*)

Nagy, Imre, 7, 172, 182
Nam Tha, Laos, 159
Napoleon Bonaparte, 192
Nasser, Gamal Abdel, 50, 80, 192; Eisenhower view of, 77, 82, 170–71, 190
National Liberation Front, South Vietnam, *see* Viet Cong
National Revolutionary Party (PNR) of Dominican Republic, 89
nationals, protection of, 9, 10, 12, 17, 20, 21; in Dominican Republic (1965), 64, 65, 66, 89, 90, 123, 124; in Korean War, 43, 73; in Lebanon intervention, 113, 119; in World War I, 11
naval warfare, 4, 185, 189; in the

INDEX

naval warfare (*cont.*)
Bay of Pigs, 175; in Dominican intervention, 63–64, 65; in Indochina War (1954), 153; in Korea, 15, 44, 45, 74, 99, 112; Laotian threats (1959–62) of, 156, 158, 159; Near East threats of, 77, 78–79; in Vietnam, 122, 128

Navarre, Henri, 53

Ne Win, 145

Near East, 10, 28, 41, 88, 170–71, 198; Fertile Crescent of, 27, 74–76, 79–80, 92, 94, 95, 114, 142, 180. *See also specific countries*

negotiation: in Dominican intervention, 18, 65, 67–68; in Indochina War (1954), 154; in Laos civil war (1959–62), 157, 158–59, 160; in Lebanon intervention, 50–52, 82; in Paraguay, 141; Vietnam War and, 18, 58

Nehru, Jawaharlal, 158, 169

Nepal, 28, 168, 210–11(*tab*)

New York Times, 84, 144, 160, 203

New Zealand, 85

Nicaragua, 6; Costa Rica and, 5, 204–205(*tab*), 212–13(*tab*); U.S. interventions in, 8, 11, 12, 220, 222, 223, 224, 225

Nigeria, 6; civil war (1966–69), 17, 28, 170, 177, 182, 214–15(*tab*)

Nitze, Paul, 175

Nixon, Richard M., 13; Cambodia and, 2, 11, 58, 59, 87, 128, 197; Indochina War (1954) and, 154; Lebanon intervention and, 95; in Venezuela, 21, 132

Nizam al-Din, 76

Nolting, Frederick, 56, 57, 58; Vietnam aid and, 120, 121

noninterventionism, 12–13, 196–97; culture and, 198, 199–200; Marine landings and, 189; operational code and, 37(*tab*);

noninterventionism (*cont.*)
post-World War II situations of, listed, 204–17(*tab*)

North Africa, 10. *See also specific countries*

North Atlantic Treaty Organization (NATO), 26, 154; Cyprus and, 167; Vietnam and, 115

North Carolina, 64, 101

North Celebes, 165

Northern Ireland, 6, 214–15(*tab*)

North Korea, 69; military strength of, 41, 99, 111–12, 117; *Pueblo* incident and, 21, 129, 132; South Korea invasion by, 31, 35, 42–44, 53, 70–71, 124–25, 126, 180, 182; Soviet troop withdrawal from (1949), 72, 94; U.S. invasion of, 4, 45, 127, 128, 131, 187

North Vietnam, 35, 69, 92, 111; Indochina War and, 7, 52, 53, 54, 85, 150, 151, 152; infiltration of the South by, 54, 55, 56, 91, 125–26, 127, 129, 181; Pathet Lao and, 155, 156–57, 159, 160, 161; U.S. attack on, 2, 4, 52, 58, 59–60, 115, 128–29, 131, 132, 186, 187, 197

Nu, Thakin, 143, 144, 145, 182

nuclear weapons, 28–29, 36, 37(*tab*), 93, 200; avoiding the use of, 29–30, 98–102, 127, 140–41, 180, 181, 182, 188; group decision-making and, 15, 192; Indochina War and, 151, 152; Laos civil war (1959–62) and, 157; official faith in deterrence value of, 95, 188, 193–94; treaties on, 30, 195

Nuri es-Said, 48, 80

oil, 83; Iran and, 146, 147

Okinawa, 10, 73, 220

operational codes, 22–24, 29, 34, 36, 69–70; change prospects for, 193–200; distortions and, 91–92, 116–17, 180; for-

operational codes (*cont.*) eign use of, 192; nonintervention situations and, 37(*tab*), 38, 93, 133, 177, 180–81; war expansions and, 74, 127, 178, 186–87. *See also specific factors*, e.g., security threats
Operation Vulture, 151, 152–53
Organization of American States, 65, 138; Council, 67–68, 88, 111
Oslo, Norway, 115
Osmeña, Sergio, 136
Overseas Press Club, 84, 152
overt military intervention, defined, 3–4. *See also* intervention

Pace, Frank, Jr., 43, 44, 96, 102, 103
Paige, Glenn, cited, 43
Pakistan, 85, 170, 212–13(*tab*); civil war (1971), 5, 6, 17, 28, 214–15(*tab*)
Palestine, 5, 170, 214–15(*tab*)
Palestinian refugees, 78
Panama, 6, 204–205(*tab*); U.S. interventions in, 220, 221, 222, 223
Panasco Alvim, Hugo, 68
Papal Nuncio, Dominican, 67–68
Paraguay, 6, 12; civil war in (1947), 134, 141–42, 177, 182, 204–205(*tab*)
Paris peace negotiations (Vietnam War), 58
Partido Revolucionario Dominicana (PRD), 61, 62, 64, 65, 67, 68
Partie Populaire Syrienne (PPS), 46–47
Pathet Lao, 58–59; civil war (1959–62) and, 155, 156–57, 158, 159, 160–61, 182
Paul, Norman, 94
peace-keeping, 17, 20, 21, 34, 177, 188, 189
Pearl Harbor, Hawaii, 12, 25

Peking, China, 12. *See also* China, People's Republic of
Pentagon, *see* United States Department of Defense
Pentagon Papers, 105–106
Pershing, John Joseph, 199
Peru, 6, 11, 142, 182, 183, 204–205(*tab*), 219
Pescadores Islands, 28, 169
Phalangist Party (Lebanon), 51, 52
Pharon, Henri, 46
Philippine Islands, 5, 165, 222, 223; Huk rebellions (1946–54) in, 134, 136–37, 185, 204–205(*tab*); Indochina War and, 85, 151; Korea and, 71, 73
Phoui Sananikone, 155–56
Phoumi Nosovan, 155–56, 157, 159, 160
piracy, 9, 218, 219, 220, 221
Plain of Jars, Laos, 156
Plank, John N., quoted, 116
Poland, 12, 172, 216–17(*tab*)
Politburo, 23
political culture, the operational code and, 33, 198–200
Pope, Allen, 165
Popular Dominican Movement (MPD), 89
Porter, David, 9
Portugal, 5, 214–15(*tab*)
Portuguese Guinea, 214–15(*tab*)
preventive-war concept, 199
Priest, J. Percy, 153
Princeton University, 113
Pueblo (vessel), 21, 129, 132
Puerto Plata, Puerto Rico, 9
Puerto Rico, 9, 27, 61, 132, 218, 219, 222
Pusan, South Korea, 45, 99
Pyongyang, North Korea, 42, 112

Qualla Battoo, Sumatra, 10
Quarles, Donald, 114
Quello, J. I., cited, 61
Quemoy Island, China, 28, 168–69
Quirino, Elpidio, 136, 137

INDEX

Radford, Arthur, 151, 153
Radio Santo Domingo, 61
radio telegraphy, 10
Rayburn, Sam, 102, 104, 105
Read, John A., 79
Red Flag Party (Burma), 143
Red River Delta, North Vietnam, 151
Reid Cabral, Donald, 60, 61, 62, 63, 117
Reinhardt, G. Frederick, 94
Republican Party (U.S.), 6, 105, 121, 139–40
restraints on intervention, *see* intervention, criteria for; *and see specific restraints on intervention*, i.e., allies; armed conflict (prior to American intervention); burden of intervention, assumption by others; intervention requests; nuclear weapons, avoiding the use of; security threats; Soviet Union, avoiding war with; veto (non-presidential)
Revolutionary Movement (Cuba), 174
Rhee, Syngman, 42, 118, 214
Ridgway, Matthew, 151
Rivera Cuesta, Marcos, 60
Roberts, Chalmers M., cited, 153
Roosevelt, Franklin D., 11, 13, 14; Indochina and, 52–53
Roosevelt, Theodore, 11
Rostow, Walt W., 120, 176; North Vietnam bombing and, 115, 129; South Vietnam mission (1961), report, 56–57, 58, 106, 115, 181
Rountree, William, 114
Rusk, Dean: Cuba and, 131, 175, 176; Dominican Republic and, 107, 116; Laos and, 158; Korea and, 43, 96, 102; Vietnam and, 55, 106, 114–15, 125
Russell, Richard, 31, 107, 153
Russia, *see* Soviet Union
Russian Revolution, 8, 224

Ruyle, Benjamin, 63
Rwanda-Burundi, 6, 206–207(*tab*)

Saigon, South Vietnam, 56. *See also* South Vietnam
Salaam, Saeb, 46
Samoa, 10, 219, 222, 223
Sandino, Augusto, 8
San Isidro air base, Dominican Republic, 62, 63, 64, 65, 67, 123, 124, 195
Santo Domingo, Dominican Republic, 60–68, 101, 116, 181
Santos Céspedes, Jesús de los, 62, 65
Saudi Arabia, 75
Savannakhet, Laos, 156
Schlesinger, Arthur M., Jr., 175, 176; cited, 86, 125, 162, 164, 169, 174, 203
security threats, 22–24, 33, 38, 69–92; containment doctrine and, 24–29, 179, 182, 190, 195–97, 200; Cuba as, 26, 131, 177; scale of importance, 25–26, 35, 36, 37(*tab*), 69–70, 180, 193–94, 203
self-determination principle, 4
Seoul, South Korea, 42, 109, 112, 181
Shanghai, China, 12
Shehab, Fuad, 46, 50–51, 52, 81–82, 113
Sherman, Forrest P., 44, 96, 102
Sihanouk, Norodom, prince of Cambodia, 59
Sikkim, 28, 168
slave trade, 9, 219, 221
Smith, Bromley, 106
Smith, Earl E. T., 139
Solh, Sami, 45–46, 47
Somalia, 5, 206–207(*tab*)
Sorensen, Theodore C., quoted, 157, 158
Souphanouvong, prince of Laos, 155, 157, 160, 161
South China Sea, 158

255

INDEX

Southeast Asia, 41; as "Communist-threatened region," 27, 84–86, 142, 153, 154, 177–78, 180. *See also specific countries*
Southeast Asia Treaty Organization (SEATO), 111, 157, 159
South Korea, 4, 41–45, 69, 127, 131; anti-Rhee demonstrations in, 214–15(*tab*); military strength of, 99, 111–12, 117, 181; North Korean invasion of, 31, 35, 42–44, 53, 70–71, 124–25, 126, 180, 182; request for intervention by, 34, 118, 122, 124; revolts of 1948 in, 208–209(*tab*); U.S. perception of security threat in, 70–74, 91, 92, 180
South Vietnam, 5, 7, 35, 52–60, 69, 131, 178, 180, 190; infiltration of, 54, 55, 56, 91, 125–26, 127, 129, 181; intervention request of, 34, 56, 58, 120–23, 124, 181; local military strength in, 55, 109, 114–17; Tonkin Gulf incident and, 132; U.S. close combat support of, 2, 4, 11, 56, 58, 94, 101, 105–106, 115–16, 121–22, 185, 186
South Vietnam Civil Guard, 55
South Vietnam Self-Defense Corps, 55
South Yemen, 6, 208–209(*tab*)
Souvanna Phouma, prince of Laos, 127, 155, 156, 157, 160, 161
Soviet Union, 19, 21, 59, 140, 167, 216–17(*tab*); avoiding war with, 29–30, 94–98, 145–46, 172–73, 194–95; Chinese border and, 216–17(*tab*); the Congo and, 149, 182; Cuba and, 26, 131–32; Czechoslovakia and, 5, 7, 17, 28, 29, 172–73; decision-making in, 23, 192; Indonesia and, 164–65; Korea and, 4, 41, 72, 73, 94, 96–98, 112; Laos civil war (1959–

Soviet Union (*cont.*)
62) and, 156, 157, 158–59, 160; Near East and, 28, 75, 76, 94–96, 133, 142, 145–48, 171, 190; Russian Revolution and, 8, 224; U.S. tacit agreements with, 29–30, 36, 93–102, 127, 145, 172, 180–81, 182, 193–95, 200; Vietnam and, 4, 111, 127
Spain, 9, 12, 214–15(*tab*)
Spanish-American War, 199, 222
Spanish Civil War (1936–39), 12
Spanish Florida, 9, 218
Spanish Morocco, 5, 214–15(*tab*)
"special interest" countries, 25, 26–27, 35; Dominican Republic as, 87–91, 92, 127, 134, 180, 181; Korea not as, 70, 71; restraints on intervention in, 29, 36, 37(*tab*), 133–42, 177, 183, 204–205(*tab*); Taiwan as, 169
Special National Intelligence Estimate on Vietnam (1961), 115
"spheres of influence" theory, 19–20, 190
Sprague, Mansfield, 94, 95
Stalin, Joseph, 145, 192
Stanleyville, Congo, 149–50
Stevenson, Adlai, 132, 175
Stump, Felix B., 169
Subic Bay, Philippines, 136
subversion, 75–76
Sudan, 5, 6, 17, 28, 206–207(*tab*), 214–15(*tab*)
Suez war (1956), 5, 110, 172, 214–15(*tab*); communism and, 170–71, 190
Suharto, 166
Sukarno, Achmed, 164, 166, 171, 192
Sumatra, 10, 219
Svoboda, Ludwig, 172
Sweden, 119
Syria, 6, 7, 10, 11, 171, 206–207(*tab*), 212–13(*tab*); Communist government in (1956–

256

INDEX

Syria (cont.)
58), 133; French occupation of, 110, 214–15(tab); June war (1967) and, 5; Lebanon and, 47–48, 74–75, 76, 77, 78, 79, 81, 83, 104–105, 109, 125, 127, 181, 187, 191, 214–15 (tab)
Syrian Communist Party, 75, 77

Tachen Islands, China, 168, 169
"tacit agreements," 29–30. See also nuclear weapons; Soviet Union
Taiwan, see China, Republic of
Tangiers, Morocco, 10
Taruc, Louis, 136, 137
Taylor, Maxwell, 56–57, 58, 106, 115, 120, 181; Cuba and, 131
Teheran, Iran, 145, 146, 148
Texas, 199
Thailand, 6, 85, 206–207(tab); coup of 1951 in, 133; Laos civil war (1959–62) and, 158, 159, 160, 161; Vietnam and, 58, 84, 86
Thompson, Llewellyn, 160
Threat to the Peace, A (U.S. Department of State), 86
Tibet, 28, 168, 169, 172, 180, 210–11(tab); Khamba uprising (1959) and, 173, 216–17 (tab)
Tientsin, China, 12
Timberlake, Clair, 148
Tito (Josip Broz), 129
Tobago, 214–15(tab)
Tonkin Gulf incident, 58, 128, 132
Trieste, 168
Trinidad, 214–15(tab)
Tripoli, Lebanon, 46
troops (U.S.): "combat ready," 3–4, 63–64, 66, 67, 101, 123, 140; Dominican commitment of, 3, 60, 64, 65, 66, 67, 68, 91, 108, 116, 120, 123, 185, 186; Korean commitment

troops (cont.)
(1950) of, 3, 45, 74, 99, 103, 109–10, 112, 118, 186; Korean withdrawal (1949) of, 71–72; in Latin America (1865–1928), 10–11; Lebanon commitment, 3, 47, 48, 51, 52, 74, 79, 80, 81–82, 105, 112–13, 118–20, 185, 186; in Russia (1918–20), 8; Vietnam commitment of, 3, 56, 57–58, 59, 60, 101, 105–106, 115, 116, 120–23, 185, 186. See also air warfare; close combat support; ground warfare; naval warfare
Trujillo y Molina, Rafael, 68
Truman, Harry S., 13, 203; Burma and, 143; China and, 2, 6, 7, 139–40; French Indochina aid and, 53; Greece and, 80, 134, 135; Iran and, 145, 146–47; Korean intervention decision and, 1–2, 11, 15, 43, 45, 70, 72, 91, 92, 96–98, 99, 102–103, 108, 110, 112, 117, 118, 125; Paraguay and, 141, 177, 182; Philippines and, 136, 137
Truman Doctrine, 135
Tshombe, Moise, 148, 149
Tucker, Robert, quoted, 33
Tudeh Party (Iran), 146, 148
Tunisia, 5, 214–15(tab)
Turkey, 49, 75, 76, 111; Cyprus and, 166, 167; Eisenhower message (1957) to, 77; Soviet Union and, 95, 133
Turner Joy (vessel), 128, 132
Twining, Nathan: Lebanon and, 49, 94, 95, 96, 100, 104, 105, 114

Udorn airfield, Thailand, 158
United Arab Republic, 5, 163; Lebanon and, 47, 50, 77, 78, 109, 113, 119, 125, 191
United Nations, 6, 132; Algeria and, 163; Burma and, 144;

INDEX

United Nations (*cont.*)
Congo (Kinshasa) and, 148, 149, 182; Cuba and, 175; Cyprus and, 32, 167, 168; Dominican Republic and, 111; Greece and, 135; Guatemala and, 138; Indonesia and, 166; Korea and, 43, 44, 45, 108, 124–25; Lebanon and, 47–48, 103, 104, 105, 109, 110, 113, 119, 125; Tibet and, 173
United Nations Balkan Investigating Commission, 135
United Nations Charter, 4, 73
United Nations Observation Group in Lebanon, 47–48, 104; on United Arab Republic intervention, 125
United Nations Political Committee, 175
United Nations Security Council, 111, 149, 163, 167, 182; Korea and, 43, 44, 108, 118, 124–25; Lebanon and, 47, 48, 109, 110, 113, 119, 125
United Nations Temporary Commission on Korea, 41–42
United Press, 42
United States Air Force, 4, 161; Korea and, 43–44, 99, 103, 112; Strategic Air Command, 95, 152. *See also* air warfare
United States Army, 189; BLUE-BAT and, 105; 82nd Airborne Division, 64, 67; Eleventh Airborne Division, 79; Korean commitment of, 15, 99; Strategic Army Corps in, 100, 101; Task Force Alpha in, 81, 82. *See also* ground warfare
United States Central Intelligence Agency (CIA), 31, 38, 185; Congo (Kinshasa) and, 150; Cuba and, 7, 173–74, 175; Dominican Republic and, 66; Guatemala and, 138; Indonesia and, 165; Jordan and, 78; Laos and, 155, 156; Lebanon

USCIA (*cont.*)
and, 47, 94–95; Syria and, 76; Vietnam and, 106
United States Civil War, 10, 11, 12
United States Congress, 6, 24, 25, 31, 38, 189; Dominican intervention and, 107, 108; Eisenhower and, 75; Greece and, 135; Indochina War (1954) and, 152, 153–54, 182; Korea and, 102–103, 108; Lebanon intervention and, 95, 104–105, 107; Quemoy and Matsu and, 168–69; Vietnam and, 106, 107, 128
United States Department of the Air Force, 185; Korea and, 44, 96, 102
United States Department of the Army: Korea and, 43, 44, 96, 102, 103
United States Department of Defense, 18, 25, 31, 185; Cuba and, 175; Dominican Republic and, 66, 68, 107–108; Indochina War (1954) and, 153; Korea and, 43, 44, 96, 102; Laos civil war (1959–62) and, 155, 159; Lebanon and, 94, 95, 104, 114; Vietnam and, 57, 105–106, 121
United States Department of the Navy, 14, 96
United States Department of State, 14, 21, 25, 31, 38, 185; Cuba and, 132, 175; Dominican Republic and, 61, 63, 64, 65, 66–67, 68, 89, 107, 123, 124; Jordan and, 78; Korea and, 42, 43, 72, 96, 97, 102; Laos civil war (1959–62) and, 155, 157, 159; Lebanon and, 47, 50–51, 75, 94–95, 103, 104, 110, 113–14; Vietnam and, 54, 56–57, 84–85, 86, 106, 121, 126
United States Department of

INDEX

USBIR (cont.)
State, Bureau of Intelligence and Research, 75, 89
United States Department of the Treasury, 104, 175
United States Department of War, 14. *See also* United States Department of Defense
United States House of Representatives: Armed Services Committee of, 95; Foreign Affairs Committee of, 84, 125, 152; Indochina War and, 152, 153; Korean War and, 102–103; Lebanon intervention and, 104, 105, 125
United States Information Agency (USIA), 132, 175
United States Joint Chiefs of Staff: Cuba and, 175; Indochina War (1954) and, 151, 153; Korea and, 43, 44, 71, 72, 73, 96, 97, 99, 102; Lebanon and, 49, 79, 83, 94–95, 104, 114; Vietnam and, 106
United States Marine Corps, 10, 189, 218–25 *passim;* in China, 12, 140; in Curaçao, 9; in Dominican Republic, 4, 17, 26, 64, 66–67, 101, 108, 116, 123, 124, 185; in Laos civil war (1959–62), 158, 159–60, 161; in Lebanon, 3, 49, 51, 78–79, 80, 82, 95, 100, 101, 104, 105, 125, 185; in Nicaragua, 8
United States Military Assistance and Advisory Group: Dominican Republic and, 63, 65, 123; Indochina and, 53; Vietnam and, 120
United States Military Assistance Command for Vietnam and Thailand, 122
United States National Security Council: Korea and, 72–73, 97, 103; Laos civil war (1959–62) and, 159; Lebanon inter-

USNSC (cont.)
vention and, 95, 104, 110, 118; Vietnam and, 57, 106, 107, 115–16
United States Navy, 10; Seventh Fleet of, 156, 158, 159; Sixth Fleet of, 49, 51, 77, 78–79, 100, 104, 110, 135; Task Force 44.9, 63–64
United States Office of Emergency Planning, 106
United States Operations Mission (Laos), 155
United States presidency: Cuban "white paper" (1961), 174; group values acceptance by, 24–25, 38, 192, 195; nonpresidential veto, 30–31, 36, 93, 102–108, 127, 153–54, 181, 182, 194, 200; nuclear warfare risks and, 15, 100; personal responsibility and, 1–2, 4, 10, 11, 13–15, 21, 31, 169, 192; secret recommendations and, 57, 106, 175. *See also individual presidents*
United States Senate, 38; Dominican intervention and, 107, 108; Foreign Relations Committee of, 72, 125; Korean War and, 102–103; Lebanon intervention and, 104–105, 125
United States Strategic Air Command, 95, 152
Uruguay, 204–205(*tab*), 220
Ussuri River crisis (1969), 5

values, *see* moral values
Vance, Cyrus R., 68
Vandenberg, Hoyt S., 44, 96, 102
Vatican, the: Dominican cease fire and, 67–68
Vaughn, Jack Hood, 68
Venezuela, 6, 11, 204–205(*tab*); Nixon in, 21, 132
veto (nonpresidential), 36, 93, 102–108, 127, 153–54, 181,

259

veto (*cont.*) 182, 194, 200; adviser selection and, 30–31, 102, 175
Vienna, Austria, 159
Vientiane, Laos, 156
Viet Cong (South Vietnamese National Liberation Front), 58, 83–84; Cambodia and, 59, 87, 128, 129, 187; military strength (1961), 55, 56, 91, 109, 114–15, 117; North Vietnamese "direction" of, 55, 125–26, 129, 181
Viet Minh, 6–7, 52–54, 150, 152; Viet Cong and, 84. *See also* North Vietnam
Vietnam, Democratic Republic of, *see* North Vietnam
Vietnam, Republic of, *see* South Vietnam
Vietnam Task Force (American), 55–56
Vietnam War, 8, 15, 21, 33, 41, 52–60, 94, 108, 114–16, 117, 125–26; casualties in, 3, 69; chemical weapons in, 101, 188; expansions of, 11, 17, 32, 52, 58–60, 105–106, 109, 127–29, 131, 161, 177–78, 185, 186–87, 197; Indochina War and, 6–7, 52–54, 84, 180; negotiation and, 18, 58; nuclear risk in, 100–101, 127; public reactions to, 1–2, 107, 196–97; United Nations and, 111; U.S. security and, 4, 20, 27, 35, 83–87, 91, 92, 115, 190
Vinson, Carl, 103; quoted, 95; Lebanon and, 104, 105

Wade, Sydney S., 78, 79, 81
Wallace, George, 13
War of 1812, 15, 218
Warsaw Pact, 172, 216–17(*tab*)
Webb, James E., 96, 97
Wedemeyer, Albert C., 71–72, 140
Wessín y Wessín, Elias, 62, 65
West Berlin, 168, 184; East German threats to, 29, 32, 133, 183; symbolic importance of, 28, 170, 180
Westerfield, H. Bradford, cited, 136
"Western Hemisphere defense" doctrine, 19, 26, 27, 71; intervention restraints in, 142, 177, 183, 204–205(*tab*); Johnson on, 87–88; United Nations authority and, 111
West Germany, 27, 32, 47, 102, 163
West Irian, 5, 170, 171, 214–15 (*tab*)
Wherry, Kenneth, 103
White Flag Party (Burma), 143
Wilkes, Charles, 9–10
Williams, John, 9, 218
Wilson, Woodrow, 8
Win, Ne, 145
World War I, 8, 15, 197; casualties in, 69; U.S. entry into, 11, 199
World War II, 33; chemical warfare prohibition in, 101; China and, 139, 140; demobilization after, 98–99, 140–41; the Fertile Crescent and, 74; Greece and, 134; group decision-making and, 14–15, 30; internationalism after, 197–98, 199; Korea and, 41; military interventions before, 8–13, 16, 21, 189, 198, 199, 218–25; Philippines and, 136; U.S. "true peril" since, 25–26, 180; wars and occupations since, 1–6, 27, 36, 52, 145, 202

Yalu River, 45, 101
Yemen, 6, 170, 208–209(*tab*), 214–15(*tab*)
Yenan, China, 140
Yosu, South Korea, 42
Yugoslavia, 129, 135, 136

Zaire, *see* Congo, Republic of (Kinshasa)